'Understand it? Why, a four-year-old child could understand it!

(Aside) Go out and find me a four-year-old child, I can't make head or tail of this.'
Groucho Marx.

The Reluctant Motor Mechanic.

By John Fordham.
Designed & Illustrated by Perry Neville.

Book Club Associates, London.

This book is dedicated to Caroline and her Morgan (which
qualifies as a suitable case for treatment if ever there was one)
and to Boris and Steve of Edinburgh, who bring motor cars back
from beyond the grave and sometimes from further still.

First published 1979
Reprinted 1982, 1983

This edition published 1983 by Book Club Associates
By arrangement with
Whittet Books Ltd, The Oil Mills, Weybridge, Surrey

Printed and bound in Great Britain by
Butler & Tanner Ltd, Frome and London

Page 7.
Foreword.

Chapter One/Page 9.
How Your Car Works.
Heat Engines 9; *Petrol Engines* 11; *The Four-Stroke Cycle* 13;
The Cam: General Dogsbody 16; *Stoking It Up* 20; *Electrics & Ignition* 20; *Fuel* 31;
Exhaust Systems 38; *Cooling* 40; *Transmission* 40; *The Clutch* 43;
The Gearbox 46; *Final Drive & Differential* 54; *Lubrication* 54; *Types of Bearing* 56;
Oil Pressure 58; *Greases & E P Oils* 58; *Getting Under Way* 58; *Wheels & Tyres* 60;
Brakes 60; *Suspension* 62; *The Tin Can: Bodywork* 67; *P.S.* 67.

Chapter Two/Page 69.
How To Buy A Good Car.
Choosing The Right Sort 69; *The Sales Pitch* 70; *Where & How* 72;
The Once-Over 72; *Buying Second-Hand* 73; *Checklist For Used Car Buying* 80.

Chapter Three/Page 83.
Setting Up A Home Workshop.
Tools 86; *Keeping Entropy At Bay* 90; *Workshops & Equipment* 96;
Tools & Spares To Carry In The Car 98.

Chapter Four/Page 101.
How To Fix Breakdowns.
Car Will Not Start 101; *Faults On The Road* 111; *Troubleshooting Guides* 112.

Chapter Five/Page 125.
Keeping Your Car Healthy.
Every Week 125; *Every 3,000 Miles* 128; *Every 6,000 Miles* 142;
Every 12,000 Miles 145; *Periodic Maintenance* 146; *The M.O.T. Test* 148;
Coachwork 148; *Beyond Servicing* 152; *Major Work* 156.

Appendix/Page 173.
Advanced Engine Testing.
Testing Procedure 175; *Examination Of Plugs* 176; *Compression* 176;
Vacuum Reading 177; *Battery & Starter* 178; *Fuel System* 178;
Ignition System Electrics 179; *Ignition System Tuning & Advance Mechanism* 180;
Carburettor Mixture 181; *Valve Clearances* 182; *Tuning Up* 182.

Page 185.
Index.

Foreword.

Keeping the wolf from the door has almost thrown me to the tender mercies of a career in the motor trade more times than I could keep a count of. Only a weakness when it comes to business and early rising, a conviction that there ought to be a close season for manual labour in the winter, and a succession of would-be partners who shared my enthusiasm for board meetings in the local diverted me, but it was a near thing.

Perhaps writing this book has been a way of laying the ghost, though it's really intended to tell people a few things I wish I'd known before I started tearing motor cars to bits. The reader will soon rumble the sentimental preference I have for the machinery and the motoring lore of the '30s and '40s; though this book doesn't deal with those days at all, the way that the early motorist went to work has influenced its direction a lot. Not only did the cars look prettier, but the explanations of how they worked were written for normal human beings and not for trainee cosmonauts. The old manuals hinted that, like lion-taming, the trick with cars is to show no fear. The trick is also not to underestimate your own inexperience of course, and if *The Reluctant Motor Mechanic* has a theme, it's about the art of getting confidence and caution into balance.

The book is an attempt to pass on a little bit of what I and various foolhardy acquaintances have learned through experiences alternately bitter and exhilarating. Through it you might avoid too many of the pitfalls in coming to grips with that most infuriating and seductive of luxuries, the motor car. It doesn't seek to be comprehensive; it could hardly be when you consider the multitude of styles and models on the road. There are instruction books and workshop manuals for that, and massive tomes perched on library shelves for the serious student; what I have tried to do is to fill some gaps by telling a series of stories about how things work on cars, how you can manipulate the ways that they work, and most importantly how to make the best use of the more methodically presented and specialized information available elsewhere. This book can't sidestep the indispensability of the workshop manual for your particular model. With a bit of luck it might make the assumptions of the manual clearer.

I've started with a long section on first principles. It's perfectly possible to learn to fix a component without knowing *why* you've fixed it of course, just as it's possible to get a handful of sentences in a foreign language word perfect without having a clue what they mean. The first chapter is intended to provide the basis of the vocabulary of auto-language, and some of the grammar as well. We have begun where any half-informed motoring buff would find it derisory to begin, with a description of the principles of the internal combustion engine and examples of petrol engines that are hardly as sophisticated as something you might find in your lawnmower, let alone that elaborate mechanism in your garage. But how the gadgets under the bonnet do what they do may well be fundamentally the same whether their actual workings are controlled by levers and bits of wire or by computers. So armed with this background, Chapter 2 lets you in on the secrets of buying a vehicle, Chapter 3 considers the equipment you need to set up as a home mechanic (and gingerly tangles with some attitudes of mind that might help the process too), Chapter 4 deals with fault-tracing and Chapter 5 with general maintenance.

But even if you never lay a spanner on a motor car with intent to tinker, I hope this book may shed at least a little light. And if it should help you, then you might perhaps have patience while I extend my thanks to the people who helped put this book on the road. Publisher Annabel Whittet, who suffered the megalomania, mad optimism, last minute changes of plan, white lies and downright moonshine foisted on her by the author. There is the remarkable illustrator Perry Neville who unfailingly distinguished the wood from the trees and kept several jumps ahead of all my garbled and roundabout requests. There is also Mr Spargo of Kingston College of Further Education who kindly checked the manuscript, and Chris Cullen, who first suggested the idea for this book. And lastly there are the countless mechanics whose invaluable advice over the years would probably fill half a dozen books. The jokes would be good, too. *John Fordham.*

How Your Car Works.

Understanding what goes on under the bonnet of a motor car appears to be a black art peculiar to those born with the gift for reducing machinery to bits and pieces and then getting it to work again. Its spells are cast in a language that sounds like English, but which might as well be Martian to most people, to whom it communicates not much more than a sinking feeling in the current account. As with many features of our increasingly specialized age, expertise has become needlessly mystifying. Though for most a car is probably the most complicated piece of apparatus they're likely to own, the principles on which it functions are straightforward enough. The problem is that the car is not so much a machine as a boxful of machines all doing particular jobs.

Clearly there's no mystery about what the jobs are. The vehicle should be capable of being controlled by one person sitting in one place, who doesn't need a Ph.D. in physics to make the vehicle go, stop, turn corners and see in the dark. All these requirements involve various machines designed to make them happen. An engine, and a means of transmitting the power to the wheels; a braking system; steering gear and lights. Let's deal with making it go to begin with.

The simplest way of projecting a lump of metal through space is to attach a rocket engine to it; you light a charge of fuel inside it and the hot gas produced by this combustion rapidly expands through a jet nozzle and 'blows' the rocket along. Anywhere except Daytona Flats, rockets are obviously of pretty limited use on motor cars, which has needless to say not stopped various eccentrics from trying them out.

A more sophisticated procedure would be to get this heat energy somehow to run a machine. When the fuel is ignited it expands in all directions. The 'machine' then becomes a container for this expansion; it's designed so that the expansion of the gas can exert a kind of leverage or motion.

Heat Engines.

As everybody now knows, James Watt got the idea for a heat engine by watching the lid of his grandmother's kettle bumping up and down under steam pressure. True or false, it's become a milestone in engineering history; all the subsequent developments of this flash of inspiration were put to industrial uses. It was one of those breakthroughs where the borderline between science and art becomes impossible to draw. The imagination that it took to conceive of harnessing gas pressure to produce mechanical movement was the foundation of countless more logical and hard-boiled developments made throughout the nineteenth century.

Not that there was anything particularly new about getting useful work out of natural forces — haphazardly gathered by windmills or by sailing ships. The problem with using the wind as an employee was that it only turned up when it felt like it. Equally, nobody 'discovered' steam, it couldn't help happening. Watt's innovation was that directing it under pressure into a restricted space could produce a far more precisely controlled and useful kind of movement. The steam would try to expand the space it was pushed into. If the space was made expandable by building it as a smooth-bored cylinder in which a close-fitting piston is free to slide, then the steam would force the piston along the cylinder.

So far so good. The steam will blow the piston down the cylinder once, and that's that. To make an engine out of this arrangement, and an engine that will make a shaft rotate, there will have to be a mechanism capable of transforming this up-and-down (*reciprocating*) movement into rotational movement. This is something you did from the first day you ever rode a bicycle, since your legs are engaged in nothing more or less than a reciprocating action which the design of the pedal converts into rotation of the chainwheel; if we compare a loosely translated representation of a one-legged cyclist with a cutaway picture of a piston linked to a simple *crankshaft* via a connecting rod, it's not hard to discern the similarities: the connecting rod is naturally able to swivel on bearings at the crankshaft and at the piston — the former is the 'big-end' bearing, the latter the 'small-end'.

This leaves us with the matter of getting the

HOW THE PISTON TURNS THE CRANKSHAFT

Downward pressure on pedal...

...chainwheel rotates

Gas pressure makes piston descend...

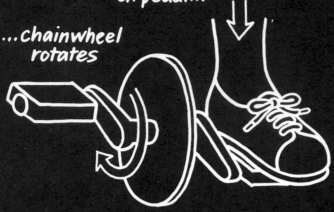

Piston

The piston is linked to the crankshaft by a connecting rod.
The moving piston turns the shaft in the same way a bicyclist's feet rotate the chainwheel.

Connecting rod

...crankshaft rotates

Little end

Big end

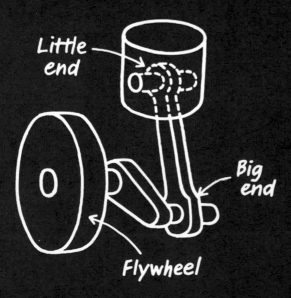

Flywheel

THE FLYWHEEL

Gas pressure makes the piston descend. The momentum of the flywheel pushes it up again.

whole contraption to keep moving for the upstroke, when the piston has ceased to be under pressure. Energy imparted to the crank by the power stroke has to be sustained by something capable of 'storing' the momentum, and a device called a *flywheel*, bolted to one end of the crankshaft, has invariably been used for this. It's heavy enough to keep the whole engine turning once it has been set in motion; on the type of inefficient single-cylinder steam engine that you find on fairground traction engines, the flywheel is a colossal affair the size of a ceremonial gong.

But as the design of engines changed to make them more efficient at power production, and the reciprocating action of the piston was smoothed out by the addition of more cylinders — like your left leg pushing down one crankpin/pedal while the right one is coming up — the flywheel was able to be considerably lightened. In fact the improved combustibility of modern fuels has meant that petrol engines that were put together in the 1930s can nowadays be run with a surprising amount of metal sliced off their original flywheels.

For the early single-cylinder stationary steam engines — called 'external combustion engines' because the high-pressure gas is cooked up in an external boiler and piped to the cylinder — there wasn't much more to be done. But the uses to which steam engines could be put were continually being extended, and by the early nineteenth century in Europe and America all sorts of bizarre fantasies were being bolted together by intrepid visionaries, most of whom have faded into obscurity. Joseph Cugnot was reputedly one of the first to power a moving vehicle with steam, building a field-gun tractor for use in Napoleon's army — though the Emperor was apparently too busy actually letting off field guns at all and sundry to attend any of the demonstrations. A man called Oliver Evans in Philadelphia built an amphibious steam vehicle in 1805, a contribution to science for which he was promptly labelled an idiot by a grateful public.

But the intoxicating notion of the horseless carriage was loose by now, despite the opposition. By 1833 Walter Hancock's steam coaches were running a bus service in Central London. It wasn't a popular departure with the punters, except as a sort of Russian roulette, since solid tyres, unmade roads, soot and noise could hardly compensate for the usurping of the horse. But clearly a quieter, smoother and more flexible source of power was going to be necessary before motor vehicles could truly stake their claim.

Petrol Engines.

Up to now we've been talking about burning fuel simply as a matter of lighting a pile of something combustible under a tankful of water to get steam. Some of the heat energy can be converted into mechanical movement, though not as much as engineers would like — a good deal of it gets lost to the atmosphere, and absorbed into the metalwork of the machinery itself. In the pursuit of improved efficiency, as well as of a power unit of compact size and reasonable quietness, the next step was to actually burn the fuel inside the cylinder itself, and burn it very rapidly at the moment when the piston was at the top of its cylinder bore. This required a much more volatile and convenient fuel than lumps of coal, and a much more concentrated and controllable means of burning it. Because combustion now takes place *within* the engine, these developments were taken to herald the arrival of the *internal combustion engine*. The 'muscles' are much the same as they were — reciprocating pistons driving a crankshaft. The 'breathing' now makes use of a liquid fuel such as paraffin, alcohol or petrol. The heat is applied electrically, by making a high voltage spark jump across a gap between a live conductor and the metalwork of the engine itself. The liquid fuel is converted to a vapour by spraying it in fine droplets into an airstream on its way into the cylinders, and this vaporizing device is the *carburettor*. There's only one other consideration to getting this contraption to deliver a reasonable amount of useful effort. The 'gas' is much more liable to impart a real kick to the piston on ignition if it has been compressed into a fraction of its original volume. So the design of the space above the piston in which the fuel is actually burned becomes a critical feature of the design of the engine. The more cramped it is, the more the *compression ratio* of the engine will be raised. This figure is simply the ratio of the volume of fuel vapour at atmospheric pressure to its final volume after it's been squeezed by the rising piston. One practical problem is that if the piston is a sufficiently sloppy fit in the bore to allow for its expansion when it gets hot, the compressed gas will leak past it. This is avoided by fitting the piston with several sprung rings *(piston rings)* just below the crown.

It's a bit out of step chronologically, but the simplest illustration of a practical petrol engine at work is the *two-stroke* engine, still in current use on everything from lawnmowers to motorbikes. Not only is it straightforward in its methods of getting fuel into the cylinder and burnt gas out, but its simplicity enables it to employ a thoroughly primitive ignition and lubrication system as well.

In the two-stroke engine, 'breathing' is accomplished by the moving piston covering and uncovering apertures in the cylinder wall, rather as if you were playing a penny whistle. As the piston rises, it acts as a suction pump and draws in its wake through the lower right hand hole on the illustration fuel which has been turned into vapour by the

THE TWO-STROKE CYCLE

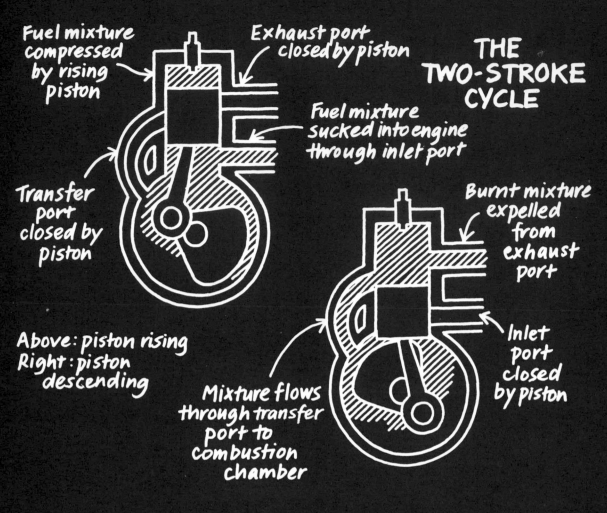

Fuel mixture compressed by rising piston

Exhaust port closed by piston

Fuel mixture sucked into engine through inlet port

Transfer port closed by piston

Burnt mixture expelled from exhaust port

Above: piston rising
Right: piston descending

Inlet port closed by piston

Mixture flows through transfer port to combustion chamber

SECTION THROUGH TWO-STROKE ENGINE

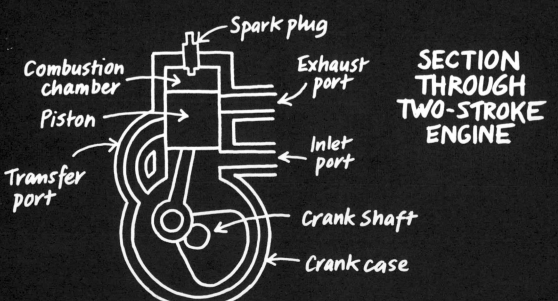

Spark plug

Combustion chamber

Exhaust port

Piston

Inlet port

Transfer port

Crank Shaft

Crank case

carburettor. At the same time, the rising piston is compressing fuel already admitted to the space above the piston crown (*combustion chamber*); when the spark ignites that compressed fuel and the piston is driven to the bottom of the bore, the carburettor inlet is closed over, the transfer port on the left and the exhaust port at top right are opened, and gas is pumped up from crankcase to cylinder.

The piston then rises once again, compresses the fuel vapour, the plug fires and the cycle is repeated. From the design point of view the beauty of this arrangement is that the gas flow pretty well takes care of itself, simply being pulled and pushed by the reciprocating piston. In any mechanism, the less moving parts, the better. There's less to wear out, and there's less hardware to be driven off the crankshaft since an engine of this design doesn't need mechanically operated valves.

The trouble is, this kind of engine isn't so attractive off the drawing board; though it's firing at every up-stroke of the piston, it doesn't develop a great deal of power, hence its application to lightly loaded vehicles. It's not very hard to see why. Since the ports are only open for brief periods, the available time for getting gas in and out of the engine is severely restricted — and the fact that the admission of fresh fuel through the transfer port is used to 'scour' or push the burnt gas out through the exhaust inevitably means that the engine is throwing out the baby with the bathwater to some extent. It's far more desirable to make use of the *full* stroke of the piston, whether in the role of a suction pump to pull the fuel in, or as a means of compressing it and expelling it.

The Four-Stroke Cycle.

In the internal combustion engine there are always four operating stages to be passed through — getting the air and petrol vapour into the cylinder in the first place, compressing it, burning it and then expelling the waste. In the two-stroke engine, these manoeuvres are telescoped into two movements of the piston by crafty positioning of the ports that let the gas in and out. If we want to disentangle all these activites so that each one has a full stroke of the piston to itself, then we get a more efficient operating cycle, but not without sacrifices.

The piston makes two strokes for every full revolution of the crankshaft — one downward, levering the *crankpin* through 180° from its topmost position again, with the piston at *top dead centre* or 't.d.c.' as it's known to the trade. Naturally then, in a four-stroke cycle there can only be a power or firing stroke once every *two* revolutions of the crankshaft, so the flywheel now has the job of keeping up the momentum of the crankshaft in between firing strokes rather than simply returning it to t.d.c.

Since the full stroke of the piston is to be used for all the operations rather than a partial stroke that can cover and release ports in the cylinder wall, the ports now have to be positioned at the top of the bore — either in the 'roof' of the combustion chamber or alongside the piston crown. Mechanically operated airtight gates or *valves* open and close the ports to control the gas flow. So the four-stroke or 'Otto' cycle works like this:

1. The piston starts to descend, with the *inlet valve* open. The suction created by its descent draws petrol vapour into the cylinder. This is the *induction stroke*.

2. Once the piston is at the bottom of its stroke (bottom dead centre or *b.d.c.*), the inlet valve closes and seals the combustion chamber. The spinning flywheel pushes the piston up to the top of its stroke again — and on this *compression stroke* the gas reaches a pressure established by the size of the combustion chamber space.

3. The compressed gas is now sparked off by the ignition system. A *sparking plug* screwed into the combustion chamber passes a high voltage pulse between a central live conductor and the earthed metalwork of the engine itself. The resulting bang heats up the air in the chamber which expands rapidly and pushes the piston downward on its *power stroke*.

4. At bottom dead centre again, the valve covering the exhaust port opens, the flywheel heaves the piston back up and the burned gases are pushed out into the exhaust.

The valves used in automobile engines have almost always been *poppet valves*, shaped a bit like a long thin mushroom. The stems slide in tubular guides, and the mating faces where the edges of the valve seal the holes in the combustion chamber have to be very accurately machined so that the valves don't leak when they're shut. Later on we'll be explaining the mechanism that gets the valves to open and close.

A swarm of new practical problems had to be faced to make the most efficient use of the revolutionary four-stroke principle. What would be the ideal type of fuel to use, and how could it be most efficiently burned? What kind of ignition system to burn it? How could the opening and closing of the fuel ports be most effectively synchronized to the various stages of the operating cycle? And, since a series of controlled explosions was obliged to take place within the engine itself, how best to keep the whole thing from going up in smoke?

Benz's experience of engines was mostly based on stationary single-cylinder models of the day, run on paraffin oil or coal gas. He had opted early on for a mixture of petrol and air, formed in a small external tank called the carburettor. And from the beginning he was set on electric ignition to fire the

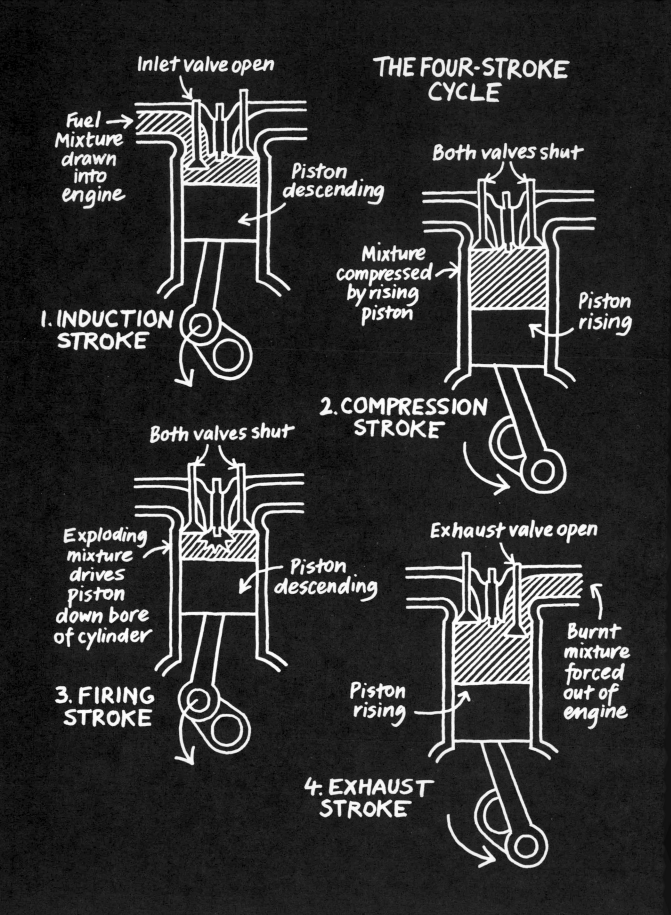

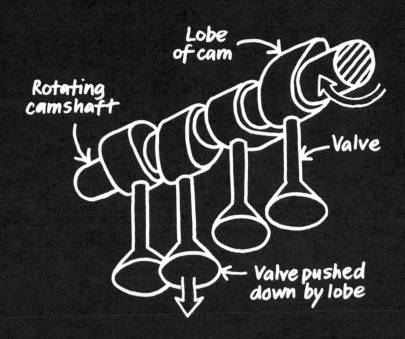

Lobe of cam

Rotating camshaft

Valve

OPERATION OF CAMSHAFT

Eccentric cams push valves open, springs (see below) push them shut

Valve pushed down by lobe

OPERATION OF VALVES

Right: valve in situ in cylinder head (cutaway)

Below: how fuel mixture flows past valve

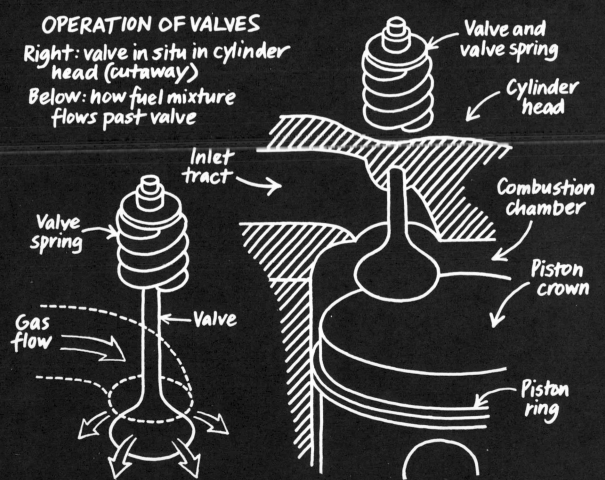

Valve and valve spring

Cylinder head

Inlet tract

Combustion chamber

Piston crown

Valve spring

Valve

Gas flow

Piston ring

mixture, although an alternative method did exist and was used by Gottlieb Daimler for a while. This was the 'hot-tube' method, whereby petrol vapour was passed through a platinum tube, kept white-hot by a blow torch.

The Camshaft: General Dogsbody.

Valves are going to solve the business of ensuring that gas gets into the combustion chamber when we want it to, and leaves when it's done its bit. But how to get the valves open and shut? Clearly, whether we employ the poppet valve directly above the combustion chamber, or at an angle to it, or upside down in the base of it, some kind of lever must bear on the stem of each valve, pushing it a few milli-metres clear of its seating when it needs to be open and allowing the coil spring to close it the remainder of the time. And not just a lever, but a row of eight levers on a four-cylinder engine, each one coming into operation in strict rotation. The *camshaft*, a slave or subsidiary shaft of the engine that takes care of the valve operation is, put crudely, a row of levers.

At the start of this injudicious intrusion into the private life of the petrol engine, we saw how a simple engineering principle such as the crank was able to turn reciprocating (up-and-down) movement into rotational movement. If our slave-shaft is rotating in harness with the crankshaft but is required to perform a reciprocating action such as pushing the valves open, another equally simple principle is introduced to reverse the process.

In all machinery, one of the most regularly featured devices for making things open and shut is the *cam* or *eccentric*. It's called an eccentric because it's a bit warped — it uses protrusions around a shaft to vary the behaviour of any moving bits and pieces it comes into contact with. Generally a cam is a raised portion at some point on the circumference of a spindle, and any mechanism bearing on it will be levered to one side as the highest point of this *cam lobe* turns to meet it, and fall back to its original position as the cam turns away. Depending on how sharp an apex the eccentric comes to, the degree of opening or *lift* can be accurately controlled in the design.

From the sketch of the basic idea, it's easy to see how this principle can be used when it comes to the operation and synchronization of our valves. First of all, we design a shaft with a number of cams along its length, the lobes all facing in different directions according to the opening and closing sequence the valves are supposed to follow in the cycle. This design can be modified according to whether there's one cylinder in the engine or any number at all, though the arrangement of the cams

will depend on what order the cylinders are supposed to fire in. Then we can either suspend the camshaft on brackets immediately above the valves themselves (with a metal cushion or *tappet* in between the lobes and the valve stems so that the swiping action of the rotating cam lobe doesn't bend the stem), or we can position the camshaft somewhere lower down in the cylinder block, operating the valves remotely through a system of pushrods and levers. The camshaft can then be run off the crankshaft itself, either by linking the two directly with gear-wheels, or hitching them up with a device more or less like a strengthened bicycle chain.

There's a catch to this, naturally. The four-stroke cycle obliges the crankshaft to completely rotate twice for the sequence of induction, com-pression, explosion and exhaust to be complete. The camshaft on the other hand, if it's to impart all the 'information' about valve operation to the whole of the valve gear, needs to rotate just once per cycle. So it can't be driven directly off the crankshaft, but needs to run at *half* the crank's rotational speed. This can be arranged by a simple gearing system, so that one turn of the crankshaft's gearwheel only turns the camshaft gearwheel half a turn.

So we now have a greatly simplified single-cylinder four-stroke piston engine with camshaft-operated valves, coil springs to keep them shut when they're supposed to be, and a pushrod and rocker arrangement to lever the valves open, as shown in the diagram. If the camshaft and crank-shafts were positioned much further apart — which they generally are — then the timing gears would be toothed sprockets instead, linked together with a chain.

All manner of variations are possible on this basic design, depending on the requirements of the engine and the restlessness of the designer; Benz's original engine had the cylinder laid flat and the crankshaft vertical. Volkswagen Beetles use hori-zontal cylinders in two pairs either side of a horizontal crankshaft. Many American engines, which go in for designs involving six or eight cylinders, set them up in a 'V' arrangement with three or four cylinders on each 'bank' — this is partly because eight cylinders in a straight line would mean a bonnet length that would take up two parking meters.

Valve design varies too. The simplest version involves positioning the valves upside down next to each cylinder — this was known as the *side-valve* design and is more or less obsolete. An overhead valve design like the one above has the valves side by side in the flat 'roof' of the combustion chamber. Sports engines frequently use a domed combustion chamber, and sometimes a domed piston crown as well, with the valves inclined on either side of the 'slope'. How fast the gas gets in and out is a vital

THE CRANKSHAFT

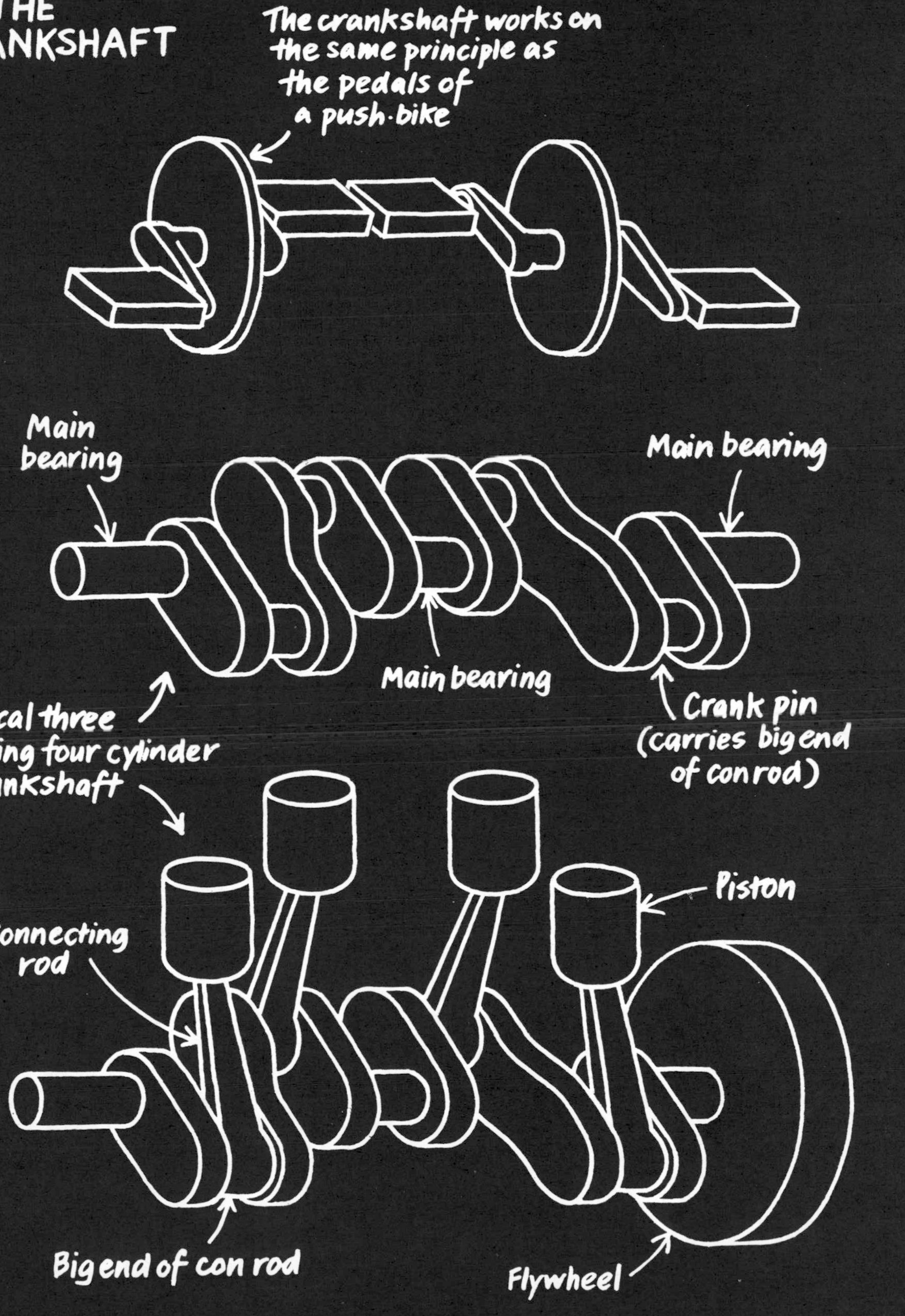

The crankshaft works on the same principle as the pedals of a push-bike

Main bearing

Main bearing

Main bearing

Crank pin (carries big end of con rod)

Typical three bearing four cylinder crankshaft

Connecting rod

Piston

Big end of con rod

Flywheel

SIMPLE SINGLE-CYLINDER ENGINE

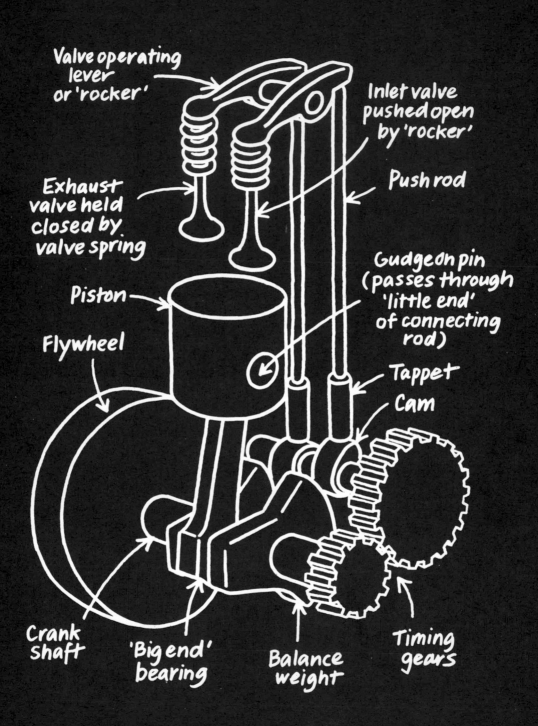

Valve operating lever or 'rocker'

Inlet valve pushed open by 'rocker'

Push rod

Exhaust valve held closed by valve spring

Gudgeon pin (passes through 'little end' of connecting rod)

Piston

Tappet

Cam

Flywheel

Crank shaft

'Big end' bearing

Balance weight

Timing gears

EXPLODED VIEW

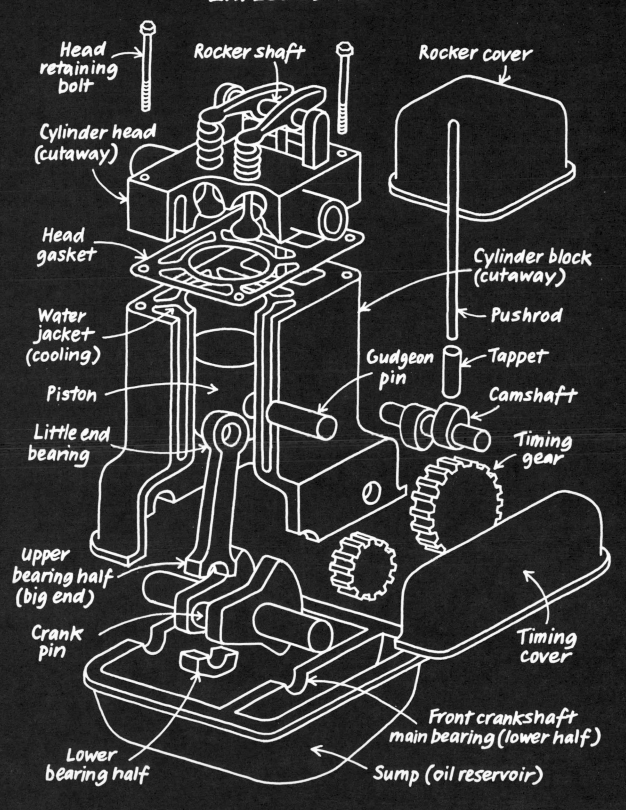

Head retaining bolt

Rocker shaft

Rocker cover

Cylinder head (cutaway)

Head gasket

Cylinder block (cutaway)

Water jacket (cooling)

Pushrod

Gudgeon pin

Tappet

Piston

Camshaft

Little end bearing

Timing gear

upper bearing half (big end)

Crank pin

Timing cover

Lower bearing half

Front crankshaft main bearing (lower half)

Sump (oil reservoir)

consideration in engine performance — efficient 'breathing' is the most challenging aspect of the engine designer's work.

For the sake of easy maintenance, our rudimentary engine would be fitted together more or less like this. The carcase or *crankcase* of the engine is a casting in aluminium or iron. The upper casting is the *cylinder head*, with the combustion chambers, cooling water passages, oilways and gas passages machined into it. The valves and their operating gear are assembled to the head, as is the earburettor and the exhaust system. The lower casting is the *cylinder block* and *crankcase*, with similar oilways and waterways and a cast-iron *liner* which forms the barrel in which the piston travels. The head bolts down directly to the cylinder block — both surfaces have to be perfectly flat to ensure that nothing leaks, either water or oil or gas pressure. In between the two is a compressible *gasket* which forms the seal. The crankshaft runs in bearings machined into the front and back of the crankcase, and an oil pan called the *sump* bolts on to the bottom of it.

Stoking It Up.

This isn't a book about the history of motor-car design, but the early pioneers genuinely did manage to crack most of the fundamental problems of operating the horseless carriage, and their prototype design is a virtually perfect practical illustration of principles that remain unchanged today. Starting from that, all the paraphernalia that you find heaped under your bonnet remains a series of refinements, though very sophisticated ones.

Imagine an orchestra, all set to play a symphony to an expectant audience, unaware that someone's pulled a Chico Marx on them and shuffled the scores with various unscheduled additions such as bits from 'Tubular Bells', 'Yankee Doodle Dandee', 'Jerusalem', the Ethiopian National Anthem and the like. Everybody's playing like true professionals should, there isn't a bum note or a missed beat to be heard but it all comes out sounding like a wagonload of drug-crazed monkeys. The design of the engine is like the score that they should have had in the first place — the idea is to get a whole collection of independent activities to happen in the right place at the right time. If the engine wears out, or gets out of adjustment, you get the wagonload of monkeys; appropriately, mechanics talk about 'tuning' an engine to get things happening in the right place at the right time again.

We've seen a simple representation of the single-cylinder engine, cranking its heavy flywheel, which lends a bit of muscle to the business of keeping the piston going. We've also seen that three out of the four strokes of the petrol engine's cycle are taken up with sucking in fuel (down), compressing it (up), and expelling it through an exhaust (also up), and only one with actually imparting a kick to the crankshaft. So the flywheel is saddled with the job of keeping the whole thing pumping for three strokes out of four, which is a considerable task for it, particularly in arduous road conditions. When Benz first got the hang of the idea, one or two horse-power was reckoned to be quite enough for any sane traveller's needs. But clearly the sensible course would be for one piston in the engine *always* to be on its power stroke while the others are busy with sucking, compressing and expelling gas. In other words, the ideal arrangement would have *four* cylinders instead of one or two, each piston taking it in turn to be on its power stroke. The flywheel could then be lightened, the flow of power would be virtually continuous. This smoothness could be further improved in six- or eight-cylinder engines — much more popular in the '20s and '30s when we didn't have to keep sending so many of those IOUs in the general direction of the Middle East.

Going back to our push-bike, it's easy to see how the crankshaft would have to be designed to cope with these additional cylinders. Imagine a three-legged race for cyclists, with two bicycles hitched together side by side like the sketch on p. 17; then take away the chain-drive and support the centre pedals on an additional bearing and you have a four-cylinder three-bearing crank-shaft, of a type to be found in many family saloons. It doesn't look much like a shaft, since it's more bent than straight, but you can see how the downward thrust of the pistons will operate a rotational pull around the centre-line. For the four-cylinder engine, two of the pistons will be at the top of their bores while the other two are at the bottom — one of the top two being on compression, the other on exhaust, one of the bottom two having just completed its induction stroke, the other its power stroke. Most modern engines arrange their 'firing order' so that the power stroke is performed by each piston in the succession of 1 (at the front of the engine) — 3 — 4 — 2; a sequence that has been found to work with the greatest smoothness and freedom from vibration.

Electrics & Ignition.

The 'nervous system' of the modern motor car is its electrical rig, and it's a much more varied and complex system than anything you'd ever find under the floorboards of your house. The back of a motor car's dashboard looks like spaghetti thrown at a wall.

Electricity is used to energize all manner of gadgets and switches on the car, including lamps, screenwipers, horns, various meters and gauges that let you know what the machine is up to. Most

BASIC AUTOMOBILE ELECTRICS

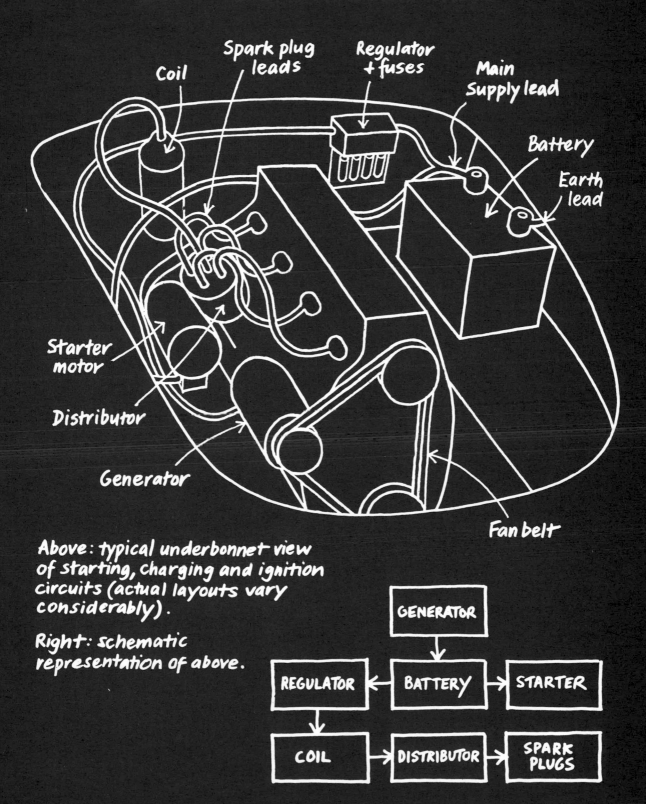

Coil · Spark plug leads · Regulator + fuses · Main Supply lead · Battery · Earth lead · Starter motor · Distributor · Generator · Fan belt

Above: typical underbonnet view of starting, charging and ignition circuits (actual layouts vary considerably).

Right: schematic representation of above.

GENERATOR

REGULATOR ← BATTERY → STARTER

COIL → DISTRIBUTOR → SPARK PLUGS

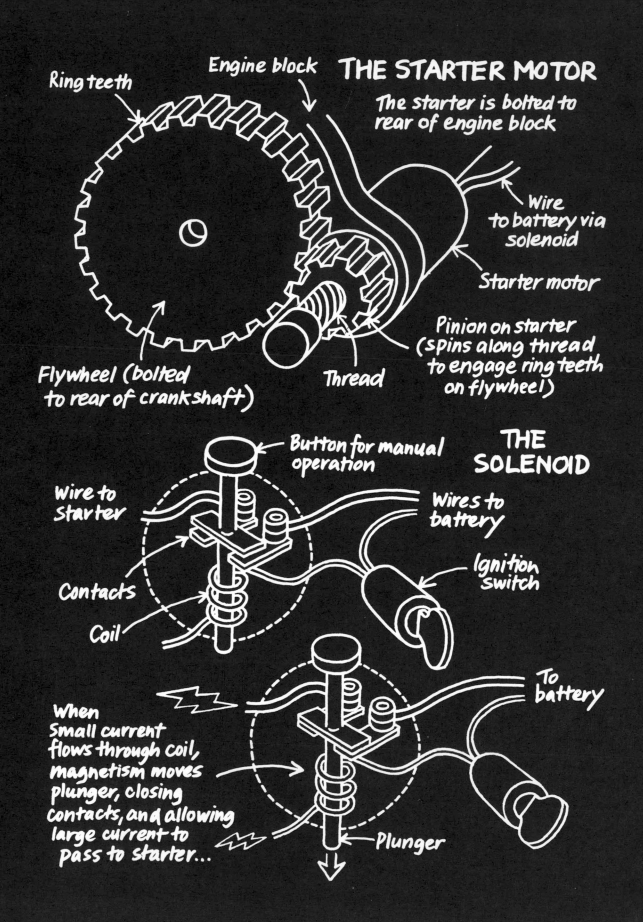

Ring teeth

Engine block

THE STARTER MOTOR

The starter is bolted to rear of engine block

Wire to battery via solenoid

Starter motor

Pinion on starter (spins along thread to engage ring teeth on flywheel)

Flywheel (bolted to rear of crankshaft)

Thread

Button for manual operation

THE SOLENOID

Wire to Starter

Wires to battery

Ignition switch

Contacts

Coil

To battery

When small current flows through coil, magnetism moves plunger, closing contacts, and allowing large current to pass to starter...

Plunger

significantly from the point of view of getting around, it provides the means by which our compressed gas is ignited.

We've already looked at the four-stroke cycle and the way in which the gas is sparked off in one cylinder after another so that a progressive flow of power is applied to the crankshaft. Depending on the number of cylinders and the design, there is an ideal 'firing order' for every kind of engine. So one of the tasks of an electric ignition system is to ensure that the production of the spark is synchronized precisely to the position of the pistons — we want it to happen when the piston is coming to the top of its compression stroke. The other job of the ignition system is to generate a spark of very high voltage from a low voltage source.

Since you can't plug your car into the mains and drive about on a cable, a lead-acid 'wet' battery is stowed somewhere on the car — it's generally a 12-volt battery these days, though some continental cars such as VWs and Renaults used 6-volt systems until recently. The battery has to be capable of providing a very high current for a short period to perform its hardest task — getting an electric motor to spin the deadweight of the crankshaft and pistons until the latter are sucking enough fuel through the carburettor for the engine to run by itself.

Batteries of course lose their power after a while and have to be recharged. For reasons we don't need to bother with, an electric motor will spin round if an appropriate current is supplied to it. If that motor is revolved by some external means, the effect will be reversed and it will *supply* a current instead. A motor used in this way is described as a *dynamo* or *generator*, and it's mounted somewhere on the carcase of the engine where it can be driven by a pulley belt off the crankshaft. This *charging circuit* is linked to a regulator that ensures that the dynamo is continually recharging the battery once the engine revolutions exceed around 1,000 per minute, but that the circuit is broken below that figure. The simple reason for this is that the battery will try to drive the dynamo as if it were an ordinary motor until the voltage from the latter is greater than that of the battery.

Modern vehicles use a more sophisticated device known as an *alternator* — producing alternating current (AC) rather than direct current (DC). The alternator provides more of a charge to the battery at the same engine speed than the dynamo, and consequently can generate current while the engine is idling. Both the alternator and dynamo produce a.c. and then rectify internally to produce d.c. and so both deliver a d.c. output.

Everything electrical travels on a sort of loop-line, though that's not perhaps the most scientific way of looking at it. But electrical energy must flow from one pole of the supply source to the other, with whatever device we want to be activated connected in between. In your home, electricity flows from the positive terminal of a plug, through the fuse (which is simply a deliberate 'weak link' that burns out and breaks the circuit if the cable overheats) through the appliance, and back to the negative terminal. In a cramped and complicated arrangement like the motor car, it's inconvenient to have a positive and negative wire passing in and out of every component, so we have the positive or feed wire alone passing to it, and use the metal frame of the car itself to act as the common 'earth return'. A main feed cable therefore runs from the battery to the live pole of the electric starter motor, another feed runs from the battery to a central distribution point which usually incorporates a fuse-board. The other terminal of the battery is simply bolted to the chassis.

Now when you get into your car and turn on the ignition, the current passes from a feed cable running to the switch through to the ignition system and the fuel pump (if the car happens to be equipped with an electric one).

What happens next involves several operations going off simultaneously so perhaps we'd better disentangle them in the approved manner — starting with what you know is happening because you can hear it, and going on to what you don't know is happening but you'd know if it wasn't. (Hmmm)

Firstly, we have to get the engine turning. As we've already seen, the pistons have to be in motion for the petrol/air mixture to get sucked into the cylinders. So we need something to act on the crankshaft to get this to happen — which used to be a swing on the crank handle by the chauffeur, but nowadays is a powerful electric motor bolted to the side of the crankcase with a toothed pinion on its revolving shaft. The pinion is able to pass up and down the shaft (as shown in the diagram) by a variety of mechanisms we'll look at in a later chapter. The idea is simply that it should slide into engagement with a ring of teeth around the rim of the flywheel, crank the engine around until it's running under its own power, and then slide out of engagement again, so that the starter motor comes to rest. This sliding-out bit is essential, because if the engine were allowed to drive the starter motor at very high rotational speeds, it would soon burn out.

So much for the part you know about. You hear this rattling tin-cans sort of noise for a bit, and then with luck the engine starts. What is also happening when you turn that key is that a current is being supplied to a device known as the ignition coil. This is the means by which our fairly impractical 12 volts is uprated by maybe a thousand times to the 10 or 15,000-volt spark that must take place in the cylinder to ignite the mixture.

A spark occurs when an electric current jumps across a gap in the conductor. A sparking plug is

THE COIL
AND HOW IT WORKS

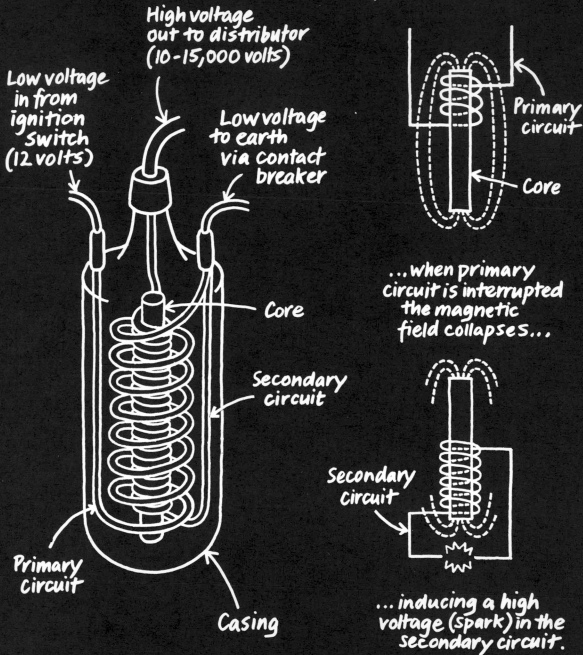

Low voltage current in primary circuit sets up field around core...

High voltage out to distributor (10-15,000 volts)

Low voltage in from ignition switch (12 volts)

Low voltage to earth via contact breaker

Primary circuit

Core

Core

Secondary circuit

Primary circuit

Casing

...when primary circuit is interrupted the magnetic field collapses...

Secondary circuit

... inducing a high voltage (spark) in the secondary circuit.

a threaded tube with a central electrode of 'live'
conductor insulated from the metal body of the plug
by a heatproof china sleeve. A brief pulse of high-
voltage electricity is fed down it. The threaded part
of the sparking plug has a small electrode positioned
something like a 25 thousandth of an inch away from
the central one, or .6 mm. The spark jumps between
the central electrode and the threaded electrode, from
which it is earthed on the metalwork of the engine.

But where do we get this high-voltage electricity
from in the first place? All we've got is a 12-volt
battery, which seems at first sight like trying to start
a fire by rubbing two sticks. The trick is to use a
device known as the *induction coil* — which consists
simply of an iron core with two coils of wire wound
around it. These are known as the *primary* and
secondary windings, the latter containing something
like a thousand times as many turns as the former.
When you turn the ignition on, a current flows
through the primary windings to earth, which sets
up a magnetic field around the core.

If we now very briefly interrupt this circuit, a
very high voltage will be momentarily induced in
the secondary windings. If we interrupt the circuit
repeatedly, like flashing a light switch on and off, we
get a regular stream of high voltage pulses from the
coil strong enough to cause a spark. If we interrupt
it at precisely the moment when each piston in the
engine is reaching its firing position, then we shall
get our regular stream of sparks exactly when required
to ignite the compressed gas.

So the principle is simple enough — an induced
high voltage or *high tension* (H.T.) spark is stepped
from a low-voltage source through a kind of trans-
former. The practical problem is how to get this
sharp interruption of the low-voltage circuit to
happen when each piston is approaching the top of
its compression stroke, and how to 'distribute' the
high voltage pulse to the right cylinders in the right
order. Both these jobs are entrusted to a device not
unreasonably called a *distributor*. This might at first
lend a bit of confusion to the proceedings, since
the low-voltage apparatus is a crucial component of
the distributor but doesn't actually have anything to
do with distributing; but for the sake of convenience,
both mechanisms have come to be described under
the same heading.

The Low-voltage Circuit.
To account for the Rapid Interruption theory, we
resort to our old engineering faithful, the cam.
What's required in this case is for a cam geared to
the motion of the engine to open and close a pair of
contacts in the primary circuit (more or less like the
contacts you find in any sort of electrical switch).
How do we gear it to the motion of the engine so
that the sparks happen when the pistons and valves
are in the right place? The crankshaft and camshaft
are the only components that 'know' all this information, so the *contact breaker* and distributor
mechanism is generally run off the latter by means
of a *skew* gear.

Clearly, if the contact breaker cam is to break
the primary circuit four, six or eight times (i.e.
according to the number of cylinders) for every
complete revolution of the drive spindle as spun
by the camshaft, its shape will have to incorporate
the appropriate number of protrusions or
lobes. In other words, for a four-cylinder engine
the cam end of the distributor spindle will be
getting on for square in section, with the lobes at
the 'corners', for a six-cylinder it will be six-sided.
The gearing of the distributor to the camshaft
is designed so that each lobe of the cam pushes
the contact mechanism (generally known as
the *points*) apart at exactly the moment when each
piston is arriving at its firing position (when the
points are apart a spark will be induced). One of the
contacts is fixed to the base plate of the distributor. The other contact is pivoted, and attached to
a fibre 'heel' that bears against the rotating cam.
When one of the cam lobes pushes against the heel,
the contact points are separated. As the cam rotates
further, the 'corner' falls away allowing the heel to
slip back under pressure from a spring blade, and the
points close. This will happen four, six or eight times
per revolution of the distributor spindle, depending
on the engine design. The gap between the contact
points when they're fully open is crucial to the
proper tuning of the engine. Clearly the further
apart they are, the longer they'll spend open, and
vice versa — though this is only a matter of fractions
of a second, too wide or too narrow a gap will
seriously affect the strength of the spark induced at
the coil, and consequently upset performance. So
'setting the points gap' is one of the familiar and
routine exercises in car maintenance.

The low-voltage circuit needs one extra gadget
to compensate for a snag in the way that the induction
coil works. That big burst of current in the secondary
windings when the spark is created sends a pulse
back down the system 'against the tide', as it were;
if this weren't suppressed somehow, there would
be a lot of extra sparking across the contact
breaker when it's not required. A device like a radio
interference suppressor called a *condenser* is therefore connected across the points to act as a buffer
against this reversing effect and momentarily 'store'
the sparks. Though the main advantage of this
arrangement is to ensure that a well-defined change in
the magnetic field at the coil occurs (establishing a
powerful spark) without a lot of subsidiary and
obstructive electrical activity flying about, the
condenser also prevents the condition of the contact
points from deteriorating too rapidly. Excessive
burning of points is almost always due to a faulty
condenser.

You should be able to follow the path of the

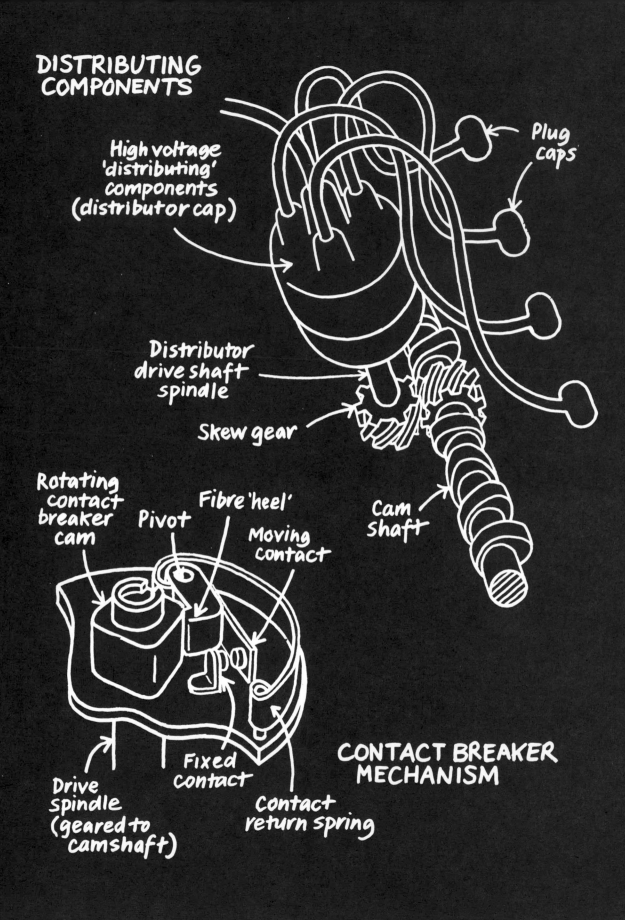

DISTRIBUTING COMPONENTS

High voltage 'distributing' components (distributor cap)

Plug caps

Distributor drive shaft spindle

Skew gear

Cam shaft

Rotating contact breaker cam

Pivot

Fibre 'heel'

Moving contact

Drive spindle (geared to camshaft)

Fixed contact

Contact return spring

CONTACT BREAKER MECHANISM

DISTRIBUTOR COMPONENTS
WITH DISTRIBUTOR CAP SUPERIMPOSED

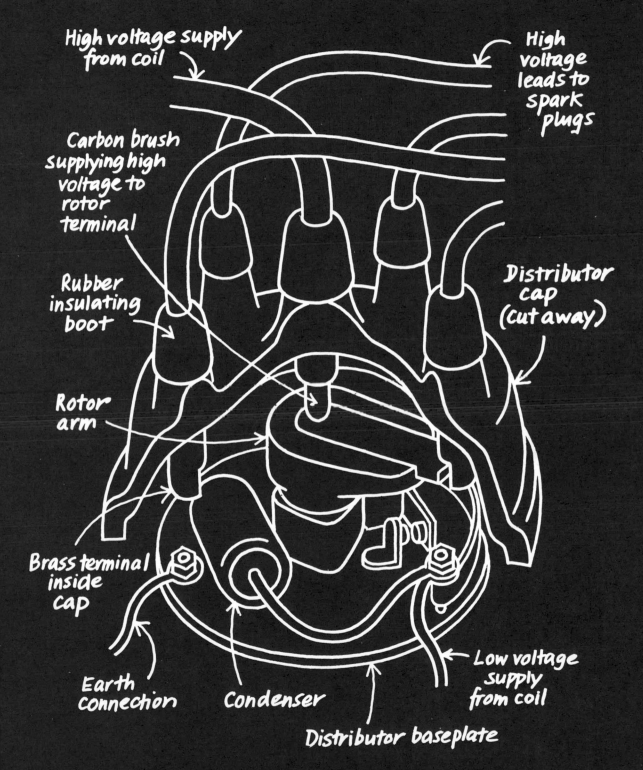

High voltage supply from coil

High voltage leads to spark plugs

Carbon brush supplying high voltage to rotor terminal

Rubber insulating boot

Distributor cap (cut away)

Rotor arm

Brass terminal inside cap

Earth Connection

Condenser

Low voltage supply from coil

Distributor baseplate

IGNITION SYSTEM CIRCUIT DIAGRAM

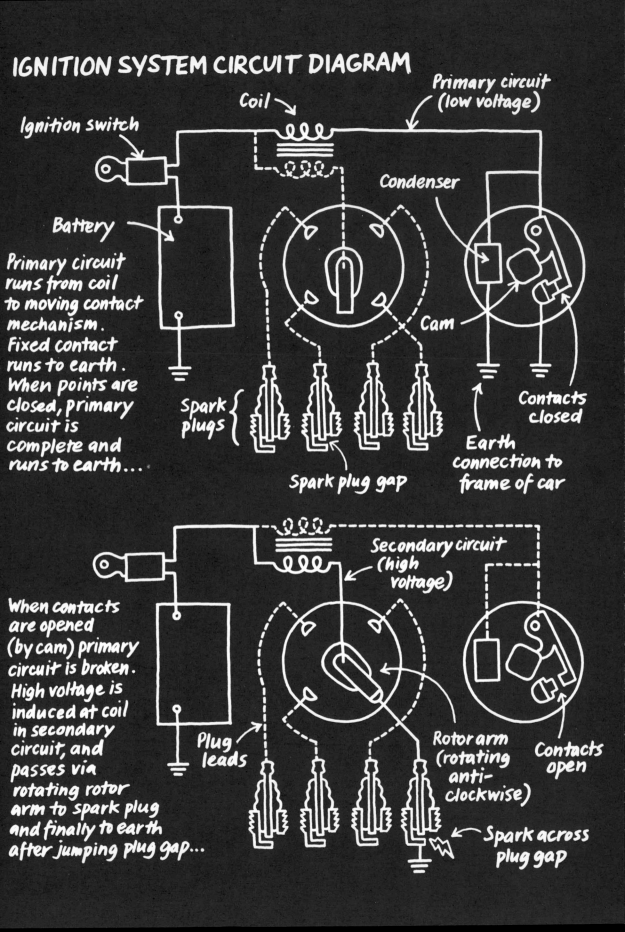

Coil

Primary circuit (low voltage)

Ignition switch

Condenser

Battery

Primary circuit runs from coil to moving contact mechanism. Fixed contact runs to earth. When points are closed, primary circuit is complete and runs to earth...

Cam

Spark plugs

Spark plug gap

Contacts closed

Earth connection to frame of car

Secondary circuit (high voltage)

When contacts are opened (by cam) primary circuit is broken. High voltage is induced at coil in secondary circuit, and passes via rotating rotor arm to spark plug and finally to earth after jumping plug gap...

Plug leads

Rotor arm (rotating anti-clockwise)

Contacts open

Spark across plug gap

low-voltage ignition circuit on the simple circuit diagram illustrated.

Big Bang Theory — The Secondary Circuit.
So the contact breaker cam is whirling round, triggering off a stream of sparks from the secondary windings of the induction coil. These sparks now need to be delivered in the correct firing order to each cylinder in turn. The most sensible way of arranging this is for the sparks to be fed to a rotating blade which can send them one at a time to a ring of contacts, each one connected to a sparking plug. Though it would be possible to have a completely separate distribution device to do this, it's much more convenient to pack it all into the same unit, since the low-voltage circuit already uses a drive shaft connected to the camshaft and making one complete revolution per cycle of the engine.

The rotating blade or *rotor arm* therefore fits on to the distributor drive spindle above the cam and contact-breaker mechanism. It's simply a bakelite moulding with a brass terminal running across the top of it. Since the whole idea is that the spark should only jump to earth when it reaches the plug in the cylinder, the rotor is naturally made of non-conductive material so that the spark doesn't earth itself down the metalwork of the distributor. (This sometimes happens if the rotor arm gets cracked. and the engine either misfires, or won't run at all.)

Clipped on top of the whole distributor mechanism, rotor and all, is a moulded bakelite cover, with a ring of brass contacts arranged around the inside, very close to the arc swept by the rotor arm. Fed into the centre of the cover is a high-voltage lead from the induction coil, which acts as the main 'spark-feed', and the sparks travel down a little sprung carbon brush which takes them on to the brass part of the rotor. Running from each terminal around the circumference of the distributor cover is another high-voltage lead which takes the spark to each plug. The ring of terminals is arranged according to the firing order of the engine. As the distributor mechanism spins, the continual interruption of the low-voltage circuit generates a stream of sparks from the coil to the central distributor terminal, and thus via the rotor arm to each sparking plug in turn.

In principle this is all there is to it. The contact-breaker mechanism establishes a fat spark at the coil from a sharp interruption of the low-voltage circuit and the distributor delivers it in sequence to the plugs when each of their pistons is at top dead centre or thereabouts.

When you get around to actually running the car, the distributor has to be a bit more flexible than this. To get the hang of the reason why, it's necessary to consider a spark as being something that takes time to do its job, rather than being such an infinitesimally short-lived event as to be not worth worrying about. Sparks across airgaps actually

happen in two stages. The first is the briefest, and called the *capacity* stage, lasting about a hundred-thousandth of a second. The second stage is the *inductive* stage, which actually makes the blue flash that you can see when testing plugs; this lasts for around a thousandth of a second. If you add this time-lapse to the amount of time that it takes for the 'flame-front' of the burning petrol vapour to consume all the compressed gas in the cylinder, it adds up to an appreciable total. If the firing of the plug were *always* at top dead centre on the compression stroke we should find that, while this might work all right at low engine speeds, once the car was travelling fast there wouldn't be enough time for the combustion of the fuel to be effective. The piston would already be halfway down the cylinder on the power stroke before a proper kick had been imparted to it by the expansion of the gas — so, as the revs increased, the engine would be progressively losing power.

So it's necessary to arrange for the spark to arrive at the plug earlier and earlier as the engine speed rises: called *advancing* the ignition timing. On early cars there was no means of bringing this about automatically, and drivers used to have a hand-operated ignition control mounted on the steering column — you would retard the ignition when climbing a hill, and advance it again once the car started to pick up speed on the flat. (When you come to think of all the things that had to be done simultaneously on veteran cars, it's a miracle their owners ever got out of their driveways.)

A simple method for getting the ignition advance to take care of itself is to fit the contact breaker cam to the drive spindle with a bit of slack in either direction so that the cam can slightly change its position in relation to the spindle. You then hook the cam to a pair of weights and — following much the same course as the conker you whirled around your head as a child — the weights swing outwards as the engine drives the distributor faster and twist the cam forward a little so that it opens the points earlier. As the engine slows, it twists back the other way to 'retard' the ignition.

Many cars are fitted with a centrifugal advance mechanism alone. Since it's designed to produce the optimum ignition advance for full throttle running, it isn't sensitive to the difference between an engine cruising at 2,000 r.p.m. in top gear with very little pressure on the throttle pedal and one slogging away at 2,000 r.p.m. up an incline with the throttle pedal on the floorboards. Because although engine speed is an important factor in determining at what point the spark ought to occur, there are others such as the amount of mixture that has to be ignited and its rate of flow into the engine, and the temperature and turbulence inside the combustion chambers. In the case of the car cruising on a flat road the speed with which the flame consumes the mixture is slowed down because *temperature and*

Cam

Contact breaker and distributor base plate

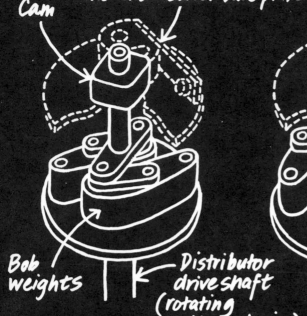

Bob weights

Distributor drive shaft (rotating anti-clockwise)

When drive shaft rotates faster, bob weights swing outwards— pulling cam round in relation to shaft.

(When shaft slows down, return springs pull weights back)

Pipe connected to inlet manifold

Contact breaker and distributor base plate

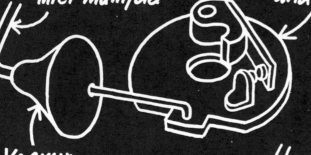

Vacuum advance diaphragm

At part throttle the pressure in the inlet manifold (and pipe) decreases...

...the suction pulls on the diaphragm...

VACUUM ADVANCE MECHANISM

...the diaphragm in turn pulls the contact breaker around in relation to the cam, so 'advancing' the spark.

mass flow are dropping — so although the centrifugal advance doesn't 'think' so, a substantial advance in the timing would help the performance.

The reason for the 'slow flame' flame spread is that most manufacturers use a lean mixture for cruise conditions — this "lean" mixture is slow burning. For this reason a suction operated or *vacuum advance* mechanism is often included as well. It's simply a lever attached to the contact breaker baseplate and pulled or released by a diaphragm attached to the inlet air pipe between the carburettor and the engine. With the accelerator barely depressed, the suction in the pipe will be high because the throttle plate in the carburettor is virtually closing the cylinders from the atmosphere. With the accelerator depressed the vacuum drops and the timing is retarded.

Fuel.

Pretty well everything liquid that's used in a motor car — except water, that is — is derived from crude oils. This is the brown muck that comes out of the ground as a hydrogen/carbon compound or hydrocarbon. Refining this stuff gives us petrol (the hydrocarbon derivative with the lowest boiling point), white spirits, gas oils and lubricating oils. The advantage of petrol is that it will vaporize easily at normal temperatures.

Not all internal combustion engines run on petrol, but the majority of conventional production cars do, and petrols are supplied in various grades according to the characteristics of your particular engine. Not that there's any such thing as cheap petrol today, but there are at least various grades of exorbitance. The variations between petrols (expressed as an octane number, or more popularly a star-rating) depend on their *resistance to detonation* — in other words, on how successful they are at avoiding catching fire of their own accord, simply as a result of an abrupt rise in pressure and consequent temperature rise. Engines with very high compression ratios (that is, with a small combustion space in relation to the volume of the cylinder when the piston is at top dead centre) need a 'high octane' fuel with a lot of resistance to spontaneous detonation. Ideal combustion circumstances would have the 'flame-front' advancing from the sparking plug smoothly across the petrol vapour, exerting a progressive push on the piston. When the petrol in use is too unstable for the engine, the mixture explodes abruptly and violently instead, and the shock wave in the cylinder can be heard as a metallic rattling noise during hard acceleration — known as 'pinking'. The petrol might of course be pre-ignited for other reasons such as local overheating, or unsuitable plugs.

Striking A Balance: Mixture Strength.
Different hydrocarbon fuels therefore have different proportions of hydrogen and carbon in their chemical make-up. When the hydrocarbons burn — and like anything else, they will only burn in the presence of air — the compound splits so that the carbon combines with the surrounding oxygen to form carbon dioxide, the hydrogen with the oxygen to form water. Without turning all this into a chemistry seminar, you can see how it might be possible for a chemist to calculate exactly how much air a hydrocarbon compound needs for all the carbon and all the hydrogen to be burned — once it's known what the composition of the particular hydrocarbon is. From the point of view of running an internal combustion engine, this means that a chemically correct ratio of fuel to air can be worked out as soon as it's been decided what type of fuel should be used. Paraffins, for instance, would generally require an air/fuel ratio of something like fifteen to one, measured by weight. Benzenes around thirteen and a half to one. Alcohols as low as seven to one. Commercial petrols are blended from these components and a ratio of between fourteen and a half to fifteen to one is generally taken to be the average for a production car. Racing fuels with much higher alcohol contents are used in much stronger — or 'richer' — mixtures, this being a case where brute force and not economy is at a premium. So while people generally think of petrol as making the bang that shoves the plug down the tube, you don't pour tumblerfuls of the stuff into the cylinders and expect anything dramatic to happen.

But in a practical motor car engine, operating under continually changing conditions of temperature and load, it would be impossible to stick to this theoretically correct mixture all the time. It would be OK for light-load running on a flat surface, but it would make the car sluggish in acceleration and impossible to start from cold.

The *carburettor*, therefore, is a sort of dietician for the engine — it stops it over-indulging, but doesn't let it starve. A device for metering the ratio of fuel to air, the carburettor is sensitive enough to changes in the running conditions to provide an appropriate mixture whether starting from cold, idling in traffic jams, abruptly accelerating or cruising on a motorway. Up to now in our consideration of the engine, we've only briefly looked at it simply as a means of vaporizing petrol. In the very early engines this was more or less what it was, but in modern engines — to combine the features of power and economy — carburettors are now among the most sophisticated instruments to be found on the car. Paul Jennings once wrote that he thought carburettors were probably made by watchmakers in their spare time, but as things have turned out, some ultra-modern fuel supply systems are more likely to have been dreamed up by Einstein's descendents. There are nowadays two principal ways in which fuel can travel to the combustion

PRINCIPLE OF CARBURETTORS

Because of the partial vacuum in the air intake, air pressure forces fuel from reservoir to intake via spray tube

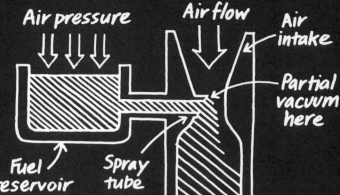

Air pressure

Air flow

Air intake

Partial vacuum here

Fuel reservoir

Spray tube

SIMPLE DOWNDRAUGHT CARBURETTOR

When the level in the float chamber drops, the float falls to allow more fuel in from petrol pump

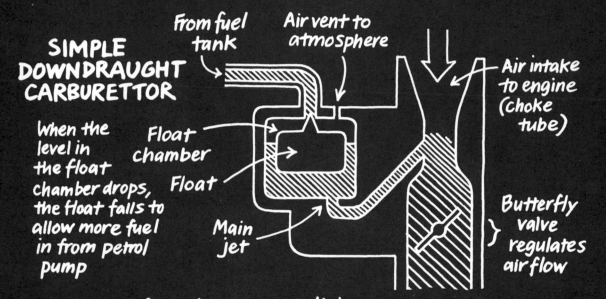

From fuel tank

Air vent to atmosphere

Air intake to engine (choke tube)

Float chamber

Float

Main jet

Butterfly valve regulates air flow

Some air enters through capacity well, and mixes with fuel

Main air flow

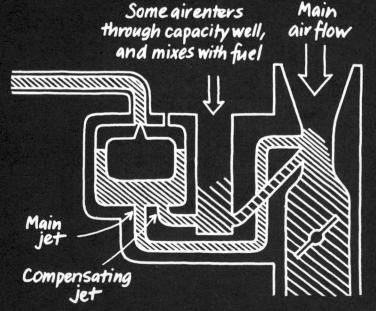

OPERATION OF CAPACITY WELL

As the engine speeds up, more air is drawn in through the capacity well, progressively weakening the mixture

Main jet

Compensating jet

chambers. One is the method of the traditional carburettor, using the action of the engine's pistons as a suction pump to draw fuel from a reservoir, the amount of fuel supplied being metered simply by the size of the aperture through which it's being pulled. The alternative is fuel-injection synchronized to the valve timing by electronics; this increases power by reducing the restrictions on the 'breathing' of the engine, and spreads the fuel more evenly between the cylinders. It's a costly gadget though, and for our purposes an understanding of a normal carburation system is quite enough.

Put at its simplest, if you introduce a small-bore tube with a constant level of fuel in it into an air-stream, the air will naturally tend to suck the fuel from the tube and atomize it into droplets. To maintain the level in the tube, you need some sort of constant-level supply system as well — exactly like the cold water tank in your house, or the cistern in your loo. The carburettor's cistern is the float chamber, a plastic float setting the level and a tapered rod or needle valve on top of it plugging up the inlet pipe once that level has been reached. In this system, as the fluid drops in use, the float goes down, more fluid is admitted until the level is restored again. All carburettors have a float chamber somewhere nowadays, almost invariably in one piece with the rest of the instrument.

Getting back to the engine, if we place a tube at the port controlled by the inlet valve, air will be sucked through it as the valve opens and the piston descends on its induction stroke. If the cylinder were 3″ in diameter and the distance the piston travelled downwards were 4″, then a typical design would make the air-tube around 1″ in diameter — the relationships between these dimensions decide what the speed of the air flow will be for any given engine speed. If the engine were running at 2,000 revolutions per minute, the velocity of the air through the pipe would be around 200 feet per second.

You still wouldn't get much suction from this situation, as far as pulling petrol through nozzles goes. So where the nozzle from the fuel supply protrudes into the air-tube, we constrict the tube to half its regular diameter. This constriction-point is called the *venturi* or *choke* — so you can see it doesn't necessarily mean the thing you pull out on the dashboard when you want to start a cold engine. The effect of this constriction is to speed up the air flow by around four times — and when you establish this abrupt stepping up of the airspeed, its pressure just as abruptly falls, which is what creates the suction over the petrol nozzle. At the other end of the fuel supply, in the float chamber, atmospheric pressure is pushing on the surface of the petrol; and when the pressure at the nozzle end gets below this, the petrol starts to flow, broken up into a fine spray. How much of this mixture gets into the engine is controlled by a hinged flap called the

throttle plate or *butterfly valve* which simply varies the size of the air intake and is hooked to the pedal under your right foot.

The nozzle is now described as the *spray tube* and the amount of petrol passing through it can be simply metered according to the designer's specification for the size of the main jet at the bottom of the float chamber. At any given running speed of the engine, there's only one way on this crude device that you could drastically enrich the mixture for cold starting — that would be by simply covering the air intake with the palm of your hand so that the engine pulls virtually neat petrol. In the good old days, this was exactly what you did, though it denied you the luxury of starting your car from the comfort of the driving seat.

You'd think perhaps that this sort of arrangement would provide exactly the sort of flexibility required by our engine in adapting to varying performance conditions. The engine speeds up, the flow of air around the jet speeds up, more fuel is drawn in to match the increased volume of air. No such luck. Due to a fiendish twist of the laws of physics, this isn't precisely what happens because the *speed* with which the air flows into the engine isn't matched by the *quantity* of air drawn in — put roughly, the velocity of the air rises faster than the density. So if we laboriously figure out an appropriate diameter for both the choke tube and the main jet so that we get our compromise mixture of 15 lb of air to 1 lb of petrol at half-throttle, we find that on opening the throttle further and speeding up the air flow, the proportion of petrol in the mixture is continually catching up on the air flow — so the ratio might change at full throttle to maybe 12:1 or richer still. Under many operating conditions, this is the reverse of what the car actually needs, since it may be more appropriate to have a rich mixture at *slow* engine speeds, and a weak one at high speeds.

The simple jet we've seen so far increases its spray of fuel as the 'choke depression' increases — a tragic-sounding condition which actually means the vacuum induced by the descending piston. The carburettor designers had to address themselves to defying apparent logic — to come up with a jet that would be inversely affected by engine speed, and actually *weaken* the mixture the faster the engine was running. The answer was for the engine to be pulling something other than 'pure' petrol — a kind of soda water of petrol and air that had already been mingled somewhere else.

The trick is to 'break' the flow between the float chamber and the choke tube with an additional chamber or 'capacity well', open to the atmosphere and consequently upsetting the potential suction pulled by the engine. In the simple main jet system, the flow of the air past the jet can pull *only* petrol from the float chamber. In the *compensating* (or *submerged*) jet system, the air flow pulls *both* petrol from the float chamber *and* more air from the intervening well, rather as if you were sucking on a straw in an almost empty glass, and as the speed rises will find it easier to suck air through the well rather than petrol through the jet. If the compensating jet and the flow behaviour of the orthodox jet are combined into one carburettor, an appropriate mixture-strength is maintained at all air flow velocities, weakening as the choke depression rises.

In this sort of carburettor, the mechanism is capable of metering the petrol flow according to the size of the jet diameters, but if it were possible also to vary the *air* flow through the capacity well it would become an instrument of much greater flexibility. Looking at the illustration, you can visualize what the effect would be if you closed off the mouth of the well — the 'flow-interruption' would be ended, the well would fill with petrol up to the float chamber level, and we'd be back where we started with the simple main jet. But if you *partially* closed it, then the petrol flow would certainly rise with the engine speed as if we were at square one but not to the same degree as in the former case; this is due to the fact that *some* air would still be mixing with it through the capacity well.

Once again, this has the makings of an ideal combination of the habits of the simple jet and the compensating jet combined into one, but the air flow through the now restricted well opening would still tend to fall behind the main flow through the choke so we'd still be stuck with the remnants of the earlier problem. So one further refinement is necessary to make this set-up the perfect compromise. Something is going to have to progressively *enlarge* the mouth of the capacity well as the engine accelerates. This is effected by means of an 'emulsion tube'. (Not a carriage full of housepainters but a tube a bit like a penny whistle with holes drilled in it at different levels.) In this arrangement, now that the nozzle of the capacity well is narrower than before (turning it into what's known as an 'air bleed') the air flow through it is slower, so the petrol level is able to rise higher in the well — though such air pressure as there is prevents it from rising to the float chamber level. As the engine speeds up and more air is pulled into the well, the petrol level there is forced to drop. This uncovers another ring of holes in the emulsion tube, so more air is able to pass through them into the mixture drawn into the engine. The flow rate is now *precisely* synchronized to engine speed, and refinements of this arrangement form the basis of all Solex and Weber carburettors, and a good many manufactured by the Zenith company.

Starting, Idling & Acceleration.

That business of putting your hand over the air intake was no joke, all the best carburettor makers incorporated it into their designs in the form of a flap or *strangler* (what you normally think of as 'the choke') which could drastically restrict the proportion of air in the starting mixture. Some Solex and Weber models use a *starter carburettor* which augments the main instrument when the engine is cold. By arranging for its spray nozzle to project into the choke tube *downstream* of the throttle butterfly — in other words between the throttle and the cylinders — the starting circuit can make use of the very considerable suction in this region when the throttle is all but shut (see p. 38 on manifold vacuum, etc.).

Additional jet and air bleed systems are built in to meter the correct mixture for the idling engine — and the design has to be very thorough to successfully bridge the gap between these 'pilot' jets fading out and the main jets coming into operation. On top of this, the carburettor generally includes an *acceleration pump* nowadays, to squirt a jet of neat petrol into the choke tube when the accelerator is abruptly snapped open and thus avoid hesitation. The pump is usually a diaphragm or a spring-loaded valve attached to the accelerator linkage.

In a carburettor like this, which requires a lot of different passages and apertures all doing a relay race with each other to keep pace with the demands of the engine, you can't make any alterations to it while driving, except by manipulating the throttle and the cold-starting device. Some carburettors greatly simplify the whole business by enabling both the size of the choke tube and the size of the petrol jet to be continually varied; in fact the petrol jet aperture can be expanded or shrunk simply by the air flow through the carburettor itself. The most famous version of this elegant idea is the S.U. sidedraught carburettor, which has followed a virtually unchanged design since W.O. Bentley's green monsters were carrying off the honours at Le Mans in the 'twenties.

Being a sidedraught design, the choke tube is horizontal or at 90° to the engine — as opposed to the *downdraught* types we've already looked at in which the choke is vertical. This is helpful for the air flow since it prevents the mixture having to turn too many corners getting into the engine. The jet is mounted in the base of the tube, and can be moved up and down by a lever attached to the rich mixture control in the car. A tapered needle sits in the mouth of the jet, screwed to the bottom of a piston, which is a close fit in the bottle shape of the suction chamber above it. A small passageway is drilled between the underside of the piston and the upper side.

As the throttle is opened, air is sucked out of the space *above* the piston through this passageway. The resulting vacuum in the upper space lets the piston rise, taking the tapered needle with it —

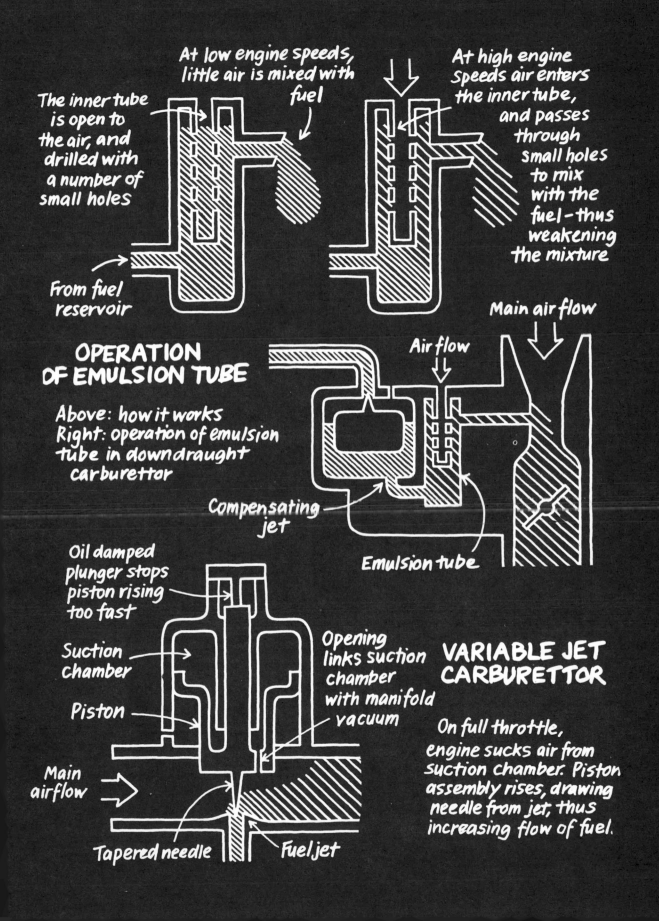

The inner tube is open to the air, and drilled with a number of small holes

At low engine speeds, little air is mixed with fuel

At high engine speeds air enters the inner tube, and passes through small holes to mix with the fuel – thus weakening the mixture

From fuel reservoir

OPERATION OF EMULSION TUBE

Above: how it works
Right: operation of emulsion tube in downdraught carburettor

Main air flow

Air flow

Compensating jet

Emulsion tube

Oil damped plunger stops piston rising too fast

Suction chamber

Piston

Main airflow

Opening links suction chamber with manifold vacuum

Tapered needle

Fuel jet

VARIABLE JET CARBURETTOR

On full throttle, engine sucks air from suction chamber. Piston assembly rises, drawing needle from jet, thus increasing flow of fuel.

this opens the aperture of the jet and pulls more fuel into the airstream.

Unlike the highly complicated fixed choke types — which actually resemble a collection of little carburettors in one instrument, each of them with an appropriate contribution to make to particular running conditions either singly or in tandem — the variable choke carburettor establishes one direct relationship between the air flow and the rate of fuel flow. The idea of the rising and falling piston is designed to stabilize a constant airspeed over the jet nozzle so that the suction effect on the jet is more or less steady regardless of the speed of the engine; so, when the engine is idling, the piston falls and restricts the bore of the choke to maintain a very high level of suction over the petrol jet. The enrichment needed for sudden acceleration is achieved by the oil-filled damper in the crown of the dome — if you snap the throttle open suddenly, the piston is prevented from rising too sharply, so you get a momentary enrichment just when you need it.

So the variable choke carburettor, with just one jet and one device to vary the constriction in the choke tube, is able automatically to provide the correct mixture for idling, acceleration and full-throttle running; the cold-start device involves simply lowering the jet assembly so that there's a greater clearance between the jet and the needle, enabling more fuel to pass. How does the S.U. carburettor overcome the earlier problem of how to get a weak mixture for high-speed cruising? A fortunate coincidence exists between the engine's natural behaviour and the design of the S.U. Remember that the vapour flow isn't going into all the cylinders at once, but one at a time in a regular pattern. This establishes a pulsating wave-formation in the passages between the carburettor and the valves. For some reason, a pulsating air flow makes the fuel flow quicker than if the air were steady. With the throttle wide open and the engine at full belt, the petrol jet is exposed to the full effect of the pulsations and a rich mixture results, which is appropriate for hard driving. With the engine running fast but the throttle partially shut and restricting the choke tube, the pulsations are effectively screened from the jet — consequently a steadier air flow passes over it and a weaker mixture ensues.

Not all engines are equally obliging in this respect — six-cylinder engines are not as good at it as four-cylinder ones. So some S.U. carburettors include a vacuum-operated economy device which reduces the air pressure in the float chamber according to the throttle position, and consequently the degree of pressure-drop between the float chamber and the jet. The result, once again, is that less fuel flows from the jet.

The Stromberg C.D. (Constant-Depression) carburettor is another popular variable-choke type,

broadly similar in operation to the S.U. The principal difference is that, while a piston rises and falls in the choke tube according to air flow rate, its movement is controlled by a flexible diaphragm mounted in the suction chamber.

Automatic Chokes.

Some cars are fitted with automatic provision for cold-starting, usually described as 'automatic chokes'. In the variation fitted to the Solex carburettor supplied for Volkswagens, the strangler-flap linkage is designed with a number of 'steps' so that the strangler can click its way through various degrees of restriction from fully closed to fully open as the engine warms up. The device is set up by depressing the accelerator once before starting the engine — this shuts the strangler. From then on a thermostatic device senses the engine temperature and progressively reopens it to allow more air into the mixture. All automatic chokes rely on a thermostat hooked to whatever cold-start arrangement the particular carburettor possesses.

Except on very high performance engines, which need the minimum possible restriction of their air flow, air cleaners are fitted to the intake of carburettors to prevent grit and dirt passing into the cylinders. Nowadays these usually take the form of a filter paper element rather like the oil filter, replaceable at service intervals. Some cars adopt the oil bath method—which consists basically of a wire strainer soaked in engine oil. The only maintenance required is to clean it out and replenish the oil periodically.

Fuel Supply.

Originally the fuel was fed from the tank to the float chamber simply by stationing the former above carburettor level and letting the one drain into the other — a 'gravity feed' system just like your household plumbing. Eventually it was concluded by a few charred experimenters that, with sparks liable to hurtle around the engine compartment if anything was amiss with the ignition system, it would be better to put the tank at the back of the car and pump the fuel to the front.

The principle of pumps is similar wherever they be. You have a pump in the space between your head and your navel, with a membrane or diaphragm stretched across the bottom of it. As you lower the diaphragm breathing in, you create an area of low pressure in your lungs — the air floating around your head being at normal atmospheric pressure, it all immediately sets off at a great rate for your lungs in an attempt to 'fill up' the space. Pumps do the same thing, but in the case of petrol the idea is to transport fluid from one place to another; fuel pumps have a flexible diaphragm too, pushed and pulled either by a lever off the camshaft of the engine or by a kind of electric motor. The pump

MECHANICAL FUEL PUMPS

When the diaphragm moves downwards, fuel is drawn into the pump through a non-return valve. When the diaphragm moves upwards, fuel is forced out of the pump through another valve.

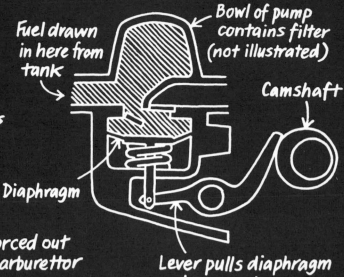

Fuel drawn in here from tank

Bowl of pump contains filter (not illustrated)

Camshaft

Diaphragm

Lever pulls diaphragm downwards

Fuel forced out → to carburettor

Spring pushes diaphragm upwards

ELECTRIC FUEL PUMPS

Electric pumps work on similar principle, except that action of diaphragm is controlled by an electromagnet instead of the cam – so pump can be positioned practically anywhere

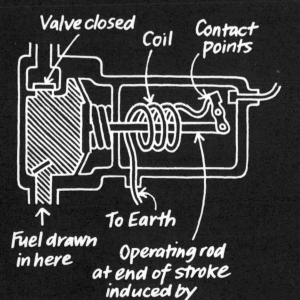

Valve closed

Coil

Contact Points

Fuel drawn in here

To Earth

Operating rod at end of stroke induced by electromagnet

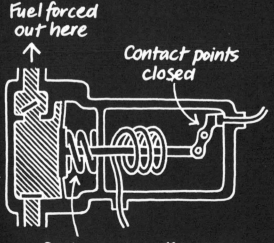

Fuel forced out here

Contact points closed

Spring pushes diaphragm forwards, also closing contact so that cycle can start again

also requires a valve in the inlet from the tank and one in the outlet to the carburettor so that the flow of petrol can't change its direction and go back the way it came.

The mechanical pump is bolted to the crankcase next to the camshaft, so that the operating lever can be rocked by the rotation of the cam. The rubber diaphragm is pulled downwards, so petrol is sucked through the inlet pipe, strained through the filter, passes through the non-return valve and, as the diaphragm rises again, it pushes the fuel through the outlet valve to the carburettor float chamber. When the float chamber is full, the pressure in the outlet pipe prevents the diaphragm from rising again; a double action lever mechanism means that the lever just flaps up and down aimlessly as the cam rotates until the diaphragm is free to rise again.

Spreading It Around.

Depending on the design, there may be one carburettor doing all this work of varying the 'diet' of fuel according to how fast the engine's 'muscles' are working, or there may be several. A single carburettor has some disadvantages, particularly on bigger engines, causing relatively poor mixture distribution between the cylinders and having insufficient capacity for high power requirements. But production engines, even big ones, don't generally have more than three carburettors. This naturally means that the flow of petrol vapour doesn't travel straight from the choke into the combustion chamber but has to travel through an *inlet manifold* which spreads the fuel more or less evenly between however many cylinders there are. It's more or less like a gallery, entered by a single door (for a single carburettor type), opening out into several rooms. This is clearly a tricky matter. If two cylinders, for instance, were receiving an 11:1 mixture and the other two were getting 14:1, the running of the engine, particularly when idling, would naturally be less than perfect.

Inside the body of the carburettor itself, we've already seen that the spray of fuel, though finely atomized, still isn't quite a vapour but more of a suspension of droplets in the airstream. We've also seen that petrol is a blend of various elements of hydrocarbons, some of them vaporizing (or 'flashing off', as the trade engagingly puts it) more readily than others. Heat naturally has a lot to do with vaporizing the petrol. So does the 'choke depression' or degree of suction pulled by the engine itself.

You only need to take an electric cleaner to a carpet to know what vacuum is. If you suck the air out of a container so that the pressure in it falls below that of the atmosphere, air is always trying to rush into it from a region where the pressure is normal. In the case of the car engine

running at medium revs with the accelerator only partly depressed, the suction created in the inlet manifold by the moving pistons isn't destroyed by the air flow coming in through the carburettor because the position of the throttle butterfly is stopping most of it from getting in. So there will be a region of high vacuum or low air pressure in the space between the throttle butterfly and the cylinders, in other words within the inlet manifold itself. These would be the sort of conditions you'd expect at a steady slowish speed on the flat in top gear. And under these conditions, petrol vaporizes easily, and the inside walls of the manifold will be dry.

If you suddenly put your foot down, the air pressure in the manifold rises rapidly because the throttle 'gate' from the outside atmosphere to the engine is suddenly swung open. The manifold walls than blot up a lot of the wet mixture flowing in, at least up to the point where they're saturated, and this momentarily starves the combustion chambers of fresh petrol. The result is a hesitation in acceleration or a 'flat spot'. Inlet manifolds between the carburettor and the valves are generally designed with sharp bends in them — to 'bounce' the fuel droplets back off the walls into the airstream. So, paradoxically, a streamlined arrangement for getting gas into the engine doesn't provide the advantage you might anticipate. It's helpful in terms of air flow but not in terms of fuel flow; which factor has the priority depends on the uses to which the engine is likely to be put.

Exhaust Systems.

Streamlining of the pipework certainly is an advantage, however, when it comes to getting the waste gases out of the engine. The faster they leave, the less contamination there is of the incoming fresh fuel. On top of that, since the 'overlapped' valve timing used on most cars means that the inlet valve generally starts opening just before the exhaust valve has completely closed, the incoming mixture can help to 'scavenge' the waste gas out of the chamber. Reducing back-pressure in the exhaust system cuts the hold-ups in this gas flow to a minimum.

Nevertheless, making a really scientific use of the relationship of the exhaust to engine performance is only fully exploited in racing vehicles, since they don't have to worry about how much row they make. Production cars are now very strictly limited by both pollution and noise regulations, so that exhaust design has become a much more considered business than it used to be.

A silencer box or muffler that will blanket the noise of the combustion process normally contains a series of strategically placed obstructions within an oblong box called the *expansion chamber* so that

INLET & EXHAUST MANIFOLDS

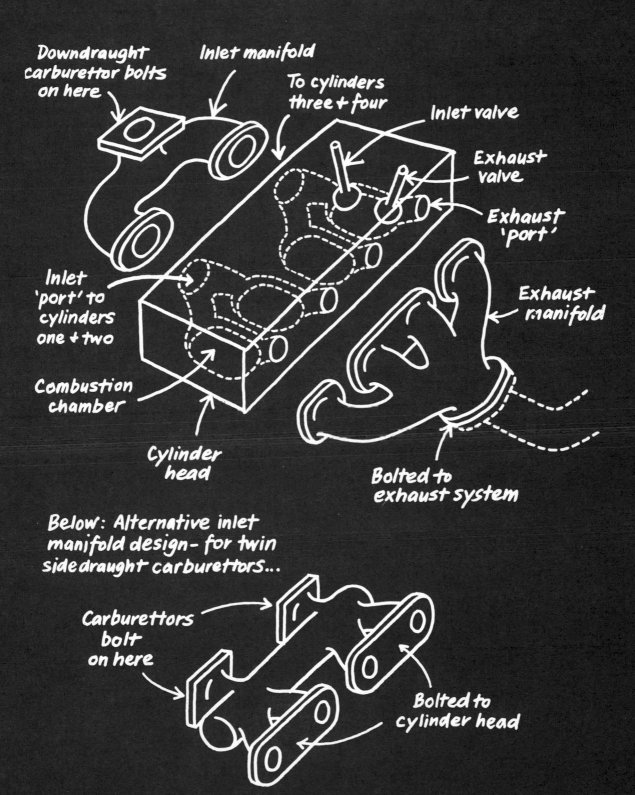

Downdraught carburettor bolts on here

Inlet manifold

To cylinders three + four

Inlet valve

Exhaust valve

Exhaust 'port'

Exhaust manifold

Inlet 'port' to cylinders one + two

Combustion chamber

Cylinder head

Bolted to exhaust system

Below: Alternative inlet manifold design - for twin sidedraught carburettors...

Carburettors bolt on here

Bolted to cylinder head

the pulsations from the engine can blow themselves out around a maze before finding their way out through the tailpipe. Straight-through silencers use no baffles, but wrap a perforated central duct with a blanket of fibreglass into which the noise of the engine can bury itself.

Silencers are regularly a problem on motor cars in everyday use, and demand frequent replacement. This is largely because all chemical reactions work faster in high temperatures, and that includes rust. The exhaust, being perfectly situated to catch all manner of road dirt and water, tends to corrode very quickly. Stainless steel silencers can now be made up for any type of car, but they're naturally fairly expensive.

Cooling.

Internal combustion engines have an innate tendency to melt, which is hardly surprising considering they're just a box in which a lot of explosions get sparked off. The temperature in the cylinder at the moment of combustion might get as high as 2500°C and the temperature of the metal around the exhaust valves is pretty hot all the time. Something has to cool the engine down.

A lot of small-capacity engines use *air-cooling* — simply blowing a draught all over the metalwork with a large fan, usually driven off the same belt that drives the dynamo. To avoid blowing this air straight out of the car rather than on to the engine, a complicated contraption of metal cowling is bolted all around the engine and directs the air on to the hot spots. Although VWs and Fiats particularly have used air-cooling very successfully, it doesn't work very well for bigger high-performance engines that generate too much heat to be dispersed this way. On top of that, it's extremely hard to service air-cooled engines, particularly if you perform some stunt like dropping one of the sparking plugs down inside the cowling, and since there's no water in the block to absorb the noise, air-cooled engines tend to make a lot more racket.

Water Cooling.
In this type of system the cylinder block and head are riddled with water passages, and the cooling water is pumped around the system so that it can absorb heat at the combustion chambers and cylinder walls and lose it again at the *radiator*. The radiator is simply a boxful of very fine brass or copper tubes which is cooled by an airflow from a fan and a blast of cold air passing through as the car is on the move. A typical layout is shown in the illustration opposite.

In a simple version of this, water would simply be drawn up through the bottom hose by the pump, circulated around the passages in the head and block and then return through the top hose to drain down the radiator tubes and get cooled. Unfortunately, it's not that simple. Everybody knows that cold engines are remarkably unhelpful; they need a lot of choke, they falter and stall, and they wear faster when hot oil isn't circulating around. To get the engine as hot as possible as fast as possible, we don't need to cool the water down until everything's well and truly woken up. This job is done by the thermostat, usually mounted in a housing above the water pump. It shuts off the outlet to the top hose when the engine's cold so the water goes through the by-pass tube straight back into the pump and misses the radiator altogether. When the engine reaches its ideal running temperature, the thermostat opens a valve to the top hose and the water starts circulating normally. If the thermostat sticks shut of course, the water will soon boil; this is occasionally a mysterious cause of overheating.

The water pump is usually driven by the fan belt and the fan is bolted to the same pulley. The diagrams show how a simple pump works.

Transmission.

Clearly the fact that the engine might be running doesn't mean that we're travelling anywhere. The transmission system, which actually arranges for the wheels to turn, can be completely cut off from the power source whenever the driver feels like it. The device that enables us to bring this about is the *clutch*. The clutch performs a kind of diplomatic role — it introduces the power of the engine painlessly to the inertia of the transmission and wheels.

People who think that driving ought to be simply a matter of sitting comfortably and not banging into things have always regarded the conventional clutch and gearbox arrangement as being something of a nuisance. For this reason all sorts of clever devices have been dreamed up to make sure that these operations take care of themselves: 'automatic transmissions', of which more later (see p. 54). Strictly speaking, the need for clutches and gearboxes derives from a weakness of the internal combustion engine itself, for reasons we went into dealing with the four-stroke cycle (see p. 13). It won't start from rest under load — where the load is the vehicle itself and the passengers — in the way that the steam engine will. As we saw earlier, this is because the steam engine only has to concern itself with delivering a power stroke to the crank, it has its hot gas delivered from an external pressure source that's got nothing to do with the movement of the pistons themselves. The petrol engine on the other hand has to use the motion of its pistons to suck its own fuel in — so that if the engine suddenly encounters conditions of heavy load, such as finding itself at the start of a steep incline, a vicious circle develops where the

THE COOLING SYSTEM

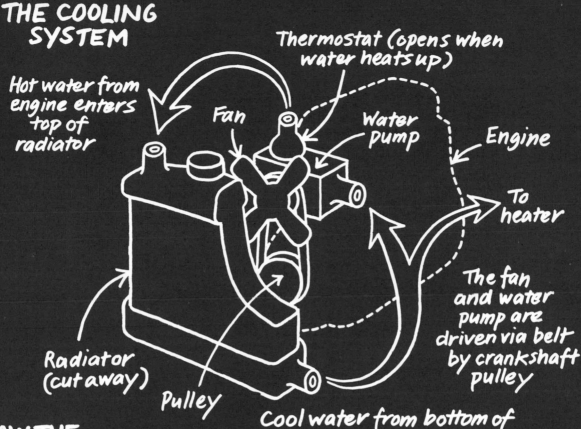

Thermostat (opens when water heats up)

Hot water from engine enters top of radiator

Fan

Water pump

Engine

To heater

The fan and water pump are driven via belt by crankshaft pulley

Radiator (cut away)

Pulley

Cool water from bottom of radiator drawn into engine by water pump

HOW THE THERMOSTAT WORKS

With engine cold (and thermostat closed) water cannot flow to/from radiator...

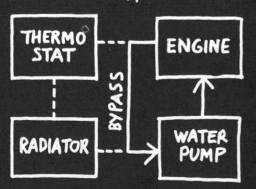

...pump circulates water within engine only, via bypass.

With engine hot, water from engine can pass through open thermostat...

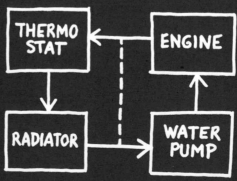

...pump draws water from foot of radiator.

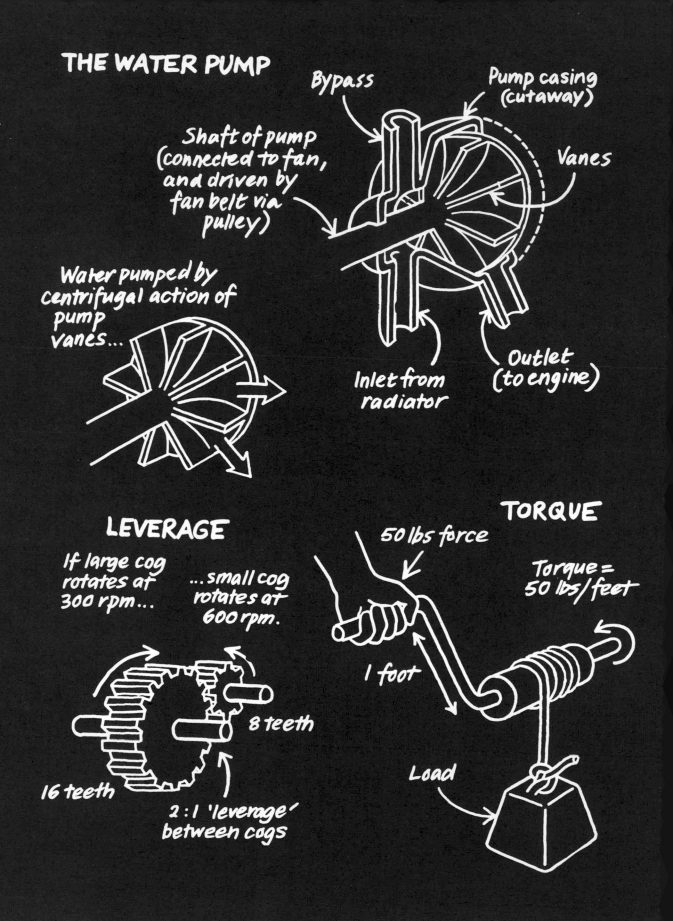

THE WATER PUMP

Bypass

Pump casing (cutaway)

Shaft of pump (connected to fan, and driven by fan belt via pulley)

Vanes

Water pumped by centrifugal action of pump vanes...

Inlet from radiator

Outlet (to engine)

LEVERAGE

If large cog rotates at 300 rpm...

...small cog rotates at 600 rpm.

8 teeth

16 teeth

2 : 1 'leverage' between cogs

TORQUE

50 lbs force

Torque = 50 lbs/feet

1 foot

Load

roadwheels are rapidly dragging down the engine revs and the flow rate of the fuel goes down with them.

The same thing happens when the engine has to be coupled to the load to start the car from rest; in this case if the coupling happens too abruptly the flow rate will be so reduced that the engine will simply falter or stall. If you've ever performed this trick by bringing the clutch up so fast that the car takes off like an overweight kangaroo, the phenomenon won't need undue elaboration. Unfortunately it isn't possible to go into the reasons for a motor car's transmission taking the form that it does without groping around a few principles of applied mathematics — but they aren't particularly abstruse ones.

Imagine an engine that idles at 800 r.p.m. and will accelerate to 5,000 r.p.m. without coming apart at the seams. We've already seen that for a four-cylinder engine each piston will complete the Otto cycle once every two revolutions of the crankshaft — in other words *two* of the cylinders will go through their firing stroke for every complete revolution. So at 800 r.p.m. the engine is firing 1,600 times a minute. But at 5,000 r.p.m. it's firing *10,000* times a minute, and consequently developing a great deal more power.

If the engine were *directly* linked to the roadwheels, then the only time you'd get that power out of it would be when the car was running flat out. With the roadwheels running slowly — for starting, or traffic driving, or hillclimbing — the engine would be developing only a fraction of its potential. And since you frequently do need considerable engine power at low roadspeeds, walking would clearly be a more effective way of getting about.

So a mechanism has to be devised that will permit the engine to run fast while the wheels run slowly — in other words to convert the crankshaft's rotational speed so that the speed at the wheels is proportionately reduced. It would also be handy to have a number of different reductions to choose from, to suit varying roadwheel speeds. So motor cars are equipped with *gearboxes*, through which a number of alternative ratios can be chosen to suit the conditions. Generally *top gear* is what's known as *direct drive* — the rotational speed transmitted to the final drive or rear axle is the same as that of the engine. *Bottom gear*, the one used for overcoming the deadweight of the car when starting from rest, has a ratio of around 3½:1. The crankshaft therefore turns three and a half times for one turn of the output shaft from the gearbox.

The reason for all this elaboration is to do with a phenomenon of spinning shafts known as *torque,* a word that you might frequently hear in motoring circles. Looking at the diagram of the winch, if you push the lever down with a force of 50 lb. and the lever is a foot long, then the torque or twisting effort is described as being 50 lb./feet (i.e. pounds

x. feet. It's sometimes expressed in lbs/inches and nowadays of course in things like kilograms and metres). So torque is a measure of leverage. When the motor car engine turns, one way of measuring its efficiency is the amount of torque it can apply in levering its load, which is of course a spinning axle. So whatever torque is required at the wheels to start the car from rest can be produced either by the use of a very large engine and a gearing system not far off being direct drive, or a small engine whose output torque is modified by suitable gears. It's easy to see how two gearwheels of different sizes represent the leverage idea in the sketch.

In addition, the car gearbox also needs a reverse gear which can invert the direction of the engine's rotation through the box. This is used for low-speed manoeuvring alone.

The Clutch.

The clutch is the means by which the power of the engine can be gradually introduced to the gearbox so that the load of the stationary car doesn't unduly slow the engine down. It's also used to disengage the power from the gearbox when a change is being made from one ratio to another. If this was done with the power applied, the gearwheels would be rotating at such unequal speeds that they couldn't be meshed with each other.

The illustrations cover several views of the single dry-plate friction clutch in action, progressing in complexity from difficult to very difficult. Actually, there's nothing to it. The mechanism is contained in a housing bolted to the flywheel and rotating with it. The *friction plate* or *centre plate* is a steel disc lined with friction material (generally some sort of derivative of asbestos), mounted so that it can slide along the front end of the input shaft to the gearbox. This plate is pushed firmly against the flywheel face when the car is being driven normally, and the pushing is done by a spring-loaded *pressure plate*. The result is a kind of sandwich of flywheel, centre plate and pressure plate which transmits the rotational movement of the crankshaft and flywheel to the gearbox and eventually the road wheels. When the clutch pedal is depressed, the pressure plate is levered back slightly, allowing the centre plate to slip and disconnecting the drive. The whole mechanism is revolving on the flywheel and the withdrawal operation is effected by a stationary pedal linkage, often a thick carbon ring which encircles the spinning gearbox shaft without touching it. The ring moves forward as the pedal is depressed, this forward movement being reversed by three pivoting *release levers* that pull the pressure plate back towards the driver.

Modern clutches have tended to abandon a ring of coil springs in the clutch cover in favour of a single large disc spring, or diaphragm.

LOCATION OF CLUTCH

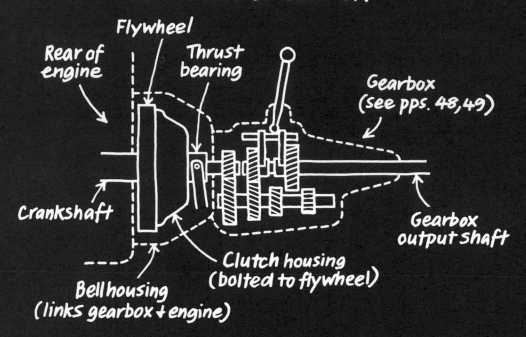

Rear of engine

Flywheel

Thrust bearing

Gearbox (see pps. 48,49)

Crankshaft

Gearbox output shaft

Clutch housing (bolted to flywheel)

Bellhousing (links gearbox + engine)

CLUTCH COMPONENTS

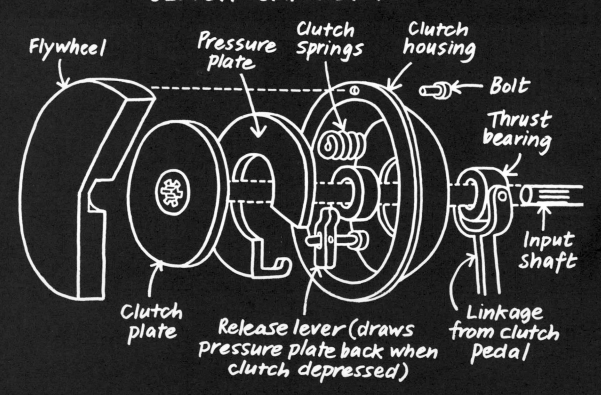

Flywheel

Pressure plate

Clutch Springs

Clutch housing

Bolt

Thrust bearing

Input shaft

Clutch plate

Release lever (draws pressure plate back when clutch depressed)

Linkage from clutch pedal

CLUTCH ENGAGED

All shaded components driven by engine...

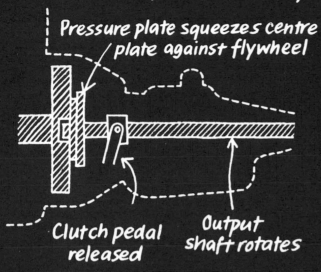

Pressure plate squeezes centre plate against flywheel

Clutch pedal released

Output shaft rotates

CLUTCH DISENGAGED

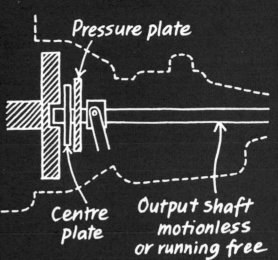

Pressure plate

Centre plate

Output shaft motionless or running free

CLUTCH OPERATION

Flywheel + clutch cover (including springs, release levers + pressure plate) revolve together as unit...

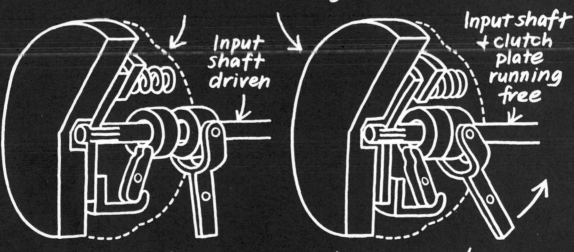

Input shaft driven

Input shaft + clutch plate running free

Clutch pedal released, clutch plate engaged (pressed against flywheel by springs)

Clutch pedal depressed, clutch plate disengaged (thrust bearing acts via release levers to draw pressure plate from flywheel)

Automatic clutches.

Automatic clutches take a variety of forms, but all of them 'sense' either the engine speed and road speed, or the driver's intention to change gear. Many years ago Automotive Products came up with the 'Manumatic' clutch, which made use of the vacuum being pulled by the engine itself, exactly as the carburettor makes use of it. A vacuum pipe is taken from the fuel intake manifold on the cylinder head, and led to a 'servo mechanism' which can disengage the clutch by itself. An electric contact in the gear shift lever is closed as soon as the lever is moved, this in turn operates a vacuum valve which actuates the clutch. Moving away from rest, when the clutch is required to engage itself gently, a centrifugal mechanism comes into operation — just like whirling a conker around your head, a contraption in the flywheel moves toward the rim of the wheel as the engine speed rises, gradually engaging the clutch.

Fluid Flywheels.

This is exactly the same principle, only what you might call a 'wet' version of it. The part of the flywheel driven by the engine contains a number of rotor blades, and spinning free within the rotor casing is a *runner* which drives the gearbox. As the engine speeds up, fluid in the centre of the rotor is flung out towards its outer rim, catching in pockets or cells on the runner and driving it round as well. As the engine slows, the fluid drains back out of the cells toward the centre and the runner comes to a halt. This arrangement was used a good deal on earlier cars such as Armstrong Siddeleys, Rileys and Lanchesters, often in conjunction with a preselector gearbox. But because the churning of the fluid absorbs a good deal of the engine's very expensive power, the device has ceased to be very attractive.

Nevertheless, various developments of the fluid flywheel or 'fluid coupling' have been made to suit modern automatic transmissions such as the 'Hydramatic' system described later (see p. 54). A more subtle kind of fluid flywheel is the *torque converter*, nowadays in very widespread use. A refined kind of turbine, the torque converter enables a very high degree of leverage or *torque* to be delivered from the engine to the transmission when the former is revving and the latter is stationary (the conditions you get when moving the car from rest), gradually becoming reduced as the rotational speed of the engine and the transmission get closer and closer into balance.

The Gearbox.

The principle on which a gearing system works is logical enough. If you feed 3,000 revs to a shaft carrying a gearwheel with 20 teeth on its circumference, and that gearwheel is meshed to a larger one with 30 teeth on it, then the *second motion shaft* driven by the larger gear will run rather slower than 3,000 r.p.m. In fact the gear reduction is 30 to 20, or 1.5 to 1. In other words, the second motion shaft is rotating at 2,000 r.p.m., so we have achieved a substantial reduction in output speed without the engine losing momentum. If we then repeat the process, with a very small gearwheel further down our second shaft, driving a very large gearwheel at a ratio of say 15 teeth to 35, the reduction has been increased by another 2.33 to 1. So the overall reduction on a shaft driven by our 35-tooth wheel is the two reduction figures multiplied together — a total gear ratio of 3.5 to 1.

This arrangement gives us the sort of gear reduction we need for the first or starting gear of a motor car, providing low speed at the roadwheel, but high power. In the average car, a fairly small engine is required to propel a relatively heavy vehicle so the first gear ratio would normally be pretty much like the example here, of the order of 3.5 to 4 to 1. To adapt the engine revolutions to as wide a variety of road conditions as possible, the designer aims for a *wide ratio* gearbox, and the engine is built to pull reasonably hard at fairly low speeds so that normal flat-road running can be achieved at moderate engine revs for the sake of petrol economy. *Close ratio* gearboxes, with a very different selection of ratios, are built for competition work, the idea being a very dramatic power output at high engine speeds, but nothing very striking when the engine is dawdling. Road cars that have been designed with a lot of racing experience only really give of their best when accelerating hard in each gear. Unlike a bread-and-butter car not built for such treatment, they don't sound as if they're heading for a coronary when you put your foot down. (It's you that gets the coronary when you look at the fuel gauge.)

So the gearbox is a means whereby a number of alternative relationships of engine speed to road speed can be established, and the transfer from one ratio to another is effected by sliding the gearwheels on the first and third motion shafts back and forth into various collaborations with fixed gears on the second motion shaft or *layshaft*. Sometimes the layshaft is actually cut from a solid chunk of steel, though this naturally does mean that none of the layshaft gears are individually replaceable if they suffer any mishaps.

Although the crash box serves us pretty well for illustration, anyone who's ever tried one will tell you that getting the hang of meshing the gears silently while the car's on the move and they're all whirling around is something of a magician's accomplishment. This was why the art of 'double-declutching' became so indispensable on early cars — the clutch was brought up in between the gear-

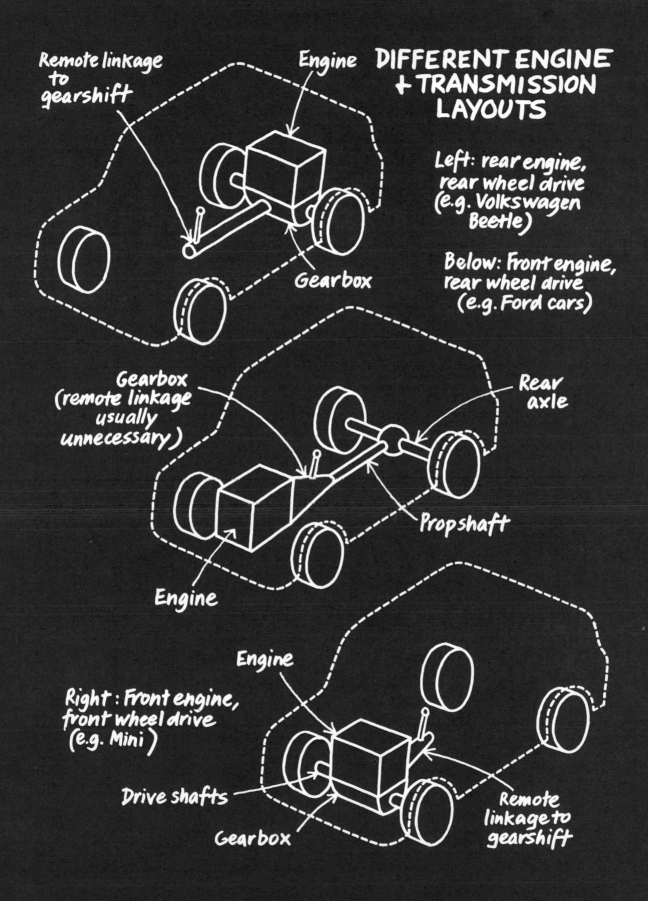

Remote linkage to gearshift

Engine

DIFFERENT ENGINE + TRANSMISSION LAYOUTS

Left: rear engine, rear wheel drive (e.g. Volkswagen Beetle)

Below: Front engine, rear wheel drive (e.g. Ford cars)

Gearbox

Gearbox (remote linkage usually unnecessary)

Rear axle

Propshaft

Engine

Right: Front engine, front wheel drive (e.g. Mini)

Engine

Drive shafts

Gearbox

Remote linkage to gearshift

SIMPLE THREE-SPEED 'CRASH' GEARBOX

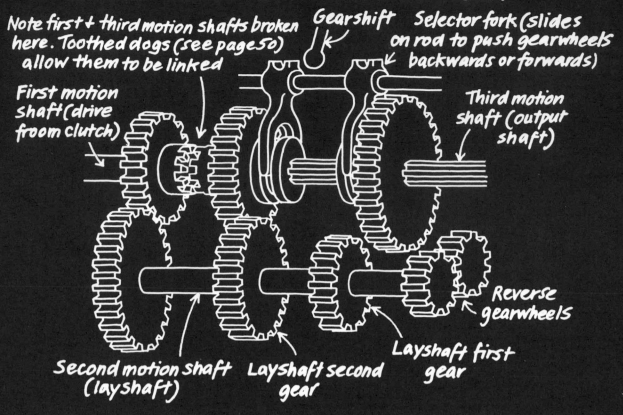

Note first & third motion shafts broken here. Toothed dogs (see page 50) allow them to be linked

Gearshift

Selector fork (slides on rod to push gearwheels backwards or forwards)

First motion shaft (drive from clutch)

Third motion shaft (output shaft)

Second motion shaft (layshaft)

Layshaft second gear

Layshaft first gear

Reverse gearwheels

TRANSMISSION PATH: FIRST GEAR

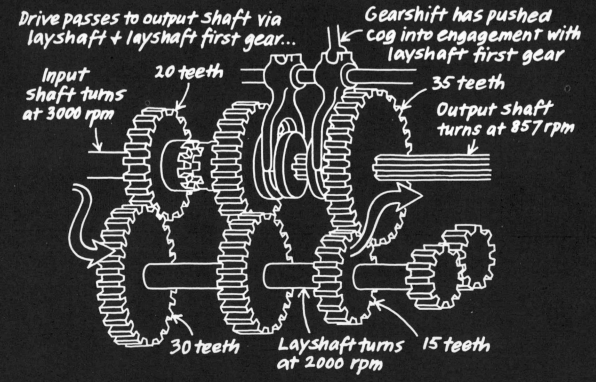

Drive passes to output shaft via layshaft & layshaft first gear...

Gearshift has pushed cog into engagement with layshaft first gear

Input shaft turns at 3000 rpm

20 teeth

35 teeth

Output shaft turns at 857 rpm

30 teeth

Layshaft turns at 2000 rpm

15 teeth

TRANSMISSION PATH: SECOND GEAR

Drive passes to output via layshaft + layshaft second gear...

Gearshift has pushed cog into engagement with layshaft second gear

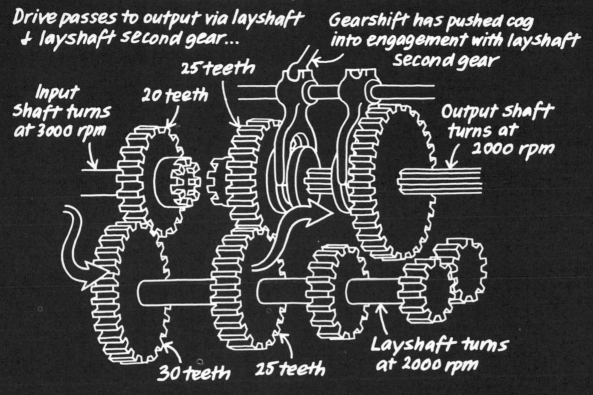

Input Shaft turns at 3000 rpm

20 teeth

25 teeth

Output shaft turns at 2000 rpm

30 teeth

25 teeth

Layshaft turns at 2000 rpm

TRANSMISSION PATH: THIRD GEAR

Drive passes directly to output, bypassing layshaft...

Gearshift has pushed dogs on first + third motion shafts into engagement

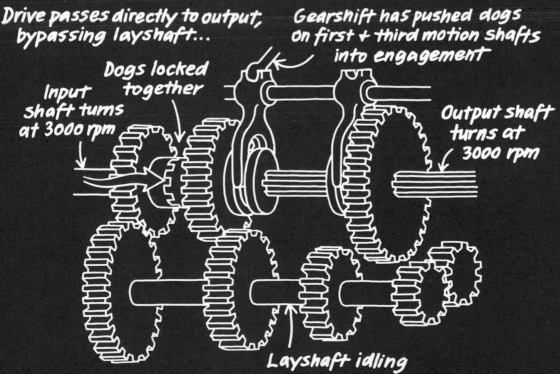

Dogs locked together

Input shaft turns at 3000 rpm

Output shaft turns at 3000 rpm

Layshaft idling

CHANGING GEAR WITH A DOG-CLUTCH

Gearshift forces sliding collar forwards so dogs engage those on input shaft...

...drive goes direct from input to third motion shaft.

Input shaft

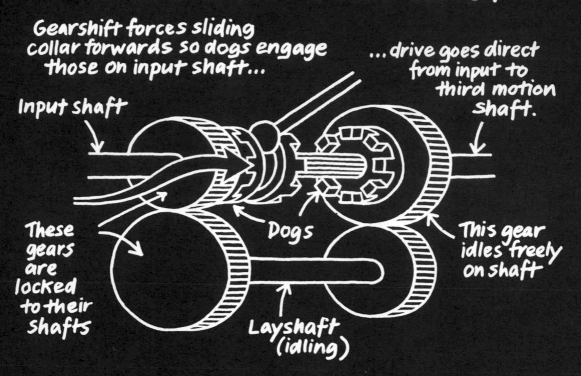

These gears are locked to their shafts

Dogs

This gear idles freely on shaft

Layshaft (idling)

Gearshift forces collar backwards so dogs engage those on (previously idling) gearwheel...

Input from clutch

Dogs

Gearwheel now locked to third motion shaft

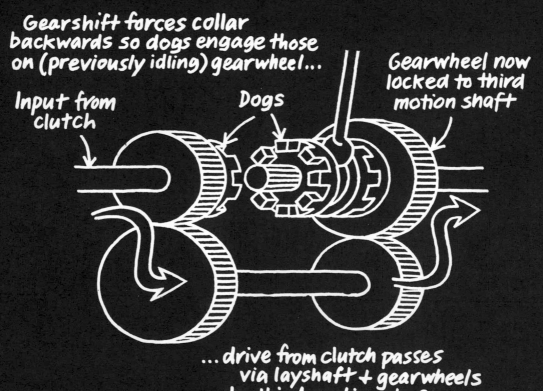

...drive from clutch passes via layshaft + gearwheels to third motion shaft.

HOW SYNCHROMESH WORKS

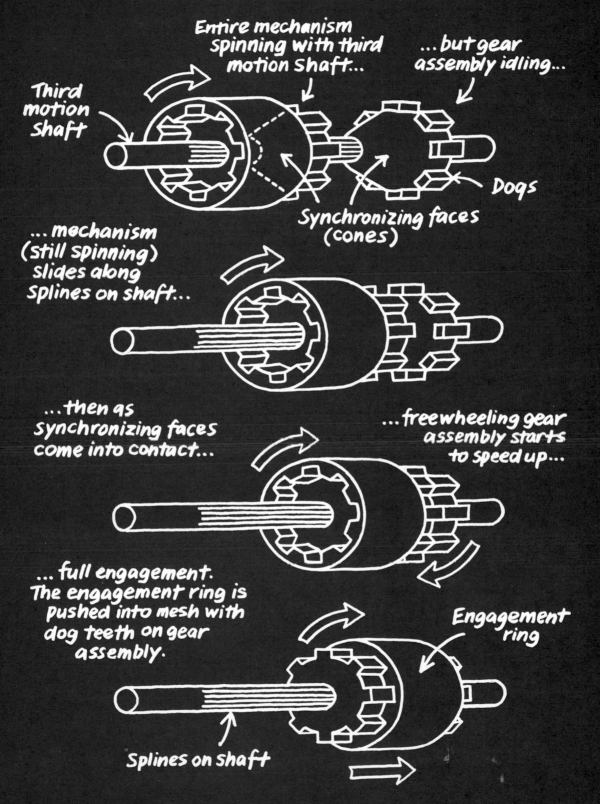

Entire mechanism spinning with third motion shaft...

...but gear assembly idling...

Third motion shaft

Synchronizing faces (cones)

Dogs

...mechanism (still spinning) slides along splines on shaft...

...then as synchronizing faces come into contact...

...freewheeling gear assembly starts to speed up...

...full engagement. The engagement ring is pushed into mesh with dog teeth on gear assembly.

Engagement ring

Splines on shaft

change so that the engine would drive the layshaft in neutral for a few moments until the driver thought that the relative speeds of the two shafts were close enough to push the gearwheels into engagement with each other. It was a haphazard business, and it depended a great deal on the skill of the driver.

A good many refinements of design have taken place since those days, which is just as well or the roads would echo to the sound of tearing metal and curses. Straight-tooth gears run very noisily at the best of times, so helical-toothed gears, with the teeth set at an angle to the rim of the wheel, were introduced — sliding them around was dispensed with, so that layshaft and third motion gears would run constantly in engagement with each other, and the method of hooking them to the output shaft was changed.

To understand the modern *constant mesh* box you have to get boned up about dogs. If you look at the top end of a rook in a chess-set, that's pretty much what a dog, or dog-clutch looks like. If you put two rooks end to end (rooks, dogs, where will it all end?) so that the turret parts slotted into each other, you would reproduce exactly the effect that dog clutches are intended to achieve. When moved into engagement with each other, they lock components together so that they revolve in tandem.

So in the constant mesh boxes you allow the first, second and third gears to spin free on the third motion shaft, and you place your dogs between the gears but lock or *spline* them to the shaft. So the dogs can slide backwards and forwards but can only spin all in one piece with the third motion shaft; the other gears can simply idle if they're not engaged. When you operate the gear lever, you yank the appropriate dog-clutch backward or forward so that it catches the idling gearwheel and locks it to the shaft.

Since the dog teeth would soon get pretty dilapidated by gearchanging, a method had to be devised to bring the two sets of teeth up to the same revolving speed before the final engagement was made. This was effected by a *synchromesh* mechanism — simply two friction cones in front of each ring of teeth which rub together during the early stages of a gearchange until both halves of the partnership are running at an appropriate speed for the rest of the change to be made. You often feel this slight resistance to forcing the gearchange when driving — then suddenly the resistance disappears when the matching speeds are achieved and the gearshift goes fully into engagement. The gear lever is linked to the top cover of the gearbox in such a way that the appropriate manipulation will hook it into whichever dog clutch mechanism is required — they're generally grouped in two pairs, one operating first and second gear, the other third and top. So once the lower joint of the gear-shift is engaged in the third/top dog clutch assembly, simply sliding it forwards or backwards will effect the necessary change from one gear ratio to another.

Overdrives.

You might not imagine that it's possible to have a higher gear than top, the point at which the drive from the engine and the output shaft from the gearbox are directly hitched together and spinning at the same revs. But there is an additional gearing reduction at the point where the drive is finally transmitted to the roadwheels (see p. 54). If this is of a particularly high ratio then the engine might have to be running uncomfortably fast (remember high ratio = low gear and low ratio = high gear) to get a respectable road performance at all. This is where the *overdrive* comes in, an extra set of gears which are normally engaged when the car reaches a certain speed. Basically it's a 'cruising' gear for economical fast driving under light load — in other words, on a flat surface. The effect of the overdrive is to make the gearbox output shaft run *faster* than the engine — so that it might be possible to get the same road speed as with a conventional top gear but with a 20% decrease in engine revs. Everything then runs more quietly and cheaply. Over-drives aren't much use for sharp acceleration though, so they're disengaged for overtaking or climbing hills.

Epicyclic Gears.

Not all gearboxes work on the pattern of sliding gearwheels or sliding hubs. Epicyclic gearboxes are commonly used in automatic transmissions because different ratios can be obtained simply by 'braking' or locking various revolving parts of the mechanism instead of moving them backwards and forwards with levers. Because of their smooth and silent operation, epicyclic gearboxes have been extensively used on automatic transmission systems.

This is what's known as an epicyclic geartrain. The input shaft from the engine drives the *sun wheel,* and both the annulus carrier and the planet carrier can be linked to the output shaft. If the outer ring or annulus is locked so that it can't revolve, then the sun wheel will drive the planet carrier around at a reduced speed, depending on the relative sizes of all the gearwheels. If the planet carrier is locked on the other hand, and the annulus released, then the sun wheel will drive the annulus at a reduced speed *anticlockwise,* so we get a reverse gear. This locking of different bits and pieces of the epicyclic gear train is achieved by frictional brake bands and small clutches (which might be manually or automatically operated) and sometimes by electromagnets. A number of different gear ratios are established by coupling a series of epicyclic gear trains together and operating them by locking each annulus in turn.

One advantage of this type of gearbox is that

MAIN COMPONENTS OF AN EPICYCLIC GEARBOX

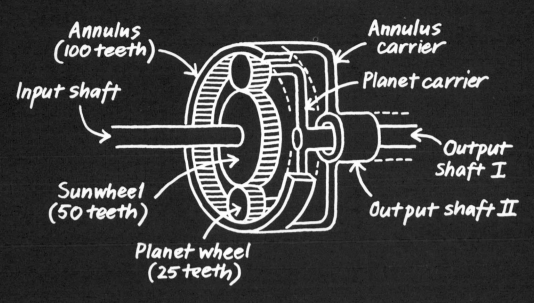

Annulus (100 teeth)

Annulus carrier

Input shaft

Planet carrier

Sunwheel (50 teeth)

Output Shaft I

Output shaft II

Planet wheel (25 teeth)

FRONT ENGINE/REAR WHEEL DRIVE TRANSMISSION LAYOUT

This the classic arrangement. The engine, clutch and gearbox are at the front of the car, with a propeller shaft driving a 'live' back axle.

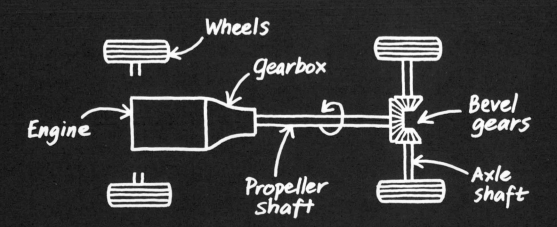

Wheels

Gearbox

Engine

Bevel gears

Propeller shaft

Axle shaft

it isn't necessary for lumps of metal to be struggling to get into engagement with each other while everything's spinning round. Consequently the clutch doesn't have to uncouple the engine from the transmission completely during the course of a gear-change.

In an automatic transmission system using an epicyclic box, it's possible to arrange for the selection and locking of the appropriate annulus gears to take place through a hydraulically operated servo or 'slave' mechanism which is sensitive to road conditions and engine speed. Ideally, a mechanism like this would be able to change the gears more or less at the same instant that the driver would choose to effect it.

Hydramatic Transmission.

This set-up, in conjunction with a centrifugally operated *fluid coupling*, is the basis of the Hydramatic transmission system developed by General Motors before the war, and used initially in the Cadillac. Rolls Royce have used a modified form of the same design. It uses an epicyclic gearbox with three geartrains, two of them providing a pair of forward ratios each, the third providing reverse. Selection and locking of various components of the train is by friction brakebands and small plate clutches. It's brought about by a gearchange control unit mounted on the side of the gearbox — simply a hydraulic mechanism linked to the accelerator control and a manual selector on the steering column.

Borg-Warner Transmission.

Borg-Warner transmission, another American design now widely used in Europe, also features an epicyclic gearbox but in conjunction with a highly sophisticated turbine-like fluid flywheel called a *torque converter*. The torque converter will provide an adequate gearing-down of the engine speed automatically — so that in partnership with the regular gearbox it will enable the car to move away smoothly from rest. If the engine is big enough, it's possible for the gearbox to be considerably simplified and its functions virtually taken over by the torque converter, which is in effect a gearbox without gears.

The device has also been used by British Leyland in a transmission system of their own, specially designed for use in the transverse-engine cars. Some manufacturers have adopted partially automatic systems; in the Volkswagen Beetle, for instance, the drive is taken up from rest by a torque convertor, but subsequent changes through a 3-speed gearbox are effected by a conventional gearstick. The difference is that there isn't a clutch pedal — moving the stick in the direction of the required gear triggers off a servo that automatically disengages the clutch.

Final Drive & Differential.

As the line in the film goes, you've got two chances of understanding how a differential works: slim and none. Not because there's anything particularly complicated about one of its functions — that of changing the direction of rotation from being parallel with the sides of the car to parallel with the axles. This is simply a matter of using cone shaped bevel gears, and isn't actually a 'differential' function at all.

The 'differential' has got nothing to do with 'bending' the drive through 90°. It has to do with balancing up the rotational speeds of the driven wheels when the car is cornering. If you think about it, on a tight bend one roadwheel will be revolving faster than the other, so the two axle shafts (half-shafts, since they're two halves of the same axle) have got to be able to revolve at different speeds while the 'feed' from the gearbox to the axle is maintaining the same speed. So we need an arrangement whereby one axle shaft can 'idle' while the other one speeds up, and vice versa.

(You don't, of course, need either of these provisions at the non-driven wheels because since these are free-running and independent of each other they can adjust to appropriate cornering speeds of their own accord.)

Up till now, none of this has had anything to do with the way that the power gets from the gearbox output shaft to the axles — we're simply dealing with the rotation of the axles themselves. Now, hold on tight while we add a couple more gears, and then the agony's over. One is a bevel gear that goes on the end of the *propellor shaft* and brings the power from the engine. The other is a very large bevel gear or *crownwheel*, that turns the drive into rotation of the axles. We mount the crownwheel on the pinion cage itself, so that once the power starts spinning it the whole cage rotates, and the planet pinions pull the sun pinions around as we've already described.

With the car travelling in a straight line, both the nearside and offside halfshafts revolve at the same speed as the crownwheel. On a left hand bend, the nearside halfshaft slows down but the differential cage keeps rolling at the same speed. The planet wheels, previously stationary, now start to turn themselves, so that the halfshafts are able to rotate at different rates until the equilibrium is restored; the planet wheels, having 'absorbed' the difference without the crownwheel having been affected at all, slow down to a halt again.

Lubrication.

You could hardly call squirting a few drops of Three-In-One into your lawnmower a lubrication

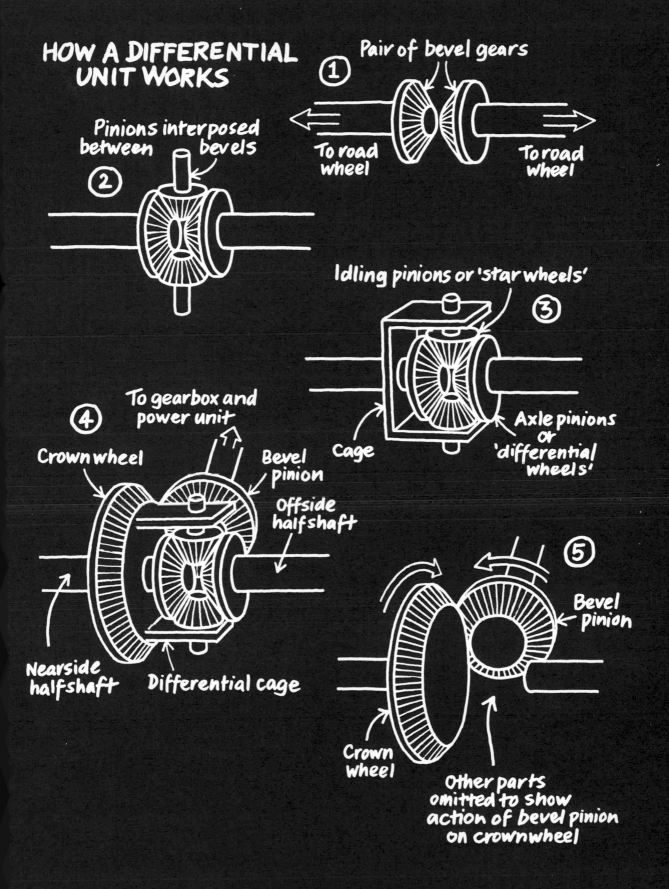

HOW A DIFFERENTIAL UNIT WORKS

① Pair of bevel gears

To road wheel

To road wheel

② Pinions interposed between bevels

③ Idling pinions or 'star wheels'

Cage

Axle pinions or 'differential wheels'

④ To gearbox and power unit

Crown wheel

Bevel pinion

Offside halfshaft

Nearside halfshaft

Differential cage

⑤ Bevel pinion

Crown wheel

Other parts omitted to show action of bevel pinion on crownwheel

system at work, except maybe that if you don't
do it regularly you'll end up rupturing yourself
trying to push it and the thing will make a noise
like a mediaeval drawbridge.

In any gadget with moving parts, lumps of
metal are going to be rubbing against other lumps of
metal, and the faster they're obliged to do it the
more disagreeable the effect. The necessary improvement is to introduce a film of something slippery
in between the surfaces. Briefly ascending into the
realms of physics, the ratio of the force needed
to shift an object to the weight of the object itself
is called the *coefficient of friction*. The idea is for
the two moving surfaces to form a sandwich with a
lubricant as the filling — and then varying levels
within the lubricant are moving against each other.

So the requirements of our anti-friction material
is that it should retain its thickness or 'body' regardless of how much of a hammering it gets when the
machine is in motion. If it's something that doesn't
move fast or get hot — such as a door hinge — then
a thin or 'low viscosity' lubricant will do the trick.
If it's subjected to considerable stresses, then a
thicker lubricant is required.

It May Just Be Oil To You.
If you walk around a motor accessory shop you
might well be a bit mystified by the ratings that
appear on different types of oil. These are S.A.E.
ratings, established by the Society of Automotive
Engineers in the States, running on a scale from five
to fifty, thin to thick. Over and above these are
Extreme Pressure or E.P. ratings for gear and transmission oils, the codings for which will run up to
140 for normal motoring use.

In the early days of motoring, you would
expect to use a low viscosity oil in the winter —
in other words a thinner oil so that the combination
of syrupy lubricant and cold weather wouldn't
make the engine too stiff to turn over — and a high
viscosity oil in the summer so that the hotter
running conditions wouldn't make the oil too thin
to do its job. An enormous amount of effort and
expense goes into oil technology as more
sophisticated machinery puts increasing demands on
lubrication systems, and nowadays most motor
engine oils are *multigrades*, combining the features
of thinness at low temperatures, and thickness in
the heat. The adverts promise you a good deal —
everything from happier family life to better petrol
consumption — but don't let the dumbness of the
P.R. men irritate you so much that you end up
thinking that cheap oil and expensive oil is basically
the same thing. Use a reputable manufacturer and
buy the best you can. An oil company that's got
the responsibility for keeping Concorde from falling
to bits, for instance, is likely to have developed a
material that will do your car quite a lot of good
as well.

In a petrol engine, particularly a high-
performance one (and even the engine in a family
saloon falls into this category nowadays by the
standards of a few years back), the requirements of
a lubricant aren't simply to stop metal surfaces
from wearing each other out. Oil comes into contact
simultaneously with both hot air and water inside
the engine; though the engine expels most of this
water, the oil can become considerably contaminated
eventually, and deposits of sludge will find their way
into all sorts of awkward places. Modern oils therefore act as a detergent as well, able to wash away
the by-products of combustion. The idea is to
break up the muck into smaller particles and carry
it around in a less harmful suspension in the oil,
or trap it in the filter.

Types Of Bearing.

Shafts revolving in a machine are carried in *bearings*
or *bushes*. If the load is very light, pretty well any
metal might do to manufacture both. Once again,
when we get to the tough requirements of automobile engines, the design and manufacture of
bearings becomes a sophisticated business. Shafts
like the crankshaft and camshaft are usually iron
castings or forgings. They run in bearing materials
that are generally much softer, often made of
bronze or various tin alloys. It might seem that
metals like these would be the worst thing you
could come up with to support high-speed moving
parts, but, as we've already seen, the metals don't
actually contact each other because of the wedge of
lubricating oil in between. The advantage of the
soft metals is that their surfaces are actually less
smooth than machined steel and they have much
more of a tendency to 'absorb' and retain the oil.
For bits such as the armature bearings on starters
and dynamos a material known as 'porous bronze'
is used. The properties of this stuff look as if they
were handed straight down from the Magic Circle —
if you take a porous bronze bush, soak it in oil and
squeeze it hard between your fingers the oil will
soak straight through the metal as if it had no more
substance than blotting paper.

To keep the oil film from breaking down,
the camshaft, crankshaft and valve operating bearings
must be pressure-fed from an oil reservoir. The
engine block itself is a warren of little oil passages
and galleries.

The engine carries its oil around in a pan bolted
to the underside of the crankcase known as the
sump. It's then pumped around the circuit by a
suction pump driven off the camshaft — sometimes
this is submerged in the oil reservoir itself, sometimes
it's higher up the system. The oil is first drawn
through a sieve attached to the pump intake, which
catches any of the larger foreign bodies floating
about in the oil, detached bits of carbon, lumps

LUBRICATION FLOW IN ENGINE

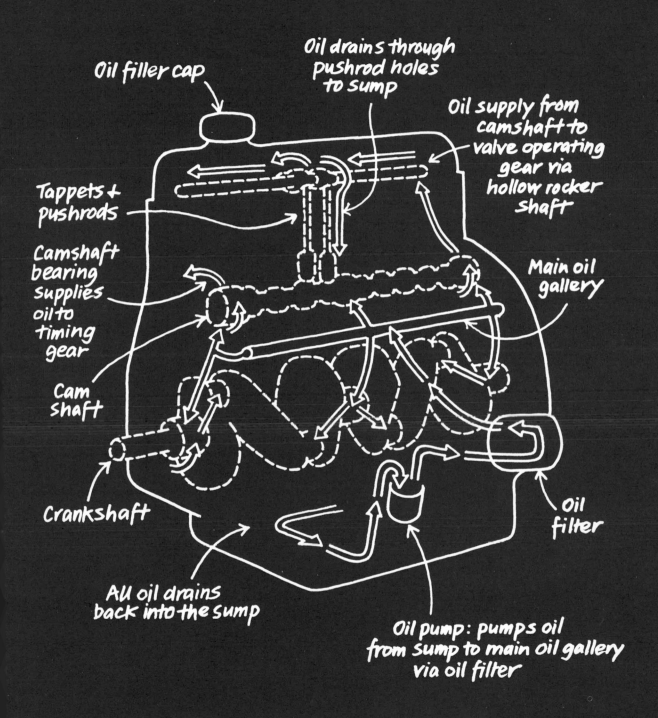

Oil filler cap

Oil drains through pushrod holes to sump

Oil supply from camshaft to valve operating gear via hollow rocker shaft

Tappets + pushrods

Camshaft bearing supplies oil to timing gear

Main oil gallery

Cam shaft

Crankshaft

Oil filter

All oil drains back into the sump

Oil pump: pumps oil from sump to main oil gallery via oil filter

Oil is pumped to the main oil gallery, from which it is distributed to all the bearings.

of sludge and so forth. Then it passes up to a canister, generally mounted on the side of the engine, which contains a cylindrical paper element. The oil soaks through this, leaving behind the smaller particles of muck, and then on to a main oil gallery running along the side of the crankcase. From here it is fed through drillings to the crankshaft bearings, camshaft and valve gear.

Some sort of fail-safe mechanism has to be incorporated in case the filter should clog. When this happens the pressure rises and a valve permits the oil to by-pass the filter altogether. Neglected maintenance is the only thing that will bring this eventuality about. It means that the engine is then running on unfiltered oil, which will play havoc with the bearings in time. This is a hobby horse to which I shall be continually reverting throughout this book.

Systematic attention to the car is vital to its long and happy life, and regular servicing as per the manufacturer's instructions. The older the car, the more important it is. The AA once proved that they could get upwards of 120,000 miles out of their minivans without an engine overhaul by a combination of good driving habits and regular servicing. Many owners content themselves with half that mileage.

Oil Pressure.

My first car was a Riley 1½ litre, a collector's piece, but I had no idea what I'd collected at the time except that garages looked at it as if it was the Missing Link. A Riley fan stopped me once in a pub car park, spouted a lot of bewildering jargon for a bit, then asked me what the oil pressure generally was. I had no notion, I didn't even know there was a gauge for it. He was appalled, and, later on, so was I. The oil pressure tells you a lot about those bits of the engine you most need to know about – the expensive bits. It's a shame that economies on modern cars have frequently dispensed with this invaluable instrument in favour of the simple warning light.

It's easy to see what its importance should be, in the light of what we've been considering about bearings and lubrication. When the engine is designed, a strict 'working clearance' is incorporated into the relative sizes of the shaft and the bearing it runs in. Enough slop to enable the oil to work effectively between the surfaces, but not so much that they start to hammer against each other and cause rapid wear and vibration. The pressure which any fluid maintains in a system of passageways depends on how much resistance it encounters in finding its way around. With the bearings in good condition and reasonably 'tight' the oil meets a lot of resistance in squeezing between the crankshaft oilway and the big-end bearing. As these surfaces

wear down, the resistance lessens; the oil pressure shown on the gauge correspondingly drops.

People jump to conclusions when the oil pressure falls. It isn't always worn bearings, though the combination of low oil pressure with an engine of known high mileage and a lot of clanking and banging from under the bonnet is fairly damning evidence. Sometimes exceptionally hot weather might do it, especially if the oil is the wrong viscosity for the car. Overheating will cause it, as will a faulty oil-pressure release valve – a mechanism designed to lower the oil pressure during cold starts when the lubricant is more than usually thick. Oil that hasn't been changed for a long time will cause it too – after a long period the oil gets contaminated with petrol and water and generally thinned out. On an engine with an acceleration pump in the carburettor and an owner who consistently pumps the throttle to start the car, a great deal of neat petrol may find its way into the sump past the pistons. Equally, a lot of 'stop start' driving may mean that combustion is never fully efficient because the engine doesn't get hot enough. Under these conditions a lot of impurities will find their way into the oil. For this reason you have to be a bit circumspect about taking advantage of modern 'long-haul' oils that claim to require less frequent replacement. If your regular mileage is low and you do a lot of short journeys, change the oil twice as often.

Greases & E.P. Oils.

With the advent of transverse engines and the tendency to put the power unit at the back, the engine and the transmission nowadays frequently find themselves perched on top of each other, and sharing the same oil – an ordinary multigrade is all right for these applications. Where the gearbox and differential are separate they use extreme-pressure oils that look like molasses – bevel gears impart much more difficult loads to the oil than a simple revolving shaft does, and the oil has to cope with conditions that render it much more prone to breaking down – in other words, no longer maintaining a film between the moving parts, so that metal starts crunching on metal.

Grease.
Greases are used for slowly moving parts, such as steering pivots, balljoints, handbrake cables and propshaft joints. Their great advantage is that they stay put, which conventional oils won't do unless continually maintained by a pressurized system.

Getting Under Way.

The Romans having unfortunately abandoned this country to its fate a long while back, all roads no longer travel in straight lines. The simplest way of

SIMPLE STEERING LAYOUT
(Seen from above)

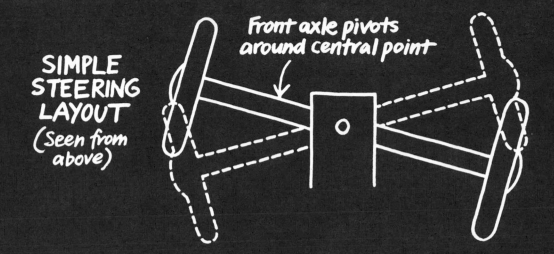

Front axle pivots around central point

MODERN STEERING
Rack + pinion steering layout (seen from above) ...

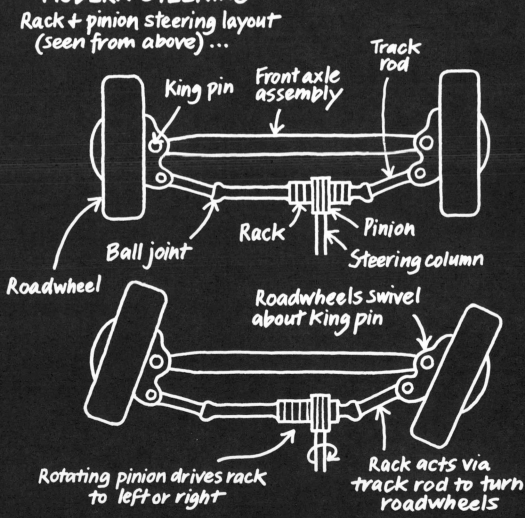

Track rod

King pin

Front axle assembly

Ball joint

Rack

Pinion

Steering column

Roadwheel

Roadwheels swivel about king pin

Rotating pinion drives rack to left or right

Rack acts via track rod to turn roadwheels

getting a vehicle to follow the bends en route is of course to pivot the whole front axle, tie a bit of string to either end of it and pull whenever a hazard presents itself. The motor industry isn't much impressed by bits of string, though it has hung on to the principle — and the rod by which the driver's evasive action is transferred to the wheels is still, not unreasonably, called the *drag link*.

This method is satisfactory for something without a body or a suspension system, because it doesn't matter that the roadwheels might move a foot or so forward or backward of their rest position in the course of rounding a bend. A much better arrangement is to swivel each wheel on the front axle beam, but, since they're now turning independently of each other, a connecting link (or *track rod*) then has to be used to get them moving in unison again. So now our drag link pulls on one wheel — generally the side the driver's sitting on — and the track rod takes care of the other.

It was hardly an insuperable problem to come up with a gearing arrangement that could transform the turning action of the driver's control of a steering *wheel* into the back-and-forth movement of the drag link.

The simplest kind of steering mechanism features a type of screw or 'worm' on the end of the steering column, with a peg on a pivoted arm running in the grooves of the worm. As the steering column is turned from the straight-ahead position, the peg runs along the worm either forward (pulling the drag link backward and turning the wheels to the right) or back towards the driver (pushing the drag link forward and turning the wheels to the left).

An alternative and more responsive arrangement is the *rack-and-pinion* steering system, originally developed for racing cars and now in widespread production use. Broadly, it takes the place of the track rod, the pinion pushing the rack to the right or the left as the steering column makes it revolve.

Basic transport like a kid's go-kart simplifies matters.

If you want to go you station yourself at the top of a hill and cross your fingers, and if you want to stop you stick one foot on the floor. At the more rarified altitudes of four-wheeled travel it becomes more urgent to add bits that don't actually change the species of the vehicle but smooth out the rough edges of its personality a bit. For instance, after a lot of use a wheel revolving on a simple spindle wears either the hole or the spindle or both until it starts to flop about in all directions. The foot-on-the-deck braking method loses its charm after the third or fourth torn ligament.

And something has to be taken on board that will dampen the worst attacks from potholes, bumps, pedestrians and other enemies of the motorist.

In effect our vehicle needs: (a) more hard-wearing and smooth-running bearings between road-wheel and stub-axle, preferably running in oil or grease, (b) a means of slowing the roadwheels by rubbing something against them that will induce a high level of frictional drag and (c) a system of springing that will enable the axles to 'float' in relation to the frame of the vehicle.

This system would be usefully augmented if the rim of the wheel were made of something absorbent as well.

Wheels & Tyres.

A tyre is simply an air cushion designed to keep the vehicle in stable contact with the road surface under a variety of conditions. It has a rubber outer cover with grooves cut into it to act as drainage channels for water on wet surfaces. Contrary to what you might expect, bald tyres provide the best grip on a dry, hard road surface, though you'd have trouble convincing a policeman of that even if you were driving on the hardest and driest road in the country. The design of the tread is a compromise to obtain the best grip possible in both the wet and the dry. The outer cover is stiffened with layers of flexible 'cords' (which might be cotton, nylon or even steel wire) which prevents the tyre from bulging under load or on corners, and the whole assembly is an airtight fit on a pressed-steel wheel. The direction in which the cords run — either directly from one side of the tyre to the other, or diagonally — determines whether the tyre is of the 'radial' or 'cross-ply' design. Recently radials have become extremely popular on both production and competition cars because their sidewalls are more flexible than those of cross-plies — this provides improved roadholding on corners, since the walls flex, and the tread remains in even contact with the road, without lifting as the turn is made. Radials are more prone to damage because of this flexibility however, and transmit a good deal more road noise at low speeds.

The pressed-steel wheel is attached to its hub by a number of nuts and studs. (These are the nuts that generally appear to have been tightened up by a Sumo wrestler when you're trying to get the wheel off after a puncture.) Wire wheels simply have one huge central nut with ears on it so that it can be hammered tight.

The hubs are actually an enclosure or cage for the wheel bearings which consist of a ring of ball or roller-bearings for smooth running and general resistance to the wheel's tendency to rock vertically, particularly when cornering.

Brakes.

Friction and motion don't naturally see eye-to-eye. If you need a mechanism that will retard motion abruptly, then the introduction of friction will

Left: Rack-and-pinion type
Below: Worm-and-peg type

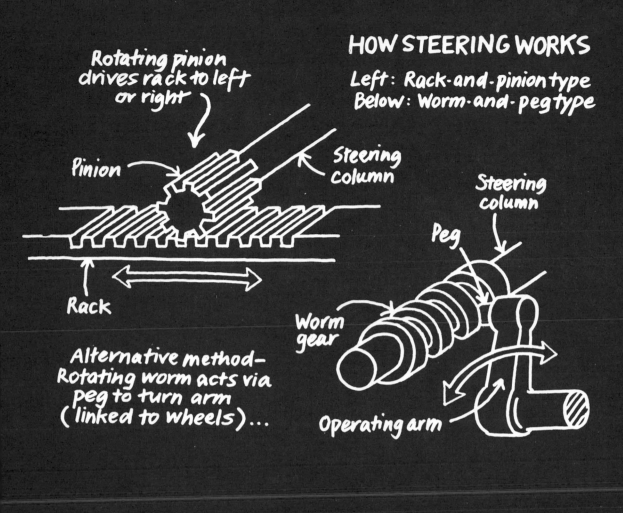

Rotating pinion drives rack to left or right

Pinion

Steering column

Rack

Steering column

Peg

Worm gear

Operating arm

Alternative method—
Rotating worm acts via peg to turn arm
(linked to wheels)...

CROSS PLY TYRES

RADIAL TYRES

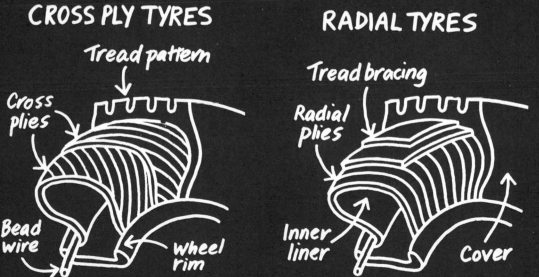

Tread pattern

Cross plies

Bead wire

Wheel rim

Tread bracing

Radial plies

Inner liner

Cover

come into it somewhere. Though unlubricated metal-to-metal friction is sometimes used as a form of braking, it causes very rapid wear of the components and makes a fearsome din. Far better to make one of your rubbing surfaces softer than the other — that way you don't wear the metal component at all, and you can replace the wearing surface of the braking device at regular intervals.

On a bicycle, the braking system is a set of rubber pads that the brake linkage pulls into contact with the inside rim of the revolving wheel. On a railway engine it's a curved shoe that follows the contours of the wheel and is pulled tight against the circumference of it when the brakes are applied. On a motor car it's the railway engine's principle turned inside out.

Bolted to the car's axle is a circular plate with two crescent-shaped 'shoes' with hardened asbestos faces attached; the shoes can be induced to move further apart in response to the compression of hydraulic fluid, which is caused by the action of your foot on the pedal. Springs pull the shoes back to their 'rest' position when the pistons retract in their cylinders. Either bolted to, or in one piece with the hub, is a cast-iron drum about the size and shape of a tambourine, and the drum, hub and road-wheel spin around the stationary brake gear. The shoes are adjusted so that in the 'rest' position they very nearly touch the inner rim of the drum, but not quite. When the brakes are applied and the wheel pistons force the shoes slightly farther apart, the asbestos linings start rubbing against the spinning drum and, if progressively applied, will eventually lock it virtually solid.

There are variations on this in the disc-brake system now in widespread use. The friction principle is the same, except that a cast-iron disc takes the place of the drum, and a 'jaw' of friction pads replaces the shoe assembly. Brake pedal action causes the pads to come together and 'bite' the disc. Disc brakes are generally thought of as preferable these days, particularly as production cars have got increasingly nippy; drum brakes have a tendency to overheat under very exacting conditions.

In the early days, the necessary leverage to get the wheel cylinder pistons pushing outwards against the shoe-ends was simply performed by levers or cables linked to the foot-pedal. Flexing of the chassis and movement of the suspension could upset these brakes, and they were eventually superceded by systems that were activated by hydraulic fluid being forced through pipes.

Overleaf, you can see how the fluid gets around on a typical hydraulic braking system, with an extra mechanical link from the handbrake to the rear shoes. Flexible hoses couple the steel tubes to the moving parts of the car, i.e. the front wheels and the rear axle. The oil or brake fluid is vegetable based and specially designed to withstand high temperature operation.

Suspension.

Even with air-filled tyres, a moving vehicle's wheels follow the hills and dales of the road surface with uncomfortable thoroughness; mounted direct to the frame of the car, naturally the whole of the bodywork and the stomachs of the occupants will be obliged to do the same. The result is that the bodywork of both vehicle and passengers will very rapidly fall to bits. The attachment of axles to the vehicle has got to be via something that will stretch.

The simplest form of road-springing is the famous 'cart-spring' which merely consists of several strips *(leaves)* of tempered steel clamped together — they're often forged in a gentle curve which flattens as the spring takes a bump but is always trying to revert to its original shape. Each end of the spring is bolted to the frame of the vehicle, and the axles are bolted across the centre of the springs. The fastening points on the frame are called the *spring shackles*, and one out of each pair is able to swing in either direction, so it can accommodate the increased length of the spring as it flattens out.

Old as it is, the leaf-spring isn't what generally comes to mind if the topic of springs is up for discussion (admittedly not a subject guaranteed to get a roomful of revellers eating out of your hand). The ordinary jack-in-the-box coil spring is the most popular member of the family and is used in vehicle suspension systems too, between an upper and lower pair of hinged suspension arms (*wishbones*) attached to the steering swivel or the hub assembly. Also used from time to time is the *torsion bar* system in which the up-and-down movement of the suspension arm simply twists a specially designed steel rod — the torsion in the rod means that it's always trying to unravel itself and restore the equilibrium before the bump knotted it up.

The leaf-spring arrangement is usually used to suspend a *beam axle*, one that is a solid piece of metal running from one side of the car to the other. Hitting a bump with an axle like this naturally tends to tip the whole assembly up and the shock is felt right across the vehicle. The coil spring and torsion bar arrangements shown here are used in *independent suspension* systems, in which each wheel has its own separate provision for springing, and is hinged to the frame of the car by something similar to the wishbone design that we've illustrated.

In the pursuit of Luxury You Can Afford, the car designers haven't stopped here of course, and have furiously addressed themselves to coming up with suspension systems that make the car float like a waterbed. Citroens have used a compressed gas system on their bigger saloons, which basically com-

Section through brake
assembly to show action
of brake linings...

HOW BRAKE LININGS WORK

Wheel
cylinder

lining

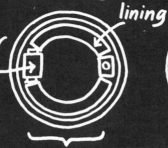

Pedal depressed,
linings forced against
drum by pistons
in wheel cylinder

Brake pedal released,
drum runs free

Axle nut

Hub

Wheel bearings

STUB AXLE ASSEMBLY

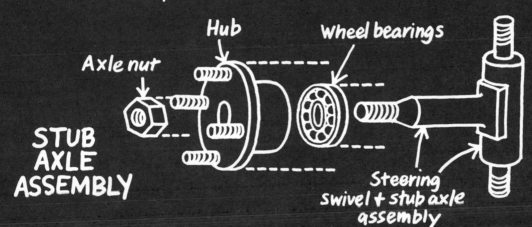

Steering
swivel + stub axle
assembly

Brake
drum

Roadwheel
studs

Hub + wheel
bearing

Wheel
cylinder

Springs

Brake lining
and shoe

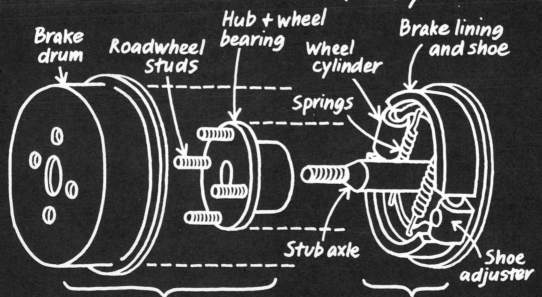

Stub axle

Shoe
adjuster

Brake drum + hub assembly
(spinning with roadwheel)

Stub axle + brake plate
assembly (fixed)

THE BRAKING SYSTEM

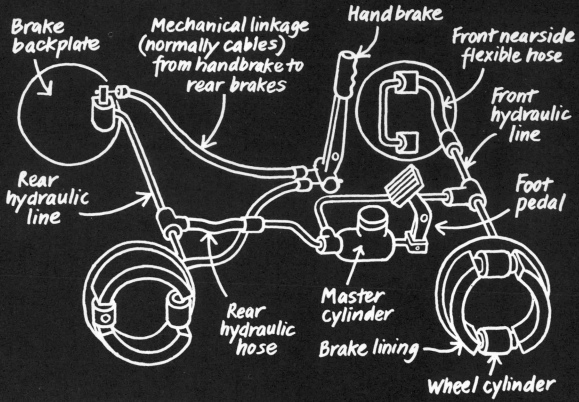

Brake backplate

Mechanical linkage (normally cables) from handbrake to rear brakes

Hand brake

Front nearside flexible hose

Front hydraulic line

Rear hydraulic line

Foot pedal

Rear hydraulic hose

Master cylinder

Brake lining

Wheel cylinder

ACTION OF MASTER AND SLAVE CYLINDERS

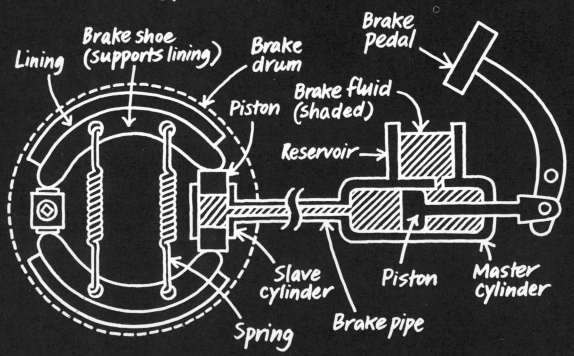

Lining

Brake shoe (supports lining)

Brake drum

Piston

Brake Pedal

Brake fluid (shaded)

Reservoir

Slave cylinder

Piston

Master cylinder

Brake pipe

Spring

COIL SPRINGS

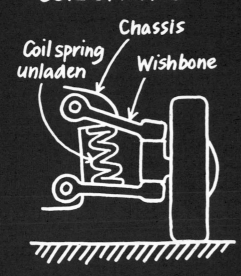

Coil spring unladen

Chassis

Wishbone

LEAF SPRINGS

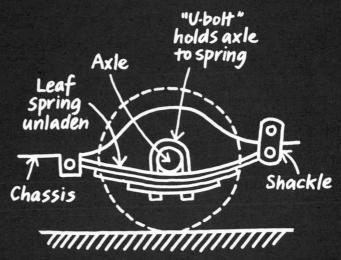

"U-bolt" holds axle to spring

Axle

Leaf spring unladen

Chassis

Shackle

Coil spring compresses under load

Leaf spring flattens under load

Shackle allows for length variation

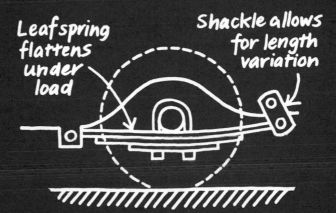

Wishbone

TORSION BARS

Wishbones pivot on chassis

This end free to twist with movement of suspension

Torsion bar

This end fixed to chassis

Torsion bars are gripped at one end and twisted at other by lever...

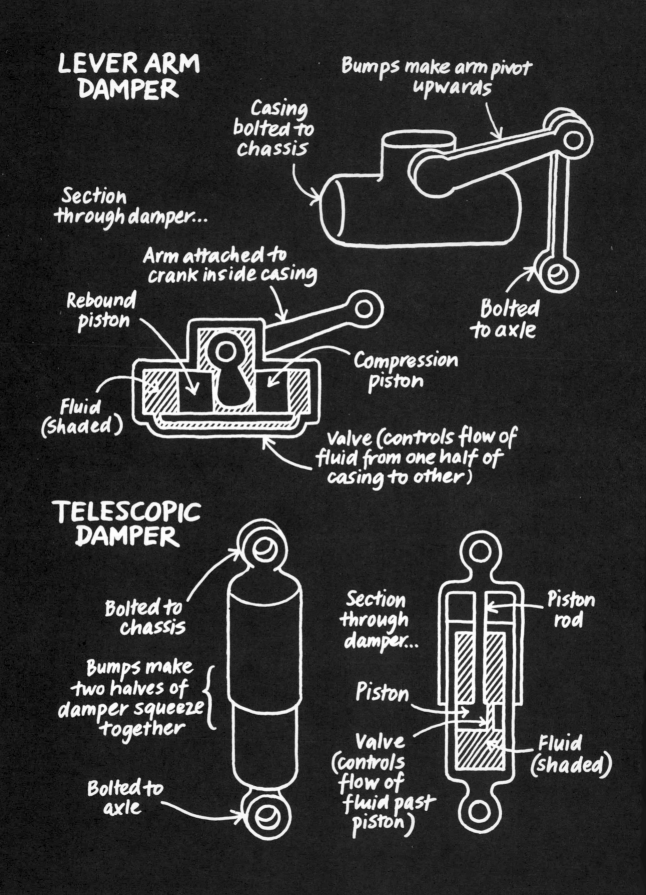

LEVER ARM DAMPER

Bumps make arm pivot upwards

Casing bolted to chassis

Bolted to axle

Section through damper...

Arm attached to crank inside casing

Rebound piston

Compression piston

Fluid (Shaded)

Valve (controls flow of fluid from one half of casing to other)

TELESCOPIC DAMPER

Bolted to chassis

Bumps make two halves of damper squeeze together

Bolted to axle

Section through damper...

Piston rod

Piston

Valve (controls flow of fluid past piston)

Fluid (shaded)

prises a piston attached to each wheel compressing the gas as the car passes over a bump. British Leyland have for some years used the Hydrolastic system (later modified to the Hydragas system) which works on much the same principle — the first version using hydrolastic fluid (non-compressible water-based liquid), the second using nitrogen. Leyland's version actually linked the springing action of the front suspension to that of the rear wheels, reducing the tendency of the car to pitch from end-to-end on its springs.

Conventional springs are pretty effective at riding the bumps, but there are side effects — like a vibrating rubber band, springs don't just twang once and then stop; they're inclined to go on oscillating long after the bump has been and gone, which makes things uncomfortable for the travellers.

Consequently *shock absorbers*, or *spring dampers* are used to control the deflections, and they're generally mounted between the point where the spring is attached to the axle and the chassis.

Nowadays shock absorbers are always hydraulic, and function by squirting oil from one chamber into another — so slow spring movements make the reciprocating action of the damper gentler. Safety valves have to be incorporated so that a sudden bang doesn't produce such a dramatic rise in hydraulic pressure as to damage the instrument.

The Tin Can: Bodywork.

Up to now we've thought of the motor car as a collection of bits and pieces, just as you might get them over the counter in the stores. Working out a way of holding them all together has occupied many drawing boards over the last half-century, though it wasn't until the 'fifties that the major design change came about that has decided the construction of most family motors up to the present day.

Until that time, the 'bodywork' of a car was always treated as something that could be added after the machine was already a road-going vehicle in its own right. A chassis was built from heavy-section steel sheet, welded together in channel-sections or box-sections. One length of this stuff would run down each side of the car, linked with several cross-braces on to which the suspension, power unit and pretty well every other mechanical device would be mounted. The problem with a chassis like this — apart from its considerable weight — was that it would quite readily twist lengthwise, setting up a good deal of creaking and groaning in the bodywork and sometimes making the vehicle difficult to steer. The light z-section chassis made by the Morgan Company were so flexible in fact that the Morgan owner's running gag is that if you park the car with one wheel up on the kerb you can't get the door open.

Under this early arrangement, bodies were quite often made by separate companies, a service that a variety of coachbuilders offered to Rolls Royce. The bodywork was constructed from a frame made of seasoned ash timber, which was then panelled in steel or aluminium. The faithful Morgan Co., determined to preserve their illustrious past, still do exactly that, on cars that are now powered by highly sophisticated modern engines.

Everybody else has gone over to the 'monocoque' construction, in which the chassis is dispensed with, or reduced to a self-contained subframe at the front and back, and the rest of the car is literally a tin box, welded together from light-gauge steel. Nothing is actually lost in structural strength, because the designers have made use of the fact that a tube or a box made from quite insubstantial thicknesses of metal is extremely resistant to bending or shock. To get the hang of the idea, try crushing a beer-can by standing it upright and stamping on the top. It's well nigh impossible to do, and the reason lies in its construction — the raw material amounts to very little. All this now means of course that every part of the car's body is intended to contribute towards its all-round rigidity — so you can't saw off the upper half of your Mini to add a soft top without winding up with a soft bottom into the bargain.

But despite their impracticality for modern production line methods and their excess weight when petrol costs a fortune, chassis-built cars have in many cases stayed on the road for half a century and monocoque cars are often written off by the M.O.T. man after ten years. Since the bodywork of the monocoque car is simply steel sheet cunningly deployed, everything's agreeable until the structure is weakened by rust. If this happens somewhere vital, such as where the wheels join the body, then the car may have passed the point where even a spot of judicious welding will help.

P.S.

You can't jump to conclusions about motor cars simply because you feel that you've grasped the rudiments of the systems that make them go. (You might not feel that now, of course, in which case we've slipped up somewhere.) Within the limits that are more or less unvarying — the way pistons and crankshafts do their jobs, for instance, the way ignition systems work, the way gears vary the speed between inputs and outputs — there are nevertheless a million and one subtleties introduced by individual manufacturers, all attempting to make their particular product more attractive, more reliable, easier to service and so forth. You are now ready for the next step, and, if you buy the book of information about your car (the workshop manual), you should have the basic knowledge to understand it.

Thus prepared, as Baden-Powell would wish, we can actually insert a toe gingerly into the water.

Chapter Two

How To Buy A Good Car.

This chapter serves a dual purpose. If you don't yet have a car and want one, we shall use what has been described up to now in a slightly different way; the book has been mostly taken up with what various bits of apparatus are supposed to contribute to the car's performance when they're all working properly. We're now going to look at exactly the same bits and pieces but in the light of what they contribute to the performance when they're working badly, or not at all. Because, when you buy a car, it's faults that you look for, not an opportunity to congratulate the vendor. On the other hand, if you're already a suffering owner, it does no harm to keep a close watch on the signs of impending mischief. Even if you do no servicing yourself, garages are far from infallible. By spotting something that your neighbourhood service station has missed, you may save your entire relationship with them a great deal of unnecessary aggravation later.

Choosing The Right Sort.

In the good old days when every car builder seemed to be able to impart a distinctive personality to even his bread-and-butter products, choosing what car to buy was a simpler business. Some people got so attached to one particular marque that they would stick with it for a lifetime. As the manufacturers have taken one another over, the names have stayed the same but the machines have grown increasingly indistinguishable; not only in appearance, but through frequently sharing identical clockwork.

Not all of this has been a regression, except in the eyes of nostalgic motoring buffs. More sophisticated engineering has meant that high performance can increasingly be combined with relatively low cost, reasonable fuel consumption and reliability. Performance has now become so good in fact, and appearances so similar, that you might as well make your choice among new models on the toss of a coin.

Whether you're buying new or obliged to find a second-hand car in as good a condition as you can get, you'll need to do some arithmetic and perusal of your bank statements first. Start with the figure that you think you can reasonably reach for the initial outlay. Then start to work out the fixed costs, which will include taxing and insuring the car, its depreciation, maybe renting a garage as well. As far as depreciation goes, you can reckon on the value dropping 30% in the first year of its life, 15% in the second and 10% annually after that, but a lot will depend on condition and what type of car it is.

Then work out the running costs. If you know the average petrol consumption of the car you want, you can get a rough figure based on an estimated annual mileage. Find out from the agents what the servicing costs will be for the car you fancy, and how often servicing needs to be carried out. By now, you'll either have unearthed enough information to have thoroughly put you off your first choice, and will be anxious to find something else that fits the figures better, or you're ready to start looking more closely at whether you and the machine will suit each other down to the ground.

Overall outlay and economy of running are probably the most important factors that will enter into the argument if you don't have the kind of budget at your disposal that would enable you to dispense with such considerations. But a car that you find awkward, cramped or unresponsive to drive can become as thoroughgoing a nuisance as one that's fun to drive but unreliable. Remember that cars are like off-the-peg suits, they're only adjustable up to a point. If you're very big or very small, you might find that some cars simply don't suit you for legroom, headroom, visibility or design of furniture. Take account of the controls of the car, particularly the ones that you need to be able to reach without taking your eyes off the road or wasting too much time. This would naturally include the gearshift, an instrument that can come in a variety of guises. The majority are positioned on the floor between the front seats, and for a four-speed gearbox the shift generally takes the form of the familiar H-pattern. On some sportier cars the gearshift may have been designed to retain the old-fashioned 'positive' feel — it's short and stubby, with a very precise movement into each gear. Some drivers can't stand any other kind of sensation than this and will dismiss a sloppier gear-change as 'like stirring porridge' or 'grabbing hold of a stick of rhubarb' or many another motoring adage frequently detected bouncing around saloon bars. There's no doubt that a more precise gearchange makes driving feel more like a craft than a convenience, but with the increasing tendency for the gearbox of the car to be stowed crosswise at the front or at the rear, the 'remote' gearshift has come to stay.

Pedals are another feature that can vary a great deal in design and convenience of use. You can find cars with all sorts of awkward idiosyncrasies in that respect that sometimes makes it seem as if the designer never actually left the drawing board. You might find your toes being struck by a universal joint on the steering column as you slip the clutch while parking, or that the accelerator pedal is placed so much further forward than the footbrake that you have to heave you leg back several inches before you can switch from one to the other – an operation that in an emergency might waste that crucial split second. Some drivers enjoy 'heeling and toeing' (using one foot on both brake and accelerator simultaneously) as well, a driving technique that enables you to double declutch whilst braking – if the pedals aren't reasonably level, it's almost impossible to do. So look for a pedal arrangement that keeps your feet from being caught up on any obstacles while you're operating them, and that isn't awkwardly offset from the line of your body so that you have to perform like Houdini to drive the car at all.

How convenient are the other driving controls? Can the inclination of the steering wheel be altered to suit the position of the driving seat, or, more to the point, the driving seat with your unique anatomy perched in it? Can you operate the headlamps, dipper switch, wipers, horn and trafficators easily while the car is on the move? Are the seatbelts comfortable?

And then there's the matter of space. Not just space for people, though that's something you'll have to consider carefully if this car is intended to be family transport, but space for luggage and for the mountains of maps, guides, manuals, parking tickets, pens, pipes, and other paraphernalia that need to be conveniently stowed in glove boxes or pouches somewhere in the car – either under the dash, or in the door trim, or behind the rear seat. The shape of the car and the disposition of its mechanics will often determine the amount of space there is for heavy luggage – boxy 'biscuit tin' kinds of cars might have quite considerable luggage space whilst being fairly small in size, particularly if they're transverse engined. (Transverse or rear engined cars also save space for the passengers too, since the 'transmission tunnel' or hump that normally covers a propeller shaft doesn't have to pass down the centre of the car from the engine to

the back wheels.) Some manufacturers have taken to saving space by stowing the spare wheel in an over-large engine compartment, thus freeing a considerable amount of boot room. With its sloping front, the Volkswagen beetle, for all its other advantages, isn't over-endowed in this respect.

The Sales Pitch.

Though you'll probably have decided at the outset the *class* of your intended purchase (babycar, light saloon, a G.T. or pepped-up version of a light saloon, or an altogether heavier, thirstier and more luxurious vehicle), different manufacturers will make use of the same basic hardware in a variety of ways. The roads are infested with 1,300 c.c. vehicles these days for instance, now that petrol has become so costly, but they vary considerably in performance and handling – according to the design of the engine and carburation, the arrangement of the gearing and the design of the steering and suspension.

Performance figures are quoted by the manufacturers in their advertising and by the motoring press in road testing new vehicles. Unless you have some idea of the relevance of these figures, the specification amounts to little more than so much blinding with science.

Much of the information supplied about the design rather than the performance isn't especially relevant to the non-enthusiast owner since the practical outcome of variations in design – performance and economy – are dealt with elsewhere in the specification. The manufacturer will quote the number of cylinders in the engine and the way they are disposed, as well as the diameter (bore) and length of piston travel (stroke) and displacement (capacity in cubic centimetres or c.c.). They will also briefly describe the arrangement of the valve gear (overhead cam or o.h.c., push rod and rockers, or whatever) the design of the carburettors and the fuel supply.

These are all explained in the first chapter, which deals with the fundamentals. Car makers will then quote a *brakehorsepower* or b.h.p. figure for the machine.

Power, in any terms other than the metaphysical, is defined as a force multiplied by the speed at which the force can be exerted. In the early days of motoring, engineers found that the pistons moved up and down at roughly the same speeds for any given engine size, and that gas pressure on the piston crowns was pretty constant too. So the only determinant of the *force* with which the piston could be thrust downward against a load would be the total area on which the gas pressure acted.

The formula for horsepower therefore involved simply multiplying the bore diameter of the engine by the number of cylinders and including a constant that would result in the horsepower figure being in the appropriate units of measurement. Now that modern lubricants and sophisticated gas flow designs have accelerated piston speeds to something like four times the old rates for the same engine size, this formula is no longer relevant. So modern testing methods result in a different kind of measurement of what is known as 'brakehorse-power' — the engine is run on a bench against a braking device.

Contrary to what you might expect, the greatest pulling ability (or *torque*) exerted by an engine isn't necessarily produced at the highest engine speeds. Torque is the twisting effort which gas pressure on the pistons generates at the crank-shaft.

Valve timing design on the average motor car is intended to ensure that at very high engine speeds the gas flow is still regular and the fuel isn't coming when it should be going or going when it should be coming. Because of this, there is inevitably a certain amount of backflow of gas at low speeds, and at the highest speeds the combustion chambers haven't time to completely fill with fresh gas. So generally the engine is working at its greatest efficiency in the middle range at around half maximum revs.

In the equation Power = Work x Speed, the work is the torque, and since it drops as the speed reaches maximum, so does the power; the torque doesn't drop proportionately with the speed increase but catches up with it eventually. So maximum torque is reached before maximum power. The graph shows how the figures for torque and brake horsepower compare for given engine speeds.

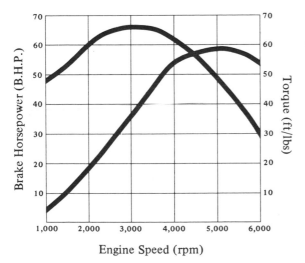

Engine Speed (rpm)

Maximum torque is closely related to engine dimensions. Mainly because the *amount* of fuel that can be burned during the working cycle is the crucial factor; though sophisticated engines with high compression ratios can develop more torque relative to their size.

B.h.p. can be quoted as if the engine were on the testbench, or as if it were in the car; gross b.h.p. refers to the former case and describes the amount of power produced by the engine at a given number of revolutions, usually between 4,500 and 5,500. *Nett b.h.p.* is a more realistic figure, since it describes the power output after it has been reduced by the presence of ancillaries such as the fan and the dynamo, and the back-pressure from the exhaust. Nett b.h.p. of, say, a baby Fiat, might be between 18 b.h.p. and 23 b.h.p. at around 4,500 revs, that for the 2 litre Lancia Beta twin cam engine 121 b.h.p. at 5,500. Some of the race preparations of the famous old Jaguar XK120 engine took the b.h.p. as high as 265, some 50% higher than standard. While semi-informed enthusiasts tend to bandy around expressions like brakehorsepower, its significance to the average car buyer is limited since what b.h.p. *means* in practical terms is expressed in other ways as a function of the car's overall performance.

The manufacturer will also specify a *torque figure* for the engine. Torque is a measure of lever-age or pulling power (as we explained on p. 43). If you're trying to exert leverage, it's obvious that there are two factors affecting the amount of effort exerted — one is the length of the lever (in this case, the stroke of the piston), the other is the amount of force applied to the end of it. So torque is measured in foot/pounds, or sometimes inches/pounds or kilogram/metres — whichever way, the figure expresses the relationship between leverage and pressure. As applied to the engine it describes the twisting force that the moving pistons are able to apply to rotate the crankshaft.

Torque actually tells you a good deal about the *flexibility* of an engine. Flexibility is generally taken to describe its behaviour when the revs drop — if the engine quickly starts labouring so that you have to change gear a lot, it's regarded as being fairly inflex-ible. Maximum torque isn't developed at the highest speed the engine will put out without blowing up, it generally appears at around half to two thirds of the maximum safe revs. If it's quoted as peaking at around 3,500 revs then the car will be of the type in which you need to 'keep the revs up', in other words do a lot of fussy gearchanging and hard acceleration in traffic, with a corresponding rise in the fuel con-sumption. If it peaks at between 2,500 and 3,000 the flexibility is good and the fuel consumption will be better. Bigger engines tend to be more flexible, but the gain in fuel consumption is cancelled out by the higher capacity. The old Rolls Royce Phantom was so flexible that you could smoothly accelerate it from walking pace in top gear.

In any country that puts a limit on high-speed driving, acceleration becomes a far more important feature of the performance of a motor car than a high top speed. The motoring magazines give acceleration figures for cars that they test and you can get hold of performance data for pretty well any vehicle that you're likely to want to buy. The experts get their 0–30 m.p.h. acceleration times under fairly tyre-shredding standing-start conditions, so the results would be better than anything you'd ever want for normal traffic driving — but the information from the middle of the speed range would be likely to be much the same as you could get yourself, and these are the figures to note. Getting good acceleration without changing down is a fuel-saving asset, so compare some results between cars of the same engine size for acceleration times between 30 m.p.h and 50 m.p.h in top gear.

Fuel consumption figures are usually quoted as overall figures simply relating the amount of fuel used to the mileage covered during the test, with a 'typical' figure included too, averaged out from a series of runs. Fuel consumption figures give only an approximate indication of running costs since a great deal depends on how the car is handled.

Handling.

Handling and roadholding will also be discussed in the test report, and the testers will have examined this feature by cornering the car at high speeds and forcing it to lose its grip. 'Understeer' and 'oversteer' are two expressions that you hear a good deal of in this context. Understeer describes the impression that some cars give you that they're always trying to take a corner wider than you seem to be inviting them to — despite your efforts at the steering wheel, the nose still runs wide. If the car tightens into the turn and appears to be changing direction more sharply than you're steering it, this is oversteer. Cars with front-wheel drive tend to the latter, rear engined cars to the former. Since oversteer if carried too far can actually result in you losing grip of the back wheels altogether, understeer is generally reckoned to be the less hazardous condition and most car manufacturers try to arrive at a design that combines a mild degree of it with the most comfortable suspension arrangement they can devise without upsetting the handling. ('Hard' suspension is generally much better suited to precise and accurate driving, but it's hardly a good sales point so the car makers have to arrive at a compromise.)

Where And How.

If you're buying new then you will normally pay a visit to one of the agencies that act as a local outlet for the car of your choice; manufacturers appoint distributors for their vehicles, who in turn supply the main dealers in particular localities; then there will be a much more extensive network of local agents who specialize in servicing the manufacturer's products and will be able to order them for you as well, even though they might not be part of the agent's regular stock.

As the Department of Trade keeps on dolefully observing, the British are turning over an increasingly large slice of the new car market to foreign competition. In recent years it's been the Italians, the French and the Japanese who have led the movement of turning innocuous looking family transport into wolves in sheep's clothing — and done it at reasonable prices as well.

You'll have to do some detective work beyond the information you can get from magazines, manufacturer's literature and test-drives; how much does the car cost to service at the recommended intervals? What's the reputation of the local agents for the car? Is it a new and unproved model, or is it an updated version of a power unit design that has already established itself?

A great many people buy new cars on the recommendations of others, and if you can collar somebody who has owned the model you want, then you can glean some information that the ads won't mention and the road tests won't have discovered about its resistance to rust, mechanical reliability and general convenience of use.

Get a quote for the regular servicing costs from the local agents. Find out if the car's first service after delivery is free, or at least involves no labour charge. Maintenance costs could be a decisive factor particularly if the cost of spares is high. Find out if the car is undersealed at the factory, or the cost of undersealing it if it isn't. (Getting this taken care of will not only spare you a lot of worry about what's happening underneath in the winter, but will help preserve the resale value of the car.) Find out how quickly it depreciates by comparing ads for cars of different years; a fast depreciating car may be expensive to run or prone to rust. Find out the cost of things you might expect to replace within the first three years or so: batteries, exhaust systems, brake relines, maybe even a new windscreen if you're unlucky enough to get yours broken.

Remember that AA members can add to their stock of background knowledge about the car they want to buy through the test reports available from that organization.

The Once-Over.

If you're buying new, naturally the problem of teething troubles is covered by the terms of the sale, though that shouldn't prevent you from making a thorough examination of the car and getting the dealer to correct any minor defects before he hands it over to you.

Most people who've previously been accustomed to heaving old ironmongery around the countryside tend to be a bit sloppy when it comes to checking over all the minor details on new models. After all, if you've spent your motoring life with cars that make a noise like a pneumatic drill and use more oil than they do petrol, who cares whether or not the cigarette lighter works? If you can overcome this understandable slackness, start looking for the various scratches and dents that new cars sometimes collect in the course of being shifted around; there may be loose trim fittings, faults in the upholstery, leaky windows, blown bulbs, stiff locks and all kinds of minor irritations.

Make sure that all the lights work, including the interior light and all the lights on the instrument panel, including the oil and ignition warning lamps. Make sure that these last two go out within a few seconds of getting the engine started — the ignition light may be on at slow idle. but should go out as soon as the throttle opening is even slightly increased. Check that the steering lock works, the heater and demister and the wipers and washers. Make sure that the gears and clutch operate quietly and smoothly and that the footbrake retards the car without the need to pump the pedal or depress it a long way. Try the window winders; they shouldn't be jerky or stiff. Check the fit of the doors, bonnet and boot and make sure that the fluid levels in the battery, brake and clutch reservoirs, radiator and engine sump are as they should be (see Maintenance, p. 126). Finally, it's ludicrous but by no means unheard of to find rust spots even on some new cars occasionally, particularly around the chrome trim, the windows and drain channels and in out-of-the-way spots like the bottom of the wheel arches. If there is any damage to the paintwork, get the dealer to correct it.

Buying Second-Hand.

If buying second-hand meant what it said, it wouldn't be so much of a tightrope walk. As it is, most people are obliged to buy third or fourth hand at some point in their motoring lives and an increasingly tremulous balance has to be struck between a bargain purchase price and the likely cost of keeping the vehicle on the road.

As before, you start with a budget. If it's a reasonably generous one — say between £750 and £1,500 — then it will definitely pay you to get a professional examination of the vehicle, either from a garage that's got nothing to do with the sale, or from one of the motoring organizations. The latter will present you with a comprehensive written report about the condition of the car, and once you've whittled down your possible choices, it's invaluable information. Naturally, since you're paying for the service, you don't want to use it for every one of the half dozen or so cars you consider buying. One golden rule of second-hand car buying is that if the seller doesn't want anybody to take too close a look at it, then you should beat a hasty

retreat, however pretty the car looks.

Get an idea about the current prices from one of the guides that are regularly published on the subject (such as *The Motorist's Guide to New and Used Car Prices*) but also get hold of several weeks'-worth of the very wonderful *Exchange and Mart*, a publication that provides you with more hours of innocent pleasure than the down-market Sunday papers. Once you've settled on a particular model, you'll be able to get a good idea of how much the prices fluctuate between several examples of the same car and the same year of manufacture — these fluctuations will of course depend on the car's condition, its mileage and how anxious the owner is to raise the money. At the same time, work out how fast the car depreciates too, by comparing the prices for several recent years with the new price. Wild extremes are suspicious; if the car is very low-priced for its year, it may be rotten or developing a serious mechanical fault. On the other hand it may simply be shabby but fundamentally sound, and the owner has thought its untidiness to be more of a disadvantage than it actually is. Very high prices may be on account of an exceptionally low mileage. Beware of a high price being asked because a car has recently had an extensive mechanical rebuild or a respray; in the first case, replacement engines and gearboxes don't actually add vast sums to the resale prices of older cars (though you should favourably regard an older car that has them) however much they might have cost the owner, unless the car has some kind of specialist or rarity value. In the second case, it would be preferable to buy something that already had well-preserved coachwork. The respray might have been on account of rusting or crash damage. If a car has been resprayed, avoid it if the colour isn't the manufacturer's original unless you're sold on it because it matches your socks; unoriginal colours are a depreciation point.

You can buy a used car from a dealer, or from an auction, or privately. Dealers generally ask the highest prices to allow for their mark-up and overheads, but you may get a guarantee and at least you're protected by the Sale of Goods Act against the dealer having kept any bad news from you. You don't get this protection with private sales so you pays your money and takes your choice; if anything falls off once the transaction is completed then you can't take off in high dudgeon and wrap it round the vendor's neck.

The safest kind of dealer is undoubtedly the large garage once again, which will be putting up for sale fairly recent second-hand cars that have been taken in part exchange for new ones. A warranty will certainly be offered in these cases.

Dealers and used-car traders are a different matter, since they often don't have the back-up of the large garage in such matters as repair work. If you buy from someone like this, make sure you

CHECKING OUT THE CAR'S INTERIOR

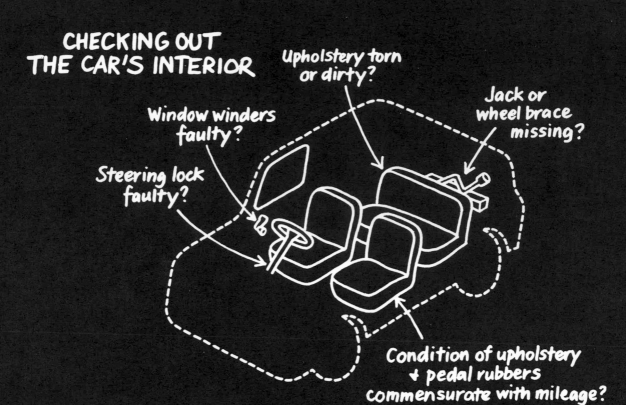

Upholstery torn or dirty?

Jack or wheel brace missing?

Window winders faulty?

Steering lock faulty?

Condition of upholstery & pedal rubbers commensurate with mileage?

CHECKING OUT THE ELECTRICAL SYSTEM

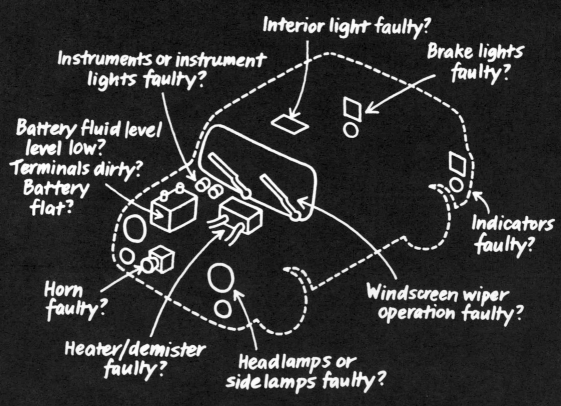

Interior light faulty?

Brake lights faulty?

Instruments or instrument lights faulty?

Battery fluid level level low? Terminals dirty? Battery flat?

Indicators faulty?

Horn faulty?

Windscreen wiper operation faulty?

Heater/demister faulty?

Headlamps or sidelamps faulty?

know exactly what the terms of the sale are; whether the guarantee he may offer will be for parts and labour, or for parts alone, or whether any corrections that you want made to the vehicle before you take it away are itemized on the order form so that he can't deny it all later on. Under the Sale of Goods Act, the dealer is obliged to ensure that his wares are of 'merchantable' quality, which means that a car has got to be able to do all the things that cars are supposed to do, and that it should meet the description he may have given of it. So anything that is likely to affect the car's roadworthiness should be fixed by the dealer as part of the sale.

You might want to put a deposit on it while you organize an expert inspection. Make sure in this case that it's in writing so that you can get the deposit back if the expert gives it the thumbs-down.

Auctions.

You can certainly find bargains at auctions and you can certainly find some of the most unspeakable heaps of scrap-iron ever to disgrace the public highways. Most of the transactions are being done by traders so you won't have their worries about what the profit margins on the deal might be; at the same time an enormous amount of junk gets pumped into the auction rooms from disbanded fleets, bodged up write-offs, and other unmentionables. Many auctioned vehicles have exceptionally high mileages for their age, and may have been used as reps' cars or minicabs. You can't road-test cars in an auction, though you might hear them running before they come under the hammer; the auctioneer will list any faults the car has, but the warranty offered may only last long enough for you to get the car off the premises and maybe drive it around for twenty-four hours. Auctions certainly put you at greater risk than any other kind of motor transaction, unless you're very experienced in the trade or have somebody with you who is.

Buying Privately.

At least in all these other possible hassles, the motor trade is now under some obligation to find out who the legal owner of a vehicle is, to tell you if it's got hidden faults, and to pick up the pieces if the sale turns out to be a dud. You don't get any of this protection privately, and, quite apart from shady vendors, a private owner may be genuinely unaware that anything drastic is wrong with the car he's selling.

So first of all you have to be sure that the car you're buying actually belongs to whoever is disposing of it. One helpful indication is whether or not you can contact the vendor again once the deal has gone through; somebody selling a car from what is obviously their own home, and possibly providing you with an office phone number as well is likely to be a safer bet than somebody who asks you to meet him at a telephone box in Chipping Norton at midnight. The registration document isn't proof of ownership, but you might make a note of previous owners, and contact them to get some idea of the history of the car. Although a finance company can't hold you responsible if you accidentally buy a car that's still under somebody else's hire purchase agreement, you want to know about such things if possible; The AA or a Citizen's Advice Bureau can help you make a check.

If you put a deposit on a car pending an investigation, get a receipt that acknowledges that the deposit is returnable if the investigation is unfavourable, and that also states the final purchase price of the car so that it can't be altered later. The law on these matters is that if you buy a stolen car, the police will arrest it as evidence as soon as the matter comes to light and then it will go back to whoever legally owned it. If the dealer sold a stolen car unknowingly, he's obliged to pay you back, but if you bought one privately you're stuck with the loss unless you can bring an action against the vendors for the money (if you can find them).

Horse-sense.

Examining used cars is a very good way to demonstrate extreme coolness and savoir faire. The hoi-polloi of course, will simply kick the tyres a couple of times, leap in, drive around the block in a cloud of dust, and say yes or no. The old hand will be distinguished by a much more leisurely approach as demonstrated in cigar adverts, guaranteed to throw scheming salesmen into confusion.

Make sure you're looking at the car in a good natural light to start with. Showrooms are extremely unhelpful for this, everything glitters like a jeweller's window. Crouch at each front wing and look along the side of the car for ripples or dents; crash damage may be glossed over by an extremely good spray job, but the number of craftsmen who can truly restore metal panels to absolute flatness is dwindling and the right light is a merciless interrogator of their skills. An aluminium bodied car that's picked up a few bangs and thumps in its life will be much more prone to rippled bodywork after repairs than a steel one. Still checking for evidence of prangs, make sure that the doors fit snugly, and the bonnet and boot, and that the car sits square on the road. If the bumpers aren't parallel to the ground, the frame may be twisted. Take a very close look at the rubber seals around headlamps, sidelamps, bonnet and boot surrounds and around the windows. If they have any traces of over-spray or paint the same colour as the coach work, then the car has been resprayed, which the dealer may not have admitted to.

The car's biggest enemy is rust, and rust that has already got an extensive hold is extremely hard to get rid of. Mostly it will form where moisture and mud can get in but not out again; so the danger spots on wings are around the headlamps, just behind the front wheels, and at the seams where various sections of the bodywork have been welded together. Lift the carpet and look for rust in the floor pan; you may find no rust but a freshly painted floor instead, which is suspicious, or burn-marks from welding. The worst nightmare in used-car buying is the 'cut and shut' job in which two halves of crashed cars of the same type have been welded together and the evidence of this should be plain once the carpets are up, either as weld-lines and burning, or a lot of heavy cosmetic work in a part of the car that in normal circumstances would never get any cosmetics.

Tap along the box sections and sills beneath the doors to see if any bits are particularly thin. Rust damage will often have been bodged with fibreglass resin; the metalwork will of course sound different when you're tapping it because it's no longer metalwork, but you can also test it with the application of a strong magnet as well. Get underneath the car as far as you can and look for rust everywhere on the underside, the sub-frames on which the power unit and suspension are mounted, and corrosion to the metal brake pipes. If the car is undersealed you're in luck. But if the underseal is very recent and the car is pretty old, then leave it alone, because underseal over existing rust is worse than no underseal at all and it may have been used to cover a lot of patchwork. Sometimes rusty metalwork will look OK at a cursory examination, but if you see one or two pinholes in a chassis or frame underneath, or pinholes and bubbles on the coachwork, don't be afraid to give it a prod with a stout screwdriver. Poke the screwdriver around any points where the suspension members, spring units or anti-roll bars are bolted to the body; rusting here can start a suspension collapse and the car will fail its M.O.T. test anyway. While you're grovelling about, look for oil leaks from the engine, gearbox and rear axle, water leaks, rusty silencers and lack of lubrication anywhere in the steering and suspension.

Fibreglass cars naturally don't suffer from rusty coachwork, but the paint finish tends to dull and occasionally goes into little cobwebby cracks if the coachwork has been in any way distorted. Checks on the underside still apply as for a conventional car, because of course the frame is a steel structure.

Examine the tyres, not forgetting the spare. Look for splits or scrubbing on the tyre walls, and make sure that the tread depth is at least 1 mm, right across the surface of the tyre. If the front tyres are worn unevenly — in other words if the inner part of the tread has worn more heavily than the outer part or vice versa, then the steering is out of alignment; possibly as a result of incorrect adjustment of the track or because the frame or suspension has been buckled in a smash.

Open the bonnet and take a look around. Look at the battery first. If the owner's been giving the same attention to his regular maintenance as we suggest you should to yours (Maintenance, p. 125) then the top of the battery casing should be clean and dry, the cells properly topped up with electrolyte and the terminals and clamps clean and not covered with that fluffy white stuff that seems to accumulate around neglected batteries. Take out the dipstick carefully; the oil level marked on it should be correct, and any evidence of foaming or water droplets in the oil should be regarded with suspicion. Water might be getting into the sump through a leaky head gasket or a crack in the block or the cylinder head. If the car has been getting regular attention to its ignition system, then somebody will have been wiping down the spark-plug leads and the distributor cap from time to time — if they're thickly coated in a mixture of grease and dust then it's also a sign of neglect and may well make the car a bad starter. Regular changing of the oil filter will also mean that the canister is likely to be cleaner than its immediate surroundings and neglect of this particular component is a bad sign for the long and happy life of the engine. Put your hand on the radiator to check if the engine's cold. Though you can't forbid the vendor to have run the car before you turn up, you can't get any idea of its cold-starting potential if it's been worked up to its operating temperature before the sale; for all you know, it might have been bump started and faulty batteries or starter motors reveal themselves much less conclusively once the engine is hot and spinning freely.

Still you don't get inside and take the test drive, which will by this time have convinced a shifty salesman that you know your business as well as he knows his, or better. See what tools are supplied with the car, which should be neatly stowed in the boot. At the least there should be a jack and a wheelbrace. Find out where the jacking points on the car are situated and jack the car up at each; you want to be sure that the jack works and that the car isn't rotting around its jacking points. While each front wheel is off the ground, grasp it at its highest and lowest points and try to rock the wheel vertically. If you can feel any slack when you do this, or worse still if you can *see* any between the stub-axle to which the hub is bolted and the swivel bearings or kingpins of the steering mechanism, then the steering or suspension is worn. Slack between the wheel and the stub-axle alone is caused by wear in the wheel bearings. These are M.O.T. failure points; if the car is otherwise sound, you might get the vendor to knock the cost of the repair off the price or get it fixed himself. Let the car back on the ground and watch the offside front wheel while you turn the steering wheel with the roadwheels in the straight ahead position. There should be no more than 1 inch of play at the

CHECKING OUT THE BODYWORK AND EXTERIOR

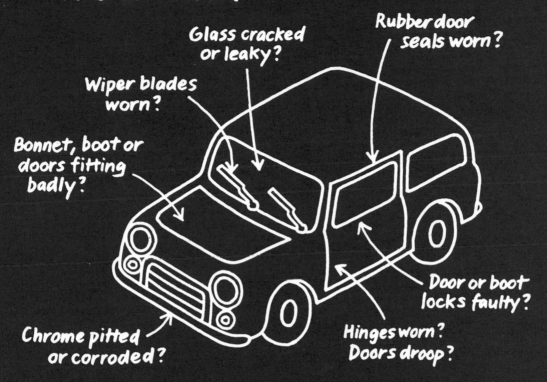

Glass cracked or leaky?

Rubber door seals worn?

Wiper blades worn?

Bonnet, boot or doors fitting badly?

Door or boot locks faulty?

Chrome pitted or corroded?

Hinges worn? Doors droop?

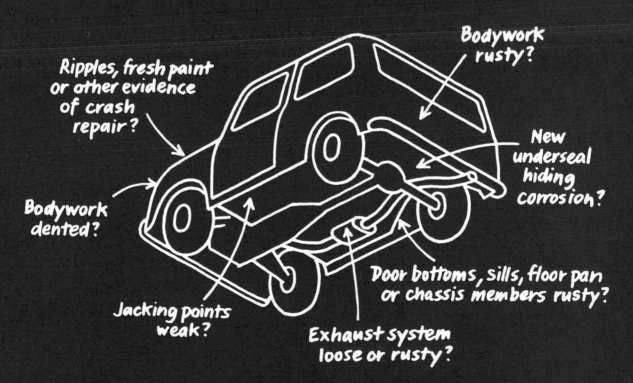

Bodywork rusty?

Ripples, fresh paint or other evidence of crash repair?

New underseal hiding corrosion?

Bodywork dented?

Door bottoms, sills, floor pan or chassis members rusty?

Jacking points weak?

Exhaust system loose or rusty?

'12 o'clock' position on the steering wheel rim before the roadwheel starts to move. Excessive slack at the steering wheel before anything starts to happen means that the steering gearbox or balljoints are worn; the car will wander on the road, and get short shrift from the M.O.T. man.

Push down on each wing of the car at a time and let the springs return it to the rest position. It should come up once and settle; if it bounces until it comes to rest, the shock absorbers are likely to be worn.

Now take to the driving seat, and check that you can adjust it into a position that's comfortable for you. Look at the mileage reading on the speedometer. What kind of a mileage you're prepared to accept depends on the price you're likely to have to pay and whether it's enough of a bargain to leave you with some spare cash for any work that becomes necessary later. A car over five years old may have done anything from 35,000 to 60,000 miles, and if the vendor can't provide any evidence of engine, gearbox or clutch rebuilds during that time, then you'll probably end up incurring some of these costs yourself. If you're not planning to keep the car long this may not be a problem. If the engine has been rebuilt or replaced, then it's a definite point in the car's favour, but don't take anybody's word for it; bills from the service station that handled the job would be a big help.

While we're on this digression, you often find that an older and cheaper car that's been carefully looked after and protected from rust and damage to its paintwork will probably have had a reconditioned engine anyway; simply because a previous owner has decided that the condition of the car is too good to let it end up on the scrap-heap. If you're buying at the cheaper end of the market — say £200 to £500 — and looking at cars that may well be seven to ten years old, then you should make a point of only answering ads that specify rebuilt engines and preferably gearboxes as well. Their mileage will be too high for the original engine to be a good risk.

If the mileage on the speedometer is low for the car's year, but the upholstery seems pretty raddled and the rubber pedal pads are badly worn, then it may be that the speedo reading is incorrect and the car has actually gone a lot further than the salesman is trying to kid you it has. Bear all these points in mind for the road test. Turn on the ignition, and make sure that the oil and ignition warning lights glow on the dashboard. Start the engine. If it's reluctant, this may be due to nothing worse than poor tune, but poor compression in a worn engine will cause it too. Take the car on to the road. If there are any complications about doing this, such as insurance or road tax problems, forget it; the only kind of car you'd buy without a road-test would be a collector's piece.

With the car on the road, check the gauges, if there are any. An oil-pressure gauge should read between 30 and 50 lb./sq. in. with the car cruising, the temperature gauge should rise gradually to the 'normal' reading but not go on into the red band, and an ammeter should read a small 'charge' current, which means a slight deflection of the needle into the + area with the engine running. If the car doesn't have any of these, make sure that the red ignition warning light and the amber oil light go out as soon as the engine is revved up, and the amber light should stay out even at idle.

Check the operation of the gears and clutch. There should be an inch or so of slack at the top of the pedal before you start to feel the resistance of the clutch springs, the gears should engage smoothly and the car move off from rest without juddering or the clutch 'snatching'. If the car only starts moving when your foot has virtually lifted the clutch pedal to its normal 'rest' position then it may be in need of adjustment or the centre-plate may be worn. You can get some further evidence of this fault if the engine speed seems to be rising faster than the car is responding, particularly on hills. Try a couple of hill-starts, to check both the efficiency of the handbrake at holding the car on a steep incline, and the freedom of the clutch from fierce operation or slippage.

Find out how well the engine accelerates in each of its gears. If any of the ratios knock or whine, the synchromesh doesn't permit smooth gear changing, or the gears jump out as you decelerate, leave the car alone. If the car has been carefully driven and you have a bit of luck thrown in, it's perfectly possible to come across very sweetly acting gearboxes, even at high mileages, so wait until you find a car that has one.

Keep an ear open for any noises that develop as you increase and decrease speed and change the load on the engine. A light tapping noise from the engine while you're accelerating hard up an incline might be an indication that it needs decarbonizing. Any hollow metallic tapping from the engine that disappears as it warms up may be piston slap, caused by the pistons being slack in their bores. If the engine rumbles during acceleration, suspect the main bearings, particularly if the oil pressure reading is low or there are oil leaks under the car. Listen for transmission noises, particularly when you take your foot off the gas when the car is cruising and it goes on the 'overrun' — a continuous graunching noise in the gearbox may be worn thrust washers, an abrupt 'clonk' at the moment you release the throttle pedal may be slack in the back axle or the drive-shaft joints. If the car is a transverse-engined, front-wheel-drive model, drive it around in a tight circle on both locks and listen for rattling or knocking from the constant velocity joints at the front end.

CHECKING OUT
THE TRANSMISSION SYSTEM

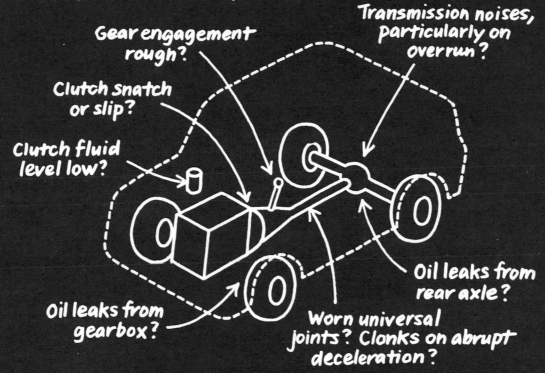

Gear engagement rough?

Clutch snatch or slip?

Clutch fluid level low?

Transmission noises, particularly on overrun?

Oil leaks from rear axle?

Oil leaks from gearbox?

Worn universal joints? Clonks on abrupt deceleration?

CHECKING OUT
THE SUSPENSION AND TYRES

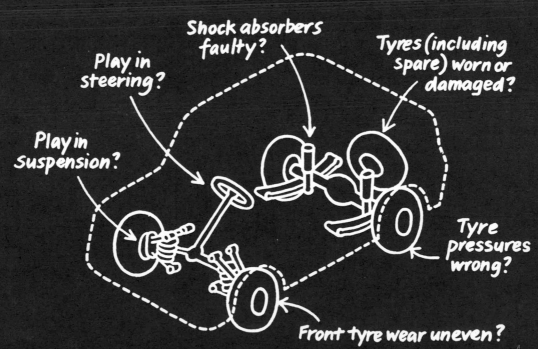

Shock absorbers faulty?

Play in steering?

Tyres (including spare) worn or damaged?

Play in suspension?

Tyre pressures wrong?

Front tyre wear uneven?

Drive over some rough ground as well as level roads. If potholes or bumps produce a real bone-shaking crash through the car, then the springs may have settled and this will be particularly likely on a heavy car with leaf-springs at the rear. With the car on a level road, momentarily take your hands off the wheel and see if it tries to pull to one side. Then try a crash stop — checking first that there's nothing behind you or it might be more of a crash stop than you'd intended — and if the brakes make the car slew or seem to be inefficient at pulling it up then suspect worn or unmatched linings, or air in the hydraulic system.

Take the car and park it, leaving the engine running. Now it should be thoroughly warm, so listen to it at idle with the bonnet up for a minute or two. Rev the engine and watch for smoke at the exhaust; black smoke may be no more than an over-rich carburettor setting, but blue smoke is a sure sign of oil burning in the combusion chambers, spelling either worn cylinders and piston rings, or worn valve guides, or both. If the engine idles very fast, and unscrewing the throttle stop on the carburettor makes it falter or stall, then there may be air leaks into the cylinders — possibly at the gaskets but most likely through a worn carburettor spindle, and new carburettors are upwards of £30 these days. You may not want to sacrifice the car for the sake of a fault like this, but make sure the vendor knows about it.

Listen at the front end of the engine for rattling at the timing cover that might indicate a worn timing chain. Rattling from within the cylinder block that gets worse when you rev the engine up to around two thirds of its maximum speed may be big end bearing noise, though it won't repeat itself when the engine is actually pulling the car at the same r.p.m. unless the wear is particularly bad. Since wear at the little-end and big-end bearings is rarely present on the full set at once, you can narrow it down a bit by lifting the plug lead off each plug in turn (protecting your hand with a rubber glove or a pair of pliers with an insulated handle) — if the bearing wear is present on only one cylinder then the rattling noise will stop when you cut the spark supplied to the faulty one.

You can do a rough compression test when the engine is hot, by putting the car in top gear and trying to push it with the ignition off. If the compressions are good and even, then pushing the car in gear will mean that you feel a definite resistance as each piston rises on its compression stroke, followed by a momentary slackness as if the engine were releasing a deep breath. You should feel this four, six or eight times in succession (depending on the number of cylinders) if you haven't collapsed gasping before you've tested the lot. A much more accurate method is to use a proper compression gauge as described in the maintenance chapter (see p. 176) — all you need is the gauge and a spark plug spanner and you can perform the test in five minutes. Make sure you know how to use the gauge though, or the results can be thoroughly misleading. The gauge manufacturer will supply a full set of instructions.

Lastly try all the electrical accessories: the horn, all the lamps, the wipers, the brake lights, and the indicators. (The last two will only work with the ignition switched on.) If after all this you're happy with the car, take a look at the registration document, make sure the vehicle has never been an insurance write-off (which will be noted on the Vehicle Registration Document), and that it carries a current M.O.T. certificate, the more recent the better.

Checklist For Used Car Buying.

1. *Loose or rusty exhaust. Blue smoke blowing on revving engine.*
2. *Worn tyres or low pressures.*
3. *Weak handbrake: won't hold the car on a steep hill.*
4. *Noisy differential gears.*
5. *Worn universal joints: 'clonk' on abrupt deceleration.*
6. *Rusty door sills, door bottoms or floor pan. Check for rust in chassis frame members and brake pipes at the same time.*
7. *Worn door hinges: doors 'drop' on opening.*
8. *Noisy gearbox, poor synchromesh or jumping out of gear.*
9. *Faulty clutch: slipping, excessive pedal travel before springs are compressed, rattle at idle in neutral, rough engagement.*
10. *Worn steering joints and suspension bushes.*
11. *Weak, snatching or unequal front brakes.*
12. *Faulty shock absorbers.*
13. *Leaky or damaged radiator core.*
14. *Battery terminals dirty, battery flat or dry.*
15. *Faulty lamps.*
16. *Slack or fraying fanbelt.*
17. *Cracked or leaky windscreen.*
18. *Slack in steering mechanism.*
19. *Faulty window winders.*
20. *Poor paintwork.*

CHECKING OUT
THE BRAKING SYSTEM

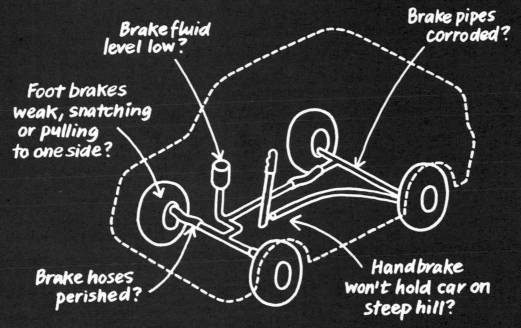

Brake fluid
level low?

Brake pipes
corroded?

Foot brakes
weak, snatching
or pulling
to one side?

Brake hoses
perished?

Handbrake
won't hold car on
steep hill?

CHECKING OUT
THE ENGINE CONDITION

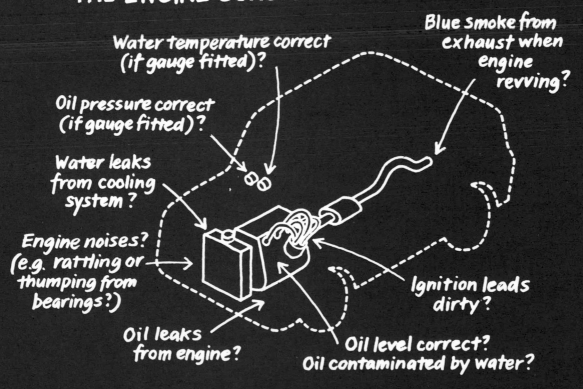

Blue smoke from
exhaust when
engine
revving?

Water temperature correct
(if gauge fitted)?

Oil pressure correct
(if gauge fitted)?

Water leaks
from cooling
system?

Engine noises?
(e.g. rattling or
thumping from
bearings?)

Ignition leads
dirty?

Oil leaks
from engine?

Oil level correct?
Oil contaminated by water?

Chapter Three

Setting Up A Home Workshop.

I once knew a man who thought that all that stuff about spanners and screwdrivers was just so much camouflage; he was sure that once the ailing machine disappeared behind those closed doors, people in pointed hats would sound off at it like Tommy Cooper and it would come out the other side with a new lease of life, as if it had just passed through some sort of transcendental car-wash. It's called 'not being mechanically minded'. A lot of people suffering from this condition fondly imagine it to be irreversible and a good proportion of them wouldn't *want* to be cured of it in any case (though they won't be reading this book).

Machines can be daunting things, and it's a temptation to feel that you can make them somebody else's responsibility not simply because you're ill-informed but because you're fundamentally ineligible. Doing things methodically is the only way to prevent the bloody-mindedness of the machine from getting on your nerves. And method is only really possible in the right conditions, and with a modicum of the right equipment.

The first step in getting this relationship off to a good start is to buy the workshop manual for whatever car it is you've found yourself in possession of. Workshop manuals and owner's handbooks are two different species. The handbook that comes with the car will explain the layout of it, where all the driving controls are, how to perform rudimentary routine roadside jobs like changing wheels and light bulbs, and often it will explain the basics of servicing, not least so you can keep some sort of check on the activities of the car's agents. It will also be littered with all kinds of reminders about things they think you ought not to touch, but unless the operation clearly does require special tools or instruments to effect adjustments, you can take some of these with a pinch of salt. Don't lose the handbook, even when you buy the workshop manual, it can often turn out to be a very handy and compact summary of routine maintenance work.

Workshop manuals on the other hand cover every aspect of the construction of the car, and they include very thorough illustrations of all the component parts, often in the form of exploded diagrams.

These are naturally technical drawings in which a great deal of detail is included, so you might find them a bit off-putting at first glance; don't try to grasp a diagram like this until you understand the principle of what it's attempting to illustrate. Have a look at the simplified drawings in the first chapter to prepare yourself.

It used to be that workshop manuals were always issued by the manufacturer of the vehicle, and they were more or less identical to the information provided to the service agencies. Manuals of this kind were very hot on technical specifications and measurements – but they naturally took a lot for granted as regards the readers' experience. In recent years, motoring publishers have been putting out their own repackaged versions of the manufacturer's data, presented with the amateur in mind; 'Autobooks' are the most comprehensive and widely available series, covering pretty well every popular car built over the past fifteen years, clearly presented and helpfully written, retailing at around £4.00. Halfords sell a range of books produced by the publishers J.H. Haynes – these adopt a slightly chattier style and a presentation halfway between that of a workshop manual and the blow-by-blow photography approach of the practical motoring magazines. The design and photography in Haynes's books have improved immeasurably since their early day, and their other advantage is that, at the moment at least, they are slightly cheaper.

Getting Acclimatized.
Don't plunge in with difficult jobs at the outset, unless your new purchase is inconsiderate enough to blow up at the first turn of the key. Get the feel of the thing with a quick weekly checkover of all the standard items like brake fluid level, water level, oil level, battery fluid level, tyre pressure checks, and so forth. Get the hang of what the car's instruments are telling you.

Then spend a few hours one weekend, preferably with someone who already understands motor cars, familiarizing yourself with the whereabouts of the more breakdown-prone components; find out where the distributor is, and the coil, and the electrical control box and fuses, and where the throttle and jet adjustments can be made on the carburettor. Find out if it's possible to get at the back of the instrument panel without crippling yourself.

Run through the roadside troubleshooting schedule we've listed in the next chapter while the car's working well, so that you know what *ought* to happen while everything's in order. Practice one or two of the simple dismantling jobs you'll need to do sooner or later; make sure you know how to get the distributor cap reclipped after you've removed it (some cars, baby Fiats in particular, can be supremely awkward in this respect and you don't want to have to discover the knack of fastening the back clip at an inconvenient time). Make sure, too, that you know how the sparking plug leads and the coil leads unfasten from the distributor cap, because it's crucial for any kind of improvised spark test that you can do this easily. If it needs a screwdriver to unfasten them, make sure you carry one of the right size. On most modern cars, the leads simply pull from the cap, but be sure that you keep them in the right firing order by labelling them with masking tape if necessary, that you press them right home when refitting them to the cap, and get the rubber sleeves properly repositioned afterwards. Learn how to remove, clean and check the gap on the sparking plugs; and one day, when you've plenty of time and aren't likely to need the car in a hurry, take the points out by following the instructions in the works manual and in Ch. 4, and replace them. You may cock it up the first time and find that the car doesn't start afterwards, but once you've solved it you won't forget again — and you can't do any permanent damage whatever happens, unless you wreck the securing screw or thread, which won't happen with care. The knowledgeable friend might be a comfort to have around while you're figuring out the whys and wherefores of contact points; panic can set in if you think you've gone wrong, instruction books or no instruction books.

Once you've acquired this kind of early experience, and a rudimentary tool kit, you should be prepared for most of the elementary on-the-road breakdowns you might be unlucky enough to encounter. When it comes to more major repair work, you have to balance a number of pros and cons. If you use the car during the working week, a weekend might not be long enough for an inexperienced mechanic to deal with a job like a clutch overhaul or a decoke, particularly if you find that you've run out of something vital after the shops have closed. You might find that your tool kit would really need some sizeable re-investments before you'd feel confident to tackle a job that might present you with stiff, rusty or inaccessible nuts, or that you'd prefer to wait for help before

you start pulling out that gearbox and discovering too late that you can't prevent its weight from distorting the clutch plate.

Mileage is a pretty good indication of how much trouble you can expect from a car that's been generally well maintained. Up to 30,000 you might expect a full brake overhaul, some replacement ignition components at service intervals, the inevitable batteries and silencers — the kind of ground covered in Ch. 5. If you are unlucky, the car might have been badly driven or used in a very hilly district and could turn out to need a new clutch plate by that time, but it would be more likely to occur between 30-50,000 miles. By now there might be a general increase in mechanical noise, though not of a very threatening kind; overhauls to the starter and dynamo and a growing lack of tone and pep from the engine. A compression test at 60,000 miles (see p 176) might confirm the advisability of removing the cylinder head for decarbonizine and attention to the valves. This is a thoroughly satisfying, approachable and not unduly frightening job for an amateur, perfectly possible with a reasonably comprehensive tool kit, and a borrowed torque wrench.

Between 60-100,000 miles you can no longer reasonably expect that the car won't cost you money, but neither need you imagine that because it's old it's liable to dump you in the back of beyond at the least provocation. It will of course be more prone to major failures, but they don't usually come without warning and will leave you plenty of time to do your sums and plan your route out of the country. There will come a point somewhere in this mileage where all the tender loving care you might expend on something like the sophisticated fault-checking procedure we go into later on will begin to be wasted, because the mechanical condition of the engine will prevent many of the adjustments from having much effect. Nevertheless, don't neglect the maintenance of an old car simply because it is old; you can greatly prolong its life by looking after it, and by keeping a regular check on the brakes (particularly the fluid level), the tyres and the running gear you may prolong your own as well.

This is always a touchy corner of home maintenance because all kinds of organizations associated with the motor trade frequently sound off about do-it-yourself car repairs leading to unsafe vehicles and a lot more work for the poor old AA. Don't give the motor agents this excuse by bodging your work, or charging off to the boozer muttering 'that'll do' with half the nuts still loose. There's absolutely no reason why someone with a modicum of brains and patience can't handle the bulk of the work taken on by trained mechanics; the difference will mainly lie in the relative speed at which you and they can work. Inexperience and rushed work is a bad combination. If you've got to work as if you

REMOVING A SPARK PLUG

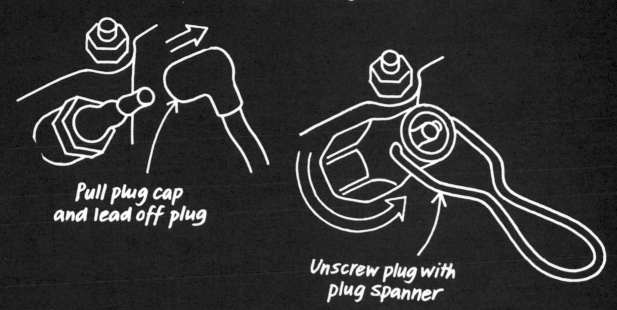

Pull plug cap
and lead off plug

Unscrew plug with
plug spanner

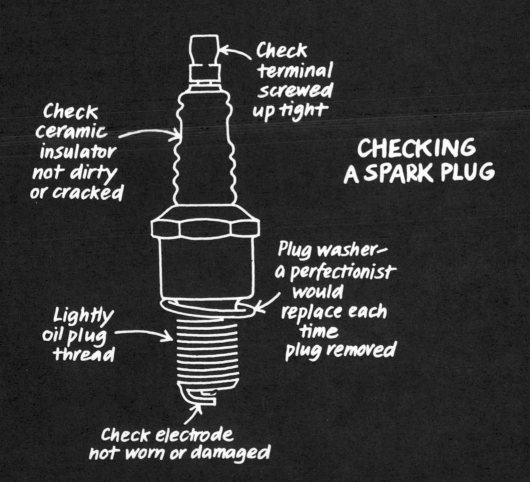

Check
terminal
screwed
up tight

Check
ceramic
insulator
not dirty
or cracked

CHECKING
A SPARK PLUG

Plug washer—
a perfectionist
would
replace each
time
plug removed

Lightly
oil plug
thread

Check electrode
not worn or damaged

were in the pits at Indianapolis, put the job off to another day or let the professional — whose speed you're paying for — deal with it this time. Dismantle things slowly, following the procedure of the workshop manual. Clean components first before you strip them down, and make a note to yourself about anything that you think might get accidentally replaced the wrong way round. Try to avoid stripping something down one week and putting it back together the next week. Check all nuts and fastenings twice, and don't ever leave out the spring washers that keep nuts from coming loose. (Better still, use new ones.) If the manual says a critical nut needs pulling up with a torque wrench, get hold of one, don't just tighten it till your sleeves bulge.

If you overhaul the steering, make sure you pay due attention to whatever method has been used to lock the nuts. This might have been by using Nyloc nuts, which have a nylon grip above the thread, in which case you *always* rebuild the thing with new ones. It might be by using split pins passed through the side of the nut and through a hole in the bolt, bent back on the other side like an old-fashioned paper clip. Get a packet of assorted split pins from the accessory shop and always rebuild the job with new ones.

Just about the best-known (and printable) inscription to decorate any shop-floor where machinery is being handled goes thus:

PLEASE ENSURE
BRAIN IS ENGAGED BEFORE
OPERATING
HAND OR MOUTH.

Put it up somewhere in your own establishment, and bow abjectly to it every time you come through the door. There's no better, or simpler, invitation to keep you on the right track. It appreciates the superficial awfulness but innate rationality of machinery; to by-pass the first and unravel the second you need only to keep a firm grip on your own powers of logic. If you reach a stage in the job where the car's obstinacy threatens to disengage your brain and send it hurtling into the ether, stop for a bit, have a cup of tea, maybe kick the cat. Don't take it out on the car; you've merely missed the short route to the solution which on reflection will seem blindingly obvious. If the problem is that you simply don't have the right instrument, then buy it or borrow it, don't go on hacking with whatever comes to hand.

This takes us to the territory of working conditions and tools: two issues that will probably determine more than anything else apart from your own temperament whether you'll remain a knowledgeable bystander or become a hardened pro.

Tools.

Paul Jennings used to maintain that the spanners issued with his lawnmower were made of lead as a deliberate piece of sabotage to undermine his relationship with the machine. Relationships with machines are certainly fragile enough, and the proper equipment for dealing with them is a crucial feature of getting things off on the right foot. This is a matter of quality, not merely comprehensiveness. There are plenty of ludicrously cheap tools on the market, many of them no doubt emanating from dark corners of the Eastern hemisphere; but you're likely to find yourself replacing them so quickly that the economy soon turns out to be a short-term one. High-quality tools for motor car applications are generally marked 'Chromevanadium' — not only is their practical quality high, but they don't rust if you accidentally leave them out in the open for a night.

As you may have noticed, most things on motor cars are held together with nuts and bolts. There are three kinds of spanners available for manipulating nuts and bolts, and as you build up your tool kit you will probably begin to appreciate the virtues of the more sophisticated kinds. The simplest are of course *open-ended spanners*, which slot over 'half' the nut — for this reason, their grip on a tight nut in an awkward position is always a bit precarious, and if they slip you may find you have rounded the flats of the nut which will make it a good deal more resistant to shifting. Though most people open their account in the tool-collecting sphere with a set of open-ended spanners, the equivalent *ring spanners* are infinitely preferable since they completely encircle the nut and the spanner stays square on it. Car manufacturers are pretty stingy about supplying tools with their vehicles these days, so you'll need to establish what sort of nuts and bolts your particular car is put together with (generally 'U.N.F.' or 'unified threads' on British cars, metrics on continental ones) and the car's local agent will be able to tell you about that. If you've invested in some sort of unlikely collector's piece then the nuts and bolts might be Whitworths, a thread type now more or less obsolete. Cars built over the last twenty years or so can generally be attended to with a set of A.F. (across flats) spanners, or a set of metric spanners if it's a continental car. A boxed set of spanners is a sensible investment, rather than collecting them individually.

The Rolls Royce of nut-tackling is the *socket set,* the most labour-saving and reliable piece of equipment you could invest in. Sockets are simply a ring-spanner's jaws embedded in a steel cylinder to which you can attach a variety of levers and braces depending on the position of the nut and how obstinate it is. Although socket sets aren't unduly

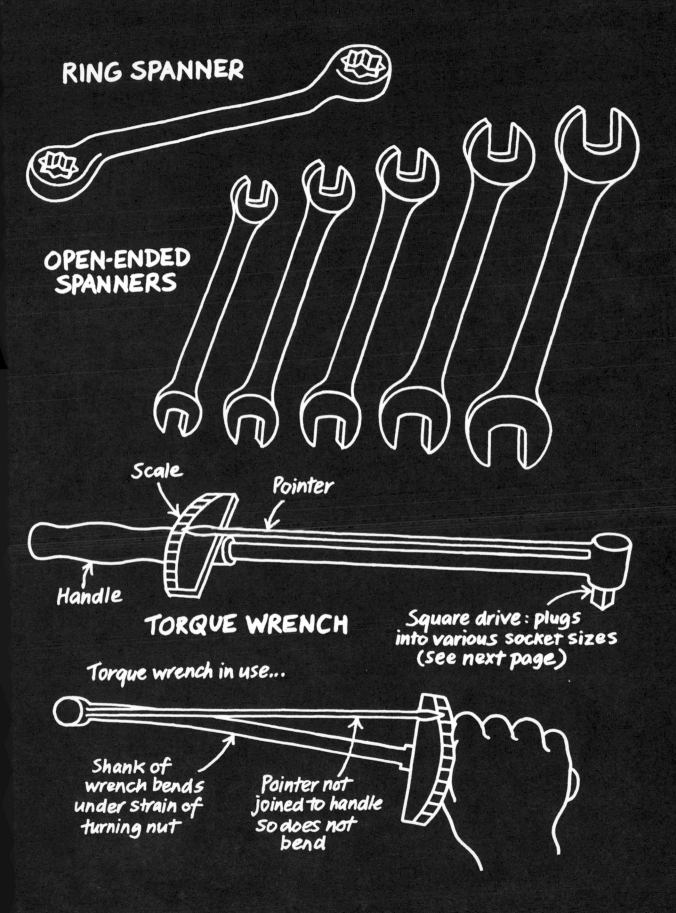

RING SPANNER

OPEN-ENDED SPANNERS

Scale

Pointer

Handle

TORQUE WRENCH

Square drive: plugs into various socket sizes (see next page)

Torque wrench in use...

Shank of wrench bends under strain of turning nut

Pointer not joined to handle so does not bend

expensive (you might be able to persuade somebody near and dear, as the manufacturers try to do, that 'they make excellent birthday presents') there's certainly no harm in building one up bit by bit since every car seems to be built in such a way that there's always one socket that does 99% of the work. (I long ago discovered that an MG TC could be stripped virtually to the chassis with a ¼" Whitworth socket.) To lever your sockets you'll need a device called a *knuckle bar,* but you'll quickly come to appreciate the advantages of a *rachet handle* and extension piece — the ratchet of course enables you to turn the nut with an easy to and froɔ pumping action rather than laboriously removing the socket from the nut and repositioning it with every half turn. A plug socket is a less advantageous device than a self-contained plug spanner with its own brace attached, and the modern ones are fitted with a rubber sleeve inside which grips the plug. This protects the insulation from clumsy manipulation of the socket, and it also holds the plug inside the socket when you withdraw it. This prevents you from dropping the plug into the bowels of the engine when you make the final turn and it's especially handy in the case of air-cooled engines like Fiats and VWs where the plug holes are obstructed by a lot of metal cowling and getting a lost plug out of there with your fingers is about as easy as getting a lost cork out of a bottle. The plug spanner is not an option, it's a must for even the most self-doubting amateur mechanic.

Hybrid Spanners.
Not all nuts and bolts have hexagonal heads. Brake adjusters, for instance, are often square in section, so you need a special brake adjusting tool for this job. Don't do it with adjustables or Mole wrenches, or you'll soon mangle the fitting altogether. Oil drain plugs on engines, gearboxes and axles come in a variety of shapes and sizes and you can either get a suitable combination spanner with several of the options included on it, or buy the appropriate spanner from the agent for the car.

The last and most luxurious item in the spanner department is the *torque wrench.* Basically a bar capable of measuring the effort applied to a nut or bolt, it can be used in combination with any socket; some torque wrenches have a pointer and scale at the handle end and you go on pulling up the nut until the pointer gives you the torque reading (in ft/lbs) specified by the car manufacturer. Others you preset to the reading you want, and they click loudly when you get there. The torque reading is simply a scientific way of expressing all that huffing and puffing you're putting into tightening up the nut. There are many applications on the car in which a torque wrench is handy but not essential; cars assembled with a lot of aluminium alloy components need care when it comes it tightening

things, because you can so easily strip threads in aluminium, and even steel will give way eventually if you and six mates are standing on one end of the spanner. Generally the length of a conventional spanner limits the amount of over-tightening you can do, but you have to take more care with sockets, where you might be tightening quite a small bolt with an excessively long knuckle bar. Torque wrenches provide you with a means of keeping all these things under control, and the fastidious amateur who regards him or herself as a species of engineer rather than a species of fitter will always make a lot of use of such an instrument.

For some jobs, the use of the torque wrench is actually unavoidable: jobs where one component is fastened by a number of bolts and the problem is not so much to avoid overstressing them, but to get all the bolts pulled up to the same tension. This naturally applies to major engine parts more than anything — things like fitting crankshaft bearings and flywheels may never intrude into your life, but fitting a cylinder head almost certainly will at some time or another. Naturally, if this is the only time you're likely to use the torque wrench, then you could hire one for the occasion. A clutch overhaul on a transverse-engined Leyland car requires one too, since there's a giant bolt in the centre of the flywheel that requires a torque reading of 110 ft./lb. Beware of this catch: some wrenches only run up to 100 ft./lb.

Screwdrivers.
For some reason screw heads seem to be much more eccentric than plain old nuts and bolts, such that however many different types of screwdriver you acquire there always seems to be a screw that needs one you haven't got. Two really hefty ones will quickly earn their keep, one straight-bladed and one cross-headed. Then a variety of others, from tiny electricians' screwdrivers for electrical components (a very small cross-headed screwdriver is invaluable for trim fittings, small jubilee clips, etc.) to medium of around six inches in length. A very short, stubby screwdriver is useful for awkward corners. Remember that screws have often been butchered by sloppy maintenance on an older car, so one of the advantages of a comprehensive set of screwdrivers is that you can often find a way out of a problem that somebody else has dumped on you. You can get a bit of help with this by using a broken piece of hacksaw blade in a pad handle and cleaning up the slot in the screw, or if it's badly damaged you might enlarge it to take a slightly thicker bladed screwdriver. There should be very little slop in the groove if the screwdriver is the correct one for the job; if it can move a lot from side to side, it's almost certain to slip and damage the head.

Apart from screws and nuts, some threaded parts of the machinery are tightened up by a kind of

SOCKET SET

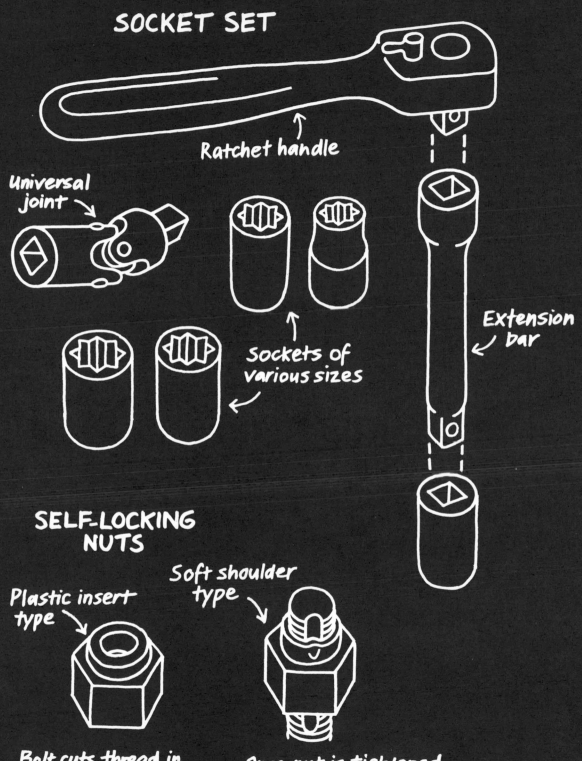

Ratchet handle

Universal joint

Sockets of various sizes

Extension bar

SELF-LOCKING NUTS

Plastic insert type

Soft shoulder type

Bolt cuts thread in unthreaded insert at top of nut

Once nut is tightened soft metal shoulder or lip is dented into groove in bolt

hexagon-headed key which fits into a suitably shaped recess in the head of the bolt. These keys are called *Allen keys*, and they range in size from '/₁₆" to ⅜" and from 1.27 mm to 10 mm. You can buy Allen keys appropriately enough in a bunch on a ring, or in a plastic pocket, but don't bother with them unless an inspection of your car has revealed something vital requiring an Allen key. Being a rather refined form of engineering, this method of fastening is often employed on more sophisticated cars.

Before we leave the subject of nuts and bolts and fastenings there is of course a problem that one doesn't confront in examining those elegant looking manufacturers' drawings but very quickly gets stumped by in real life: rust. Rust isn't simply that stuff that eats holes in your wings and door bottoms, it's the stuff that turns perfectly ordinary bolts into something close to spot-welds. Dealing with rusted fastenings requires you to examine the particular problem in the light of the job the bolt is doing, whether your tool kit is up to it, and how much time you have. Rusted bolts are of course weakened, and simply throwing a lot of weight behind a wrench may merely break the head off. There are plenty of occasions, particularly on things like exhaust mountings, where this is the ideal solution as long as you can lay hands on replacements; the condition is that both the bolt and its corresponding nut are accessible so you can get a suitable spanner on to both ends and simply over-tighten until the bolt snaps. *Don't* do it where the bolt is actually threaded into a casting or some irreplaceable component (such as for instance where a sub-frame bolt is threaded into the bodywork of the car) or you'll end up with damage that can only be repaired by tapping a new thread into whatever it is you've wrecked. This involves drilling a hole close to the bolt size and then gradually tightening a special cutting bolt called a tap into the hole to form the thread.

With this kind of problem, where a rusted bolt is clearly doing too critical a job to be merely brutalized out, a long soaking with penetrating oil ('Plus-Gas' is excellent, and can be obtained in an aerosol form) should do the trick eventually, though the application of heat from a portable blowtorch will often bring about the same result rather more rapidly. Be careful of petrol tanks and fuel lines though. If you're unfortunate enough to break the head off a screw or bolt, but you can get a wrench on to the remaining threaded part once you've removed whatever component it was holding on, then a *Mole wrench* will prove its worth. This is a kind of adjustable spanner which exerts a vice-like grip; you adjust the jaws until they're slightly narrower than whatever it is you want to shift, and than clamp the wrench on to the component. Even more effective on studs and broken bolts (in fact

anything tubular that you want to rotate) is a plumber's *Stillson* which comes in a variety of sizes and possesses the remarkable knack of gripping its victim tighter the more effort you put into shifting it. A medium size Stillson, such as a 12", is in any case a useful tool should you ever find yourself tempted into tangling with the household plumbing.

The worst disaster of the lot of course, is when you break off a bolt flush with whatever it's threaded into, so you've nothing to get a purchase on. This might seem to leave no option but drilling out the hole and re-threading it with a tap set, a laborious operation where it's difficult to be accurate if you're working in an awkward position. The last resort is the stud-extractor, which again you can obtain at all the regular High Street accessory shops; the instructions for its use are included with it. It's basically like a woodscrew threaded backwards — you drill a hole in the broken bolt, and as you tighten the extractor into the hole you begin to rotate the bolt in the opposite direction and eventually screw it out.

Keeping Entropy At Bay.

Cars are always doing their best to fall apart from the minute they leave the factory, so here are just a few refinements about the things that hold the motor car together. As we've said on the subject of spanners, nuts and bolts come in various thread sizes. Only if you have a very early car would you be likely to need Whitworth spanners; with a modern vehicle you choose between AF and metric. If you have to replace any nuts and bolts, make sure that you establish which sort you need, because if you try tightening the wrong type of bolt into a threaded hole, you could wind up with damage that might take a month of Sundays to put right.

Just tightening nuts up on to bolts doesn't stop them from falling apart. A car isn't like a piece of wrought ironwork, standing in leisurely indolence. It's continually subject to vibrations, rattles, bangs and bumps which are always doing their best to unravel all the fastenings, so engineers have developed various means of preventing this from happening. The simplest means is to squeeze something compressible under the nut, and these devices are called *spring washers*. Some spring washers have a raised serrated edge, some of them are split and slightly twisted — you can get both types in assorted packs at accessory shops and you should always replace used ones when you're making a repair.

Other ways of getting the same result are to use special *self-locking nuts*, which either have a nylon sleeve above the thread that grips the bolt, or a soft raised lip which you hammer over into a slot in the bolt.

These nuts are scrapped and replaced when they've been used once. The traditional method of

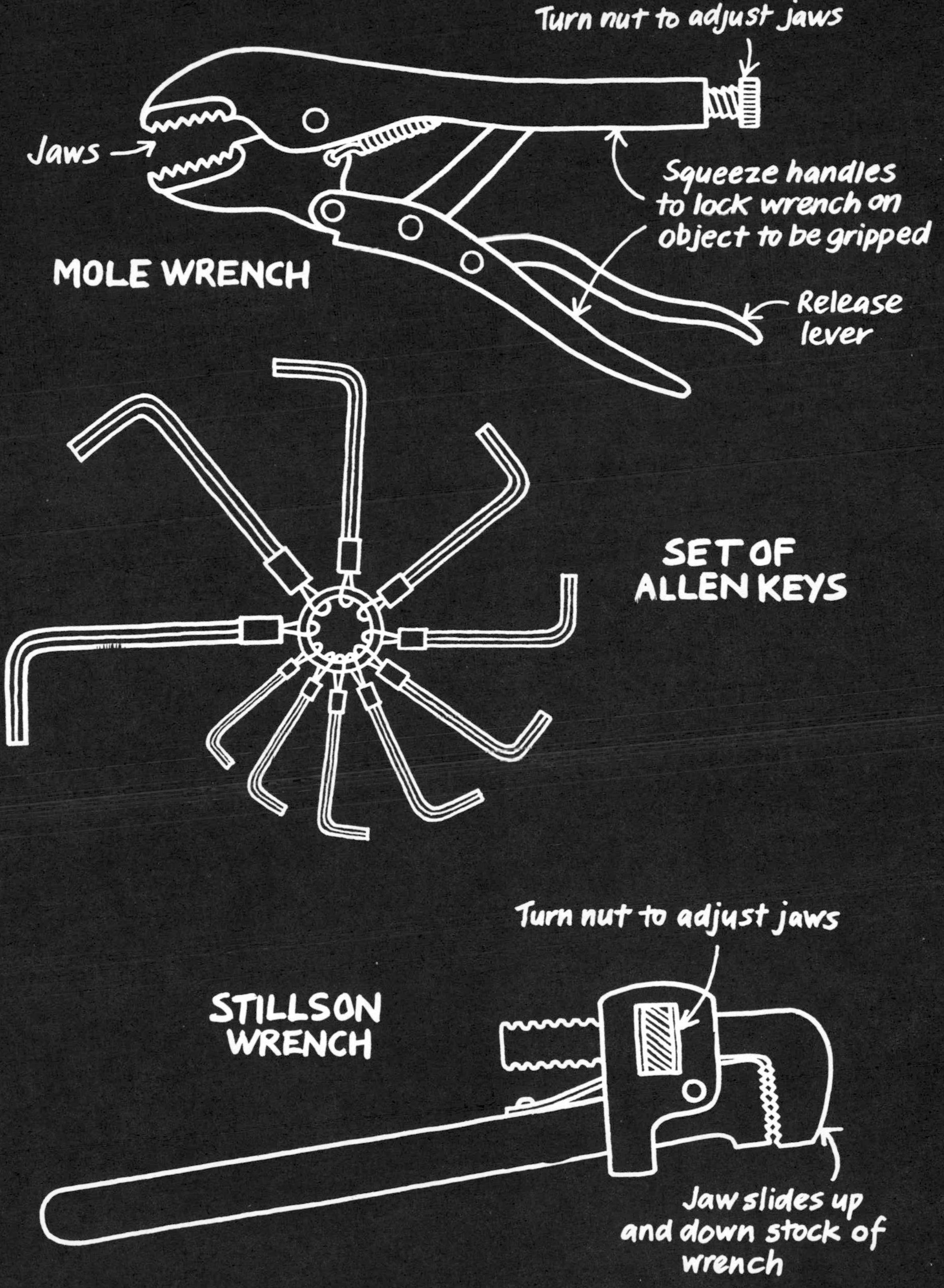

Turn nut to adjust jaws

Jaws →

MOLE WRENCH

Squeeze handles
to lock wrench on
object to be gripped

Release
lever

**SET OF
ALLEN KEYS**

Turn nut to adjust jaws

**STILLSON
WRENCH**

Jaw slides up
and down stock of
wrench

getting the same result, still often used on heavily stressed components like stub-axle retaining nuts and suspension parts, is the *split pin*. This is a device a bit like an old-fashioned paper clip, and is used in conjunction with what's called a *castellated nut*. This is simply a nut that looks as if it's got the top part of a rook from a chessboard on top of it, and it screws on to a bolt that has a small hole drilled through the threaded part near to the end. You tighten up the nut so that one of the slots in the 'battlements' lines up with the hole in the bolt. Then you push the split pin right through and spread it apart on the other side.

A method of securing nuts and bolts sometimes used on adjusting mechanisms in clutches and brake gear where something has to be screwed along a threaded rod to make an adjustment and then prevented from retreating is the *locknut*. This simply means using two nuts on top of each other. You tighten the first one up to the position you want with an open-ended spanner, keep the spanner on it to stop it turning any more, and tighten the second nut up behind it. U-bolts on leaf-springs often use this dodge as well.

Rivets are quite frequently used on motor cars and these are simply little copper plugs, domed at one end, which you push through a hole drilled to their size and hammer the other end flat. If you want to remove a rivet, just drill through it with a drill bit big enough to separate the domed head from the shank. A modern labour saver is the *pop-rivet*, which doesn't require you to wave hammers around and means you only need to be able to get at one side of whatever you want to join together. Pop-rivets are the invention of a genius, and whoever he is I hope they've been able to retire on the proceeds. They're hollow, and supplied with a steel pin passing through them that has a swollen part at the end. When fitted to the pop-rivetting gun and pushed in the rivet hole, the gun pulls the pin back through the rivet — the swollen end of the pin expands the rivet on the far side of the joint and once it's expanded enough, the pin breaks off. Once again, if you want to remove these, you just drill through them.

Hammers.

Or Birmingham screwdrivers as they're sometimes rather condescendingly known; you can't do without hammers when working on motor cars, but equally you can do more damage with them than with any other tool you're ever likely to employ except maybe an oxy-acetylene cutter. The 1 lb. ball-pein hammer is the most popular item in the tool-kit (this is a hammer with one striking face flat and the other domed) though an ordinary domestic claw hammer can turn out very useful for removing hub caps if you've lost the original wheel-brace. A mallet with a composition or soft-metal head can

also be invaluable — particularly for parting tightly fitted components that would be marked or distorted by a steel hammer. When you use a hammer, let the weight of the head do the work rather as you would the head of a golf club; if the tool is properly balanced and the correct weight for the job you shouldn't need to rip any ligaments in your arm to direct a useful blow.

Hammers for dealing with the car's bodywork are a different matter entirely, and their use in this department becomes something of an art that can't really be learned from a book. Panel-beating hammers come in a multiplicity of shapes and sizes, some for 'shrinking' or squeezing sheet metal into a smaller space as you're required to do in flattening out a bulge, some for spreading it out if the metal has been crushed by an impact.

Pliers.

Apart from the general purpose Mole wrench that we've already mentioned, you need a pair of engineer's pliers with both concave and flat gripping surfaces and a pair of thin-nosed pliers with an insulated handle. Wiring jobs on the car are best tackled with the kind of combination cutting and stripping pliers sold in electrical shops for ordinary domestic use.

Speaking of electrical jobs, the *electrical circuit tester* is such a phenomenal labour-saver once you've got the hang of its use that its inclusion in the tool-kit really should be an essential (only costing about £1); it cuts so many corners in tracing a roadside ignition failure that you wouldn't be extravagant to invest in two of them, just to ensure that one is *always* in the car. The circuit tester is simply a kind of screwdriver with a bulb in the handle and a length of wire passing to one terminal of it with a clip on the end. The clip is attached to a suitable earth point on the metalwork of the car, or to the earth terminal of the battery if it's within convenient reach. You then use the blade of the instrument to probe whatever circuit you're investigating and if the bulb glows then you know that the circuit in question is assuredly alive and kicking. Since it's sharply pointed, the blade or probe of the instrument enables you not merely to touch contacts to see if they're live, but to pierce the insulation of cables and discover whether or not they're carrying a current. You might find, for instance, that the bulb lights up down one end of the wire but does nothing at the other end, indicating that the wire has fractured somewhere. Discovering that by guesswork would take you more time than most people would care to waste on their weekends off.

Another cheap and invaluable testing device is the *hydrometer*, used for checking the state of charge of a battery. It's just like a tube with a rubber bulb at one end and a float inside. You take the plugs or the cover off the battery, squeeze the bulb,

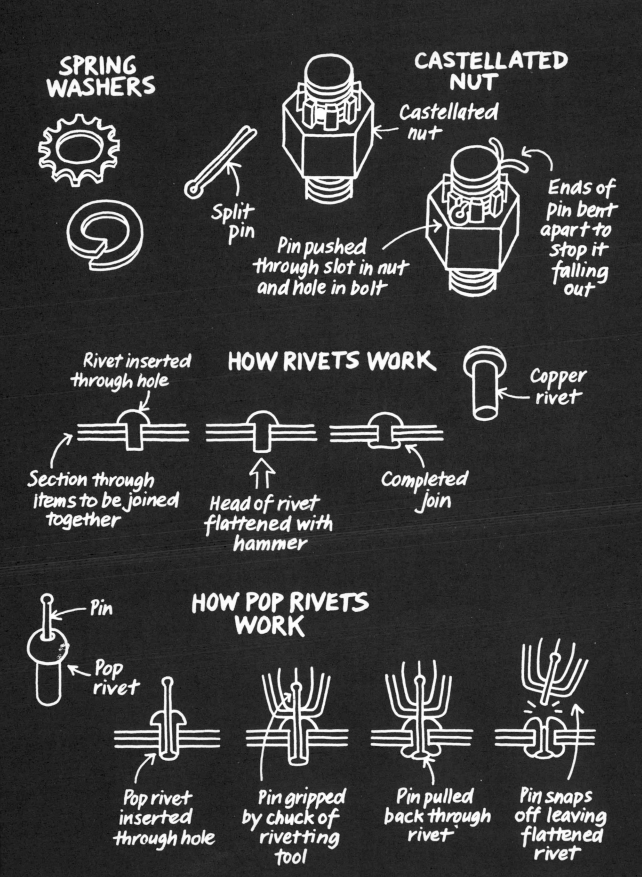

SPRING WASHERS

CASTELLATED NUT

Castellated nut

Split pin

Pin pushed through slot in nut and hole in bolt

Ends of pin bent apart to stop it falling out

HOW RIVETS WORK

Rivet inserted through hole

Copper rivet

Section through items to be joined together

Head of rivet flattened with hammer

Completed join

HOW POP RIVETS WORK

Pin

Pop rivet

Pop rivet inserted through hole

Pin gripped by chuck of rivetting tool

Pin pulled back through rivet

Pin snaps off leaving flattened rivet

stick the hydrometer in each cell and draw up the fluid. How high the fluid level rises on the float tells you the relative density of the battery electrolyte, and in the Routine Maintenance section (see p. 126) we go into interpretations of the information provided by the hydrometer. Again, don't try to do without one. If you've got a battery charger, it's ridiculous not to have a hydrometer to tell you when you need to use it. The instrument can also give a certain amount of advance warning of battery failure, particularly where one cell breaks down ahead of the others.

If you were even the most part-time of weekend carpenters you wouldn't think of doing without a steel rule; so even the most part-time of weekend mechanics can't think of doing without the spark-plug gapping tool and the set of feeler gauges. Critical distances between things are generally so small on motor cars that you can't measure them by stringing something of predetermined length across the gap because you can barely see the gap; so you measure them by pushing something of pre-determined *thickness* into the gap instead and decide whether it's too tight or too loose. Sets of *feeler gauges* are supplied both in fractions of an inch and in metric sizes, though the specifications quoted in maintenance manuals generally express the figure both ways. Feelers are used in routine maintenance for measuring the clearance between valve stems and valve operating gear (a clearance that, as we saw in the first chapter, is required to allow for expansion of the valve as the engine warms up) and for measuring contact breaker gaps and spark plug electrode gaps. Most of the important clearances required in the ignition system are also included on a tool that Champion supply which is like a boy-scout's penknife and includes a number of feelers, a fine file for cleaning points and plugs, and a bending arm for moving the outer electrode of a plug without damaging the central one. Both tools are useful, since it's unlikely that the ignition version will include the right thickness of feeler to cope with your valve gear. In any case, a full set of feelers comes in handy in a lot of other applications, from setting up the throttle interconnections on carburettors to measuring piston-ring gaps during an engine rebuild.

Other essentials for regular maintenance naturally include a tyre pump, and since you've got to have some means of measuring the air pressure in the tyre, you might as well invest in the type of pump that has a built-in pressure gauge. A *grease-gun* is an essential, too, and the handiest is one of the Tecalemit trigger-type. You load the container with whatever grease you're intending to use, clean up the grease nipple, snap the nozzle of the gun on to it and give a few pumps until fresh grease starts to squirt out of the overflow hole on the component. Sometimes the grease nipple turns out to be well and

truly bunged with grit and dried lubricant if it hasn't been attended to for a long time — you can either take the nipple out and unbung it, or substitute another one of the same type.

Sooner or later you're going to find it necessary to bleed your brakes, as explained in Ch. 5; this is a simple-sounding operation intended to expel air from the brake fluid, but it can be a great deal more awkward to deal with if you're working alone and some braking systems are in any case rather obstinate about being bled. The works manual will mention any peculiarities about the braking system that might lead it to require an unusual pumping procedure, and if you want to do the job cheaply all you really need is a length of plastic tubing to fit snugly over the brake bleed screw, and a jam jar to squirt the fluid into. Doing it this way without help, though, you need to pump the pedal to the floor, keep it there with some sort of heavy weight while you nip out to tighten up the bleed screw and stop the fluid flowing back again, then dive back into the car to let the pedal come up, and repeat this cycle until you don't see any more bubbles in the plastic tube (at the same time ensuring that the fluid level doesn't drop). An enterprising firm called Gunsons, which supplies a very useful range of tuning and maintenance equipment for cars, have now brought out a single-handed *brake bleeding kit* of great ingenuity. Retailing for around a fiver, it consists of a plastic reservoir for the fresh fluid, an adjustable cap that attaches it to several different sizes of master cylinder tank, and a hose that can be clipped on to the valve of your spare tyre. So you simply use the air pressure from the tyre to push fresh fluid into the braking system, displacing the old aerated fluid as it goes. All you have to do is attach your plastic tube and jam jar to each wheel in turn and watch until the fluid clears. Check with your supplier, though, that the kit will work on your particular car — Gunsons can supply a variety of different fittings to suit various master cylinder reservoirs.

Special tools associated with tuning and trouble-shooting we've left until the relevant chapter, since they're mostly items that you can live without, but which make the work faster and more accurate. Specialized equipment intended for the dismantling of the car (e.g. hoists for lifting engines) you might prefer to hire, since you would need them very infrequently. *Pulling* and *extracting tools* are certainly very useful items for the workshop; these come into the picture when components are not only bolted together but are what's known as an *interference fit* (in other words, so closely machined that it needs considerable mechanical effort to prise them apart). On many modern cars, you find that the rear hubs and brake drums have actually been manufactured in one piece, and that you need some form of hub puller even to be able to carry out a routine check of the brake-shoes. A suitable puller can be

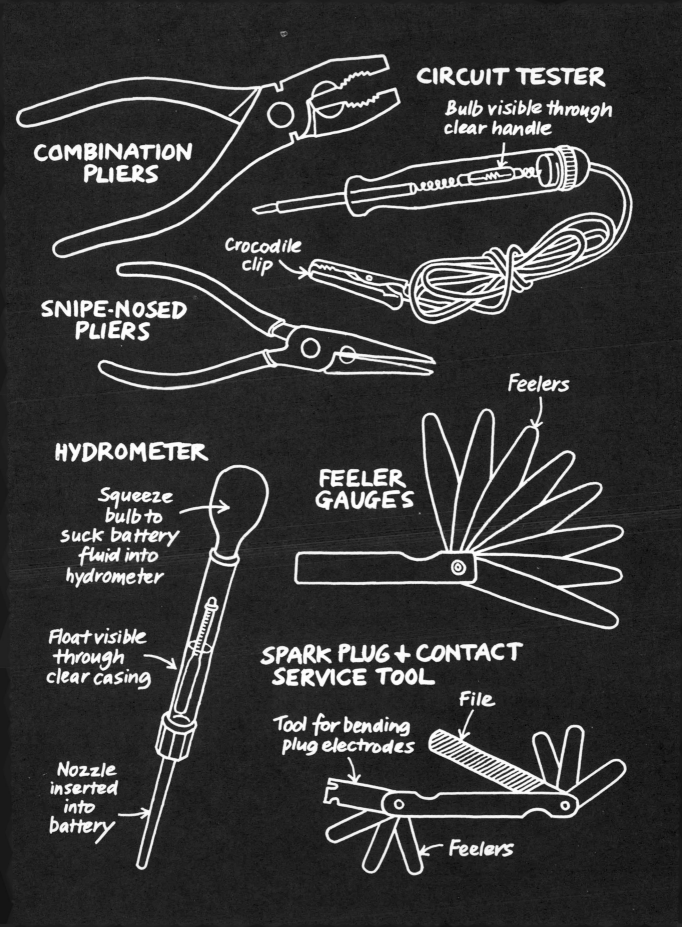

COMBINATION PLIERS

CIRCUIT TESTER

Bulb visible through clear handle

Crocodile clip

SNIPE-NOSED PLIERS

Feelers

HYDROMETER

Squeeze bulb to suck battery fluid into hydrometer

FEELER GAUGES

Float visible through clear casing

SPARK PLUG + CONTACT SERVICE TOOL

File

Tool for bending plug electrodes

Nozzle inserted into battery

Feelers

hired, but if you were performing this operation at routine services every six months or so, to invest in the appropriate puller might not be a bad idea. The Sykes-Pickavant Engineering Company market a puller system in which a basic ram or draw-bolt can be combined with many different kinds of pulling legs for different applications. This is a high-class tool and naturally expensive; much cheaper and more rudimentary versions can be found, and if you explain to your accessory shop what the application is, they'll likely be able to fix you up with something that will do the trick.

A much simpler type of extractor well worth buying is the *ball joint taper breaker*, used in dismantling steering assemblies. Ball joints can be split simply by driving wedges into them, but the device that actually forces the linkage apart as you tighten up a large bolt is the more stylish way of going about it. To hell with style, you may say, what about the money? It's certainly true that you won't find yourself needing to dismantle steering arms every other Sunday, so this is another specialized tool that you can more or less forget about until you actually find you have a worn steering joint (see p. 138 on Running Gear), and then you can decide what the most economic course would be.

Finally on the subject of tools, there are all kinds of odds and ends that you will gradually accumulate in the course of working on your car; some metalworking tools will be worth gathering together as you go along. A selection of *files* will come in handy when you least expect them. (Replacing a gearbox with an exchange unit, I once found that the clutch operating cylinder wouldn't go back where it came from because the new gearbox casting was of a slightly different shape. This was an occasion for a bit of judicious filing rather than roaring back to the gearbox supplier bristling with indignation.) A 10-inch rough flat file is a good start, with a variety of 8-inch smooth and second cut files useful in support.

A *hacksaw* will soon earn its keep, not just on the car but in a variety of household jobs. The Eclipse adjustable frame with a choice of different blade types is the most efficient and fast-working, but the Junior hacksaw is invaluable for attacking rusty bolts in difficult corners, so you should ideally have both. Remember, when replacing hacksaw blades, to keep the lie of the teeth away from you, and wherever possible set up what you're going to cut in the vice rather than have it rolling around on the bench. Blades are more inclined to jump when cutting steel than cutting wood, and they can soon make a nasty mess of your fingers.

Lastly there is the *electric drill*, which can have an enormous variety of applications on the car, from polishing, grinding and hole-cutting to cleaning up cylinder heads with a wire brush. In these burgeoning days of D.I.Y. nearly every home already has one for

some purpose or another, but if you're just about to invest in one it's handy to have a range of speeds to choose from, particularly when starting off holes in solid metal. All the major manufacturers of electric tools now supply a range of fittings such as pillar stands, bench grinders, and so forth, so the basic tool becomes a maid of all work.

Rather than have to take a trip to the shops every time you need to top something up, it's a good idea to keep on the premises a supply of whatever *lubricants* are specified for your car. Normally this will include a multigrade oil by one of the reputable manufacturers, a squeeze-bottle of transmission oil if your car has a separate transmission, and a tin of the appropriate grease for all-round lubrication, re-packing hub bearings, and so forth. An oil-can filled with a light machine-oil is handy for lubrication of locks, distributor spindles and the like. Always follow the maker's directions with respect to types of lubricant; they didn't arrive at their conclusions by guesswork.

Workshops & Equipment.

The right tools and the right surroundings are as important as each other but the realities are different. With tools, it's shortsighted to do anything less than get the best you can afford. When it comes to workshops you have to take what you can get. The home garage is the most likely option, and this will normally have been designed to accommodate a car, and just about let the owner in and out of it but not much else. You may be able to borrow a garage to work in from time to time, or you may have already decided to rent one fairly close to home to keep the car away from the elements and wandering tamperers. Wonders can be done in diabolical conditions, provided the very best use is made of those conditions by the kind of self-discipline that many home mechanics don't have.

I started taking cars to bits in the street, much to the disgust of the neighbours. (This is nothing . . . there was a drop-out law graduate of my acquaintance who at one point in his burgeoning career as a used-car salesman took to arc welding in the middle of the night in a front garden in Kilburn.) The practice isn't to be recommended. Not only do you become a sitting duck for interfering busybodies and incontinent dogs but the generally unsatisfactory nature of the proceedings can let your work down. Being anxious to get it over with as quickly as possible you can find yourself hurrying the job and skipping checks; working in the street isn't unduly uncomfortable for routine maintenance of the engine, but has limitations when it comes to jobs which require a deal of grovelling about underneath.

Anyway, this is all academic. If you've got a garage, you've got a head start. If you haven't, you're restricted, but not stymied, in the work you can undertake. Let's start with some common sense about garages. I worked for some years in a rented lockup about seven and a half feet by fifteen. There is a mysterious blight that very rapidly afflicts even the most pristine and unlumbered of garages, which is that large and cumbersome objects, often in damp and collapsing cardboard boxes, soon start congregating around any available bit of floor space so that you soon find yourself picking your way through a minefield of junk to get anywhere near the car. Some people are spared this plague, they seem to be mysteriously immunized by a mania for tidying up. If, like me, you know you're not one of those people, then keep an eye on it; once conditions deteriorate to the point where every job reduces you to a cursing, stumbling psychotic, you'd have been better off taking the car to a garage.

A rudimentary bench, or simply a sturdy table from the junkshop, is a fairly essential requirement for those jobs that have to be done on components removed from the car. If the length of the garage permits a regular workshop-size bench to be installed at the end, with enough room for you to work at it with the car already inside, then you might buy a purpose-built bench. Alternatively, if you're even marginally handy at woodwork you can build something similar to the one in the drawing, and there are plenty of other examples in the books and magazines for do-it-yourselfers. This bench is assembled with coach bolts at the joints, which are available from builders suppliers and probably from wherever you get your timber. Take your time with the measurements and the cutting, though – benches whose feet do a sort of tapdance when you start working at them are no fun. Incorporate what storage space you can into the bench, it all helps to keep things off the floor; you might build a set of drawers or at least of cubby holes underneath.

A vice is essential once you've got a bench to mount it on; stripping components is always easier if you don't have to chase them all over the garage. Vices are expensive but a good one will last a lifetime and justify itself in many other ways, apart from usefulness to the motor mechanic. Apparently indestructible lightweight vices are now marketed; they're fine if restricted to the uses for which they're made, but it's invariably a temptation to use the vice as an anvil eventually, and the alloy vice doesn't take kindly to this treatment. A four-inch hardened steel engineer's vice, preferably with a swivel base, should do the trick, and you mount it over one of the bench legs for rigidity.

You can't have too much shelving for all the tools, pots, spares, nuts and bolts and other jumble that accumulates in the garage, and a lot of the shelves will probably find their natural place behind the bench. Alternatively, hang a perforated hardboard sheet in this position, to which you can hook your tools individually.

Equipment that you might regard as standard issue whether you have a workshop or a corner of the potting shed would be a battery charger (remember to check whether the electrical rig on your car is 6 volt or 12 volt – if it's the former, you'll need to shop around for a charger that deals with both ratings). An inspection lamp is essential, and for garage use handlamps are supplied with a wire cage to protect you from the bulb and vice versa, and a rubber handle. For lifting the car it's handy to have a less tedious method to fall back on than the lightweight screw jack supplied with the car; a hydraulic bottle jack is ideal, all you do is gently swing the lever as if you were pumping water. The important proviso about using non-standard jacks is to make sure you don't have it located under something that's going to get bent or ripped through. In other words you don't jack the car by placing the jack under the floor, or under the engine sump or the transmission, or any of the steering mechanism. Place the jack under one of the subframe members, or chassis members, or possibly the reinforced bit that's already provided as a jacking point. One last check when you jack under chassis members or outriggers (chassis side-members) is that there are no hydraulic pipes or fuel lines liable to get trapped when the jack goes up.

Unfortunately, nobody's yet designed a car that requires no work to be done from underneath, so the mechanic without a hydraulic lift or a pit is forever being faced with the most undesirable feature of car maintenance there is – getting underneath the vehicle, and having enough elbow room once there to be able to get some useful work done. Ordinary jacks, even hydraulic bottle jacks, are *not* good enough on their own for this sort of activity; they're intended for raising the car so that you can get a wheel off, but they don't provide sufficient security to risk your neck. People do get killed under motor cars from time to time, and often because they put too much faith in a single jack. Remember, it might not be that the jack itself fails but that the car's weight distribution has been changed by its being tipped up at one end; if the jack slips, that's that, and there's not much you can do to keep a ton or more of steel off your chest until the firemen turn up.

So an additional method of support for the car must always be used. *Steel ramps* are available from the accessory shops. and you simply drive the car up them, once you're sure they're correctly positioned – it's wise to have a helper to tell you when you're reaching the point of no return. Or you can use *axle stands*, which are tubular tripods – you raise the car with the ordinary jack, position the axle stand under a suitably meaty bit of chassis, secure the adjustable section of the stand with a peg, then remove the jack and repeat the operation on the other side. Chock the pair of wheels that remain on the ground, so that the car can't roll away.

Best option of the lot, provided you know a friendly builder or you're trying to get your weight down, is to dig a pit in the centre of the garage floor. The ideal size of pit unfortunately requires just that fraction more spadework and application than the human constitution can normally tolerate, so people building their own pits generally give up digging halfway and finish up with one that turns you into a three foot misshapen hunchback within a few hours of working in it. Ideally you want the pit to be long enough to enable you to get in and out of it without a mountaineering operation, and it's also handy to be able to get out from under the car in a hurry should some mishap befall you like a mortal enemy accidentally dropping a lighted match into the petrol tank. A useful depth for the pit would be around five feet, so that you could stand under the car without crouching, and be in a comfortable position to actually get leverage on components rather than simply using the pit for inspection. Make some enquiries of builders before you set about an ambitious venture such as this. The pit is certainly invaluable and will save you much exasperation, cramp, minor injury and oil-sodden hair, but it loses its charm if you find you've dug through the gas main or the sewers in the course of constructing it. If you were installing one into an existing garage you would also of course need to get hold of some mechanical means of breaking up the concrete floor. Any pit should be built with a recessed cover which is strong enough to keep people and cars out. The cover should *always* be replaced after use.

Arrange some adequate lighting in your workshop, fluorescent being the brightest and the cheapest (a 40W fluorescent strip will give you a great deal more illumination than a 40W bulb), with maybe a flexibly mounted lamp above the bench. A few 13 amp power points distributed around the place avoid the danger of lots of trailing extension cables which have a sneaky habit of pulling over insecurely sealed cans of oil, but in garages you must locate the outlets at least four feet above floor level so they don't get crushed should you bump the car against the walls. Heating is always a problem particularly if your workshop is remote from the house itself; where the garage is very adjacent, you might be able to have an extra radiator plumbed off the central heating system. If not, use an enclosed electric radiator, storage heater, or the finned tubular electric heaters supplied for use in workshops and greenhouses. Exposed flames are illegal where there's petrol about, and the authorities weren't necessarily just being awkward when they penned that law, so don't risk it. On the subject of fire, make sure the garage is equipped with a foam extinguisher in good working order, and that you know how to work it without mulling over the instructions for a quarter of an hour while your trousers are on fire. Nobody needs reminding that petrol fires are both very hot and very fast, and blanketing them with foam is the only kind of discouragement they understand. A fire extinguisher is not such a bad investment to have about the house in any case.

Tools & Spares To Carry In The Car.

At one time car manufacturers sent their products out into the world complete with tool-kits respectable enough to cope with most eventualities, but this generosity is nowadays restricted to the high-class end of the market. Clearly there's no need to take up valuable storage space in the car with tackle that you would only ever use for major overhauls, but there is a bare minimum you'll need for dealing with roadside breakdowns.

All new cars come with an appropriate jack and a wheelbrace at least, but if you have a second-hand car that has lost these items somewhere in its career, make sure you provide yourself with replacements. In addition, make sure you have:

Tyre pump/pressure gauge. (You might think you can get away without this since garage forecourts all have one, but what do you do when you have to change a wheel on a sheep track in the Peak District and you want to bring the spare up to the right pressure?)

Feeler gauges.

3 screwdrivers (1 plain, 1 Phillips, 1 small electrical).

Plug spanner.

1 set open-ended Unified or Metric spanners.

Mole wrench.

Combination pliers with wire cutter.

Set of battery jumper leads.

Torch.

In addition to all this, make sure you've inspected all the likely breakdown areas of your particular ignition and carburation systems, and carry any special tools necessary for servicing them. If you own a socket set in a conveniently shaped flat box, carry it in the car.

There's a limit to how many spares it's realistic to carry on the car, but these would be the minimum that would enable you to cope with the most likely roadside emergencies:

Fan belt.

Sparking plug.

Condenser/set of contact points.

Headlamp/sidelamp/rear lamp bulbs.

Insulating tape.

Roll of copper wire (for lashing up broken exhausts, etc.).

Fuses.

Emergency plastic windscreen.

Silencer bandage.

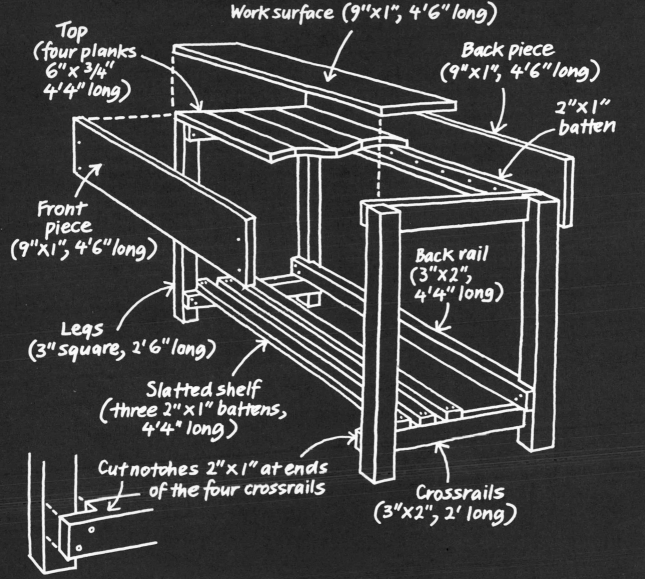

Work surface (9"x1", 4'6" long)

Top
(four planks
6" x 3/4"
4'4" long)

Back piece
(9"x1", 4'6" long)

2"x1"
batten

Front
piece
(9"x1", 4'6" long)

Back rail
(3"x2",
4'4" long)

Legs
(3" square, 2'6" long)

Slatted shelf
(three 2"x1" battens,
4'4" long)

Cut notches 2"x1" at ends
of the four crossrails

Crossrails
(3"x2", 2' long)

AN EASILY MADE WORKBENCH

Well, fairly easy. Glue and screw the various pieces together as shown in the illustration – except for the (replaceable) work surface, which should be screwed only.

Section through bench...

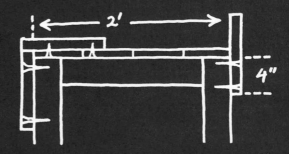

2'

4"

How To Fix Breakdowns.

Because Sod's Law applies to motoring life in no small measure, it's inclined to engender a certain amount of helpless resignation amongst owners. Everyone tells you the same story, one way or another. It broke down in a snowstorm, or a hurricane, or a traffic jam, or halfway across Exmoor, or on the way to the best business deal/assignation/football match the world has ever known. System! That's the way to beat the Fates. As Sherlock Holmes put it, when the impossible has been eliminated, whatever remains, however improbable, must be the truth.

But people are repeatedly misled by the sporadic successes of guesswork. Informed guesswork is one thing, particularly when you're stranded, uncomfortable, and in a hurry. Random guesswork is altogether something else; it's often deployed by people who want to sound knowledgeable to garage mechanics or incredulous friends. An AA publication once compared knowledge of the motor car to an earlier generation's knowledge of horse-trading; half a century ago you wouldn't ordinarily have owned a horse without knowing its tail from its teeth, and the average equestrian would at least have been able to engage in a reasonably informed dialogue with the vet.

We're going to begin by thinking of this in terms of total breakdowns as opposed to what might be called mild neuroses (on the part of the vehicle, that is, not the owner). If the patient can't tell the doctor the problem, which is basically what's happening if the engine is stone dead, then matters naturally become aggravated. Let us begin, then, with the engine that won't start, rather than the one that has broken down on the road (though many of the necessary tests can apply to either circumstance).

Car Will Not Start.

First pace around the car, eyeing it balefully. John Cleese in an episode of 'Fawlty Towers' once started belabouring his with an uprooted bush, but it's unwise to let the machine (which is simply lying low and biding its time) think that it's scored a psychological victory so early in the game. Start to consider the obvious things first, which naturally we blush to bring up.

Have you run out of petrol? The fuel gauge may be lying to you, so if you're having trouble remembering the last time you put any in, improvise a dipstick (it would have to be something flexible like a rubber tube if the intake to the tank bends around corners) and check the level. Have you overchoked the engine and flooded it? If this seems a likely possibility, push the choke in and operate the starter with your foot hard down on the accelerator to ventilate the combustion chambers.

Is the starter turning the engine fast enough, or is it turning it at all? Starters generally make a fearsome rattling noise when in operation, like somebody shifting milk-crates – if you're still doubtful, this can be verified by having somebody take a look under the bonnet while you operate the starter button or the ignition key. The fan pulley and belt will be revolving fairly smartly if the starter is working effectively. If the engine isn't being turned over at all, or only turned very sluggishly (a sort of disconsolate, apologetic noise, like a smoker's cough) then we have to look to the electrics for the fault.

Switch on the lights. If they're dim or non-existent, the battery may be flat. Check the connections to the two poles of the battery. (Most batteries are fairly obviously sited under the bonnet or in the boot – some are stowed under the rear seat.) Fluffy white corrosion on the terminals may indicate that they need to be removed, scraped clean, preferably coated thinly with Vaseline and retightened. They may be merely loose, and this is a common problem with the type that have a screw passing through the centre of the terminal into the battery post. Occasionally a sharp tap with a light hammer, or repositioning the terminals on the posts by working them gently around and retightening will do the trick. Avoid overdoing any strong-arm methods with the battery posts, though; if you snap one off the whole battery may be a write-off. Remember that the current taken from the battery in getting one small electric motor to spin all the hardware inside the engine (particularly in cold weather) is considerable; the slightest current leakage through a bad connection can have a disastrous effect. If the battery is flat and there's an alternative battery or a helpful motorist to hand, you can overcome the problem by using a pair of 'jump leads'. These are sold in most accessory shops and are likely to prove just as useful a permanent fixture on the car as the spare wheel.

Jump leads are a cinch to use if you observe these rules: Make sure you get them connected up the right way round (the *red* lead of the pair connects the positive (+) terminal of the booster battery to the positive terminal of the clapped-out battery, and the black lead connects the negatives). Don't drop one end of the live lead on to the car bodywork in the middle of this operation or you'll produce at the least a spectacular firework display of sparks, or maybe an even more spectacular incendiary bomb if there's a petrol leak anywhere in the engine compartment (it's worth noting that you should always use a modicum of common sense when it comes to manipulating electrical gadgets near petrol, even if it's to produce the innocuous looking sparks involved in plug-testing).

If you simply suspect loose connections and prefer to get home first before you sort it out, a bump start is the quickest recourse. You can bump start cars on the flat, but few people would recommend it, except perhaps the salesmen of surgical trusses. The bigger the car the harder that operation is, and bump starting down even a slight incline is much to be preferred. The driver engages third gear, turns on the ignition, declutches, and waits for the car to pick up a bit of momentum, at this point bringing the clutch up fairly sharply. When the engine starts, declutch again and rev it up. A tow from another car can be used in the same way.

Batteries.

Remember that even if the driving lights appear reasonably bright, that doesn't necessarily rule out the possibility of a loose battery connection making enough contact to pass a small current for the lights but not enough to cope with the starter. If you've ever been in a stationary bus at night while the driver starts his engine, you'll recall there's a momentary slight dimming of the interior lights while the current is being sidetracked by the starter. The same phenomenon supplies us with our next test. If the headlamps are bright, switch on the starter and see what happens to them then. *If they stay bright* and the starter doesn't respond, there must be a fault in the electrical circuit dealing with the starter.

In our initial guided tour around the automobile we looked at the job performed by the starter solenoid (p. 22), being a kind of electric motor in itself, but moving laterally instead of rotating. A live wire from the electrical distribution

box of the car passes in and out of the ignition switch and to the live terminal of the solenoid. When the key is turned and the circuit is completed, the solenoid operates to push two heavy bronze contacts together and complete the high-current circuit between the live battery terminal and the starter motor. This cable is pretty easily recognized, being about a half inch in diameter to be able to carry the starter load, and insulated by a thick black plastic cover. Check the connections of this cable at the solenoid end and at the starter motor end; the nuts might be loose or the terminals so dirty that they're introducing a high resistance into the circuit. You generally find that there's an earthing strap between the carcase of the engine and the bodywork of the car, looking something like a steel pyjama cord (this book has been written for very conservative dressers) — the connections at either end of this might be dirty or loose, preventing the starter from earthing itself. If you're fortunate enough to possess a car with a lot of space around the engine, then investigating the earth strap is easy enough, but in some of those engine compartments that look like overcrowded broom cupboards it's a tougher job.

If the lights immediately dim or get extinguished altogether when the starter is turned on and the battery and its terminals have been established as OK, then clearly the starter is receiving its current but for some reason isn't able to turn. Watch the red ignition light and turn the key. If it goes out and the starter doesn't budge, there may be a short circuit in the live lead from the battery, or a short in the starter itself. I once came across a main battery lead on a Mini which had somehow detached itself from its underfloor clips and had its insulation melted through by the exhaust. Where the battery is at the other end of the car to the engine, the lead may occasionally have chafted itself against the bodywork and worn through to the copper cable.

Starters occasionally jam when the toothed drive pinion becomes so mangled or dirty that it can't disengage itself from the flywheel ring. Some owners of vehicles prone to starter sticking go in for mugging the device with blunt instruments until it unsticks, but putting the car in third gear and rocking it backwards and forwards with the ignition off is a more reputable method. Many starters have a removable cover about the size of a thimble which can be pulled off to give access to a square plug. Turning this with a suitable spanner will often free the starter. If all else fails, the starter motor will have to be removed and replaced; it's usually secured to the flywheel flange and clutch housing with two or three large bolts.

If the starter makes a kind of despondent whirring noise but the engine doesn't run, the drive pinion is sticking — in other words, it's failing to run down the armature shaft into engagement with the flywheel. This is generally caused by muck, which might be because somebody has misguidedly tried oiling the pinion (it should only ever be cleaned with a solvent such as petrol or paraffin) or oil has got on to it from some other source, such as the rear bearings of the engine itself. Again, thumping the starter can temporarily overcome it, but the starter will eventually need to be stripped and cleaned.

Sluggish operation of the starter, as opposed to total failure, can be caused by any of the battery or terminal faults we've already considered, where a high circuit resistance is starving the motor of current; but it can be caused by internal faults. Checking the motor brushes (either for dirt or undue wear) used to be an easy enough job in the days when starters had a removable cover band so you could look at the brushes in situ, but lately the makers have taken to ensuring that you need to remove the rear bearing cover to make this check, which is only convenient to do with the starter on the bench. In any case, starter problems of this kind really fall into the category of routine maintenance. Getting yourself home with a duff starter rarely presents much of a problem, particularly if you can get some help.

The final and least comfortable conclusion to the problems of starters that don't start is that for some reason the engine itself may be too stiff to turn. This might mean that some engine component such as a piston or the crankshaft is broken or seized — you can check it by attempting to push the car in top gear.

Starter OK.
Don't flatten the battery by endless attempts. If the engine turns over normally but fails to start, then the problem broadens out somewhat. *Ignition troubles* cause more engine failures — both sudden and cumulative — than anything else on the vehicle, so they are inevitably our first suspects. If the engine has been a difficult starter all along, particularly in cold or damp weather, and if bump starting overcomes it (the ignition coil gets the full charge from the battery, instead of what's left over after the starter has done its bit) then the ignition system could probably do with some improvement. Fuel faults are inclined to introduce themselves progressively, often to the accompaniment of 'flat spots', where it feels as if you're intermittently driving the car with the brakes on.

Ignition faults are generally of two kinds: there's the type due to a spark not being produced at all, and the type due to the spark being produced but getting lost or sidetracked either en route to the sparking plugs or at the plugs themselves. Remember that the combustion chamber, pressurized upwards of 100 lb./sq. in., is the last place the spark wants to end up if it can possibly get out of it. So we need to discover firstly if a spark is being produced at all, and roughly

how strong it is — and then we need to make sure that it isn't hopping to earth somewhere further back along the line than in the cylinder head.

You don't need any apparatus for these checks, but a rubber glove or a soft rubber pad might come in handy — ignition shocks don't generally do you a great deal of harm but they can cause a fairly uncomfortable flutter in the fingertips. Failing that, a pair of plastic-handled electrical pliers will do just as well. To see if a spark is being produced, remove one of the sparking plug caps and disconnect the ignition cables from them, either by unscrewing the cap from the lead (don't twist the lead itself, see Diagram 2) if this is the method of fitting that's been used, or by pulling the cap from the lead if the latter is merely fitted with a spring clip that locates it on the plug. Then you get a grip on the lead with whatever means of protection you have to hand, hold the end of it a quarter inch or so from a suitably clean bit of metalwork on the engine (usually a rocker-box nut or cylinder-head nut — *not* the carburettor) and get someone to operate the starter. This business can be awkward if you're alone, because if you try to suspend the lead the critical distance from the metalwork, you generally find that it's meandered off like Alice's flamingo by the time you get into the driving seat to turn the key. Using the spare spark plug would be so much easier and quicker, to check the leads for continuity. Where a button-operated solenoid is situated under the bonnet, the problem is solved for you because you can turn the ignition on, get your lead suitably dangled, and still be able to reach the solenoid to turn the engine.

As the engine turns over, you should now be able to see and hear a spark jump between the end of the lead and the metalwork of the engine. It's a good idea to be doing this in shaded light where possible, because even a good spark looks fairly feeble in bright sunlight. If the spark is yellowish, intermittent, or generally makes the hop between the lead and the engine with anything other than a good sharp crack, then we can conclude that the efficiency of the ignition system could at least do with some improving. There are no hard and fast rules here. A youngish engine, in excellent mechanical condition, will start from cold more readily with a deficient ignition system than an older one that already has enough troubles of its own in the form of poor compressions, worn carburettors or air leaks. *If there is no spark at all* during this test (it's tedious to repeat it, but do make sure you have the ignition switched on, though don't leave it on without the engine running for longer than necessary), then clearly the ignition system is the culprit and needs to be checked right through, from the contact points and condenser, coil, connecting leads and distributor rotor and cap. If the spark seems all right, make a final check on the cleanliness and effectiveness of the plugs before you dismiss the complicity of the

TESTING FOR SPARKS AT PLUGS AND PLUG LEADS

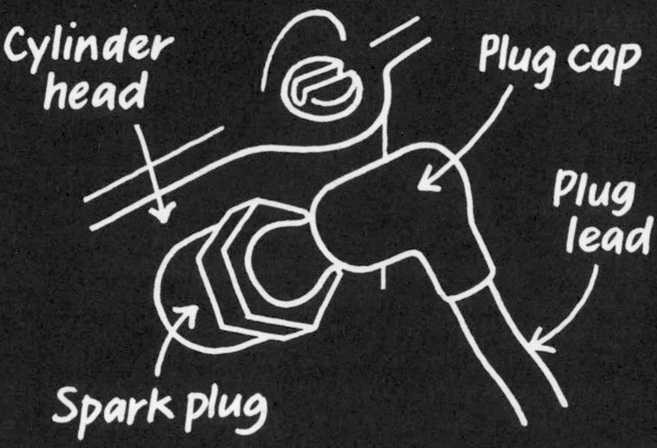

Cylinder head

Plug cap

Plug lead

Spark plug

Pull plug cap and lead off plug...

①

... remove cap from lead...

②

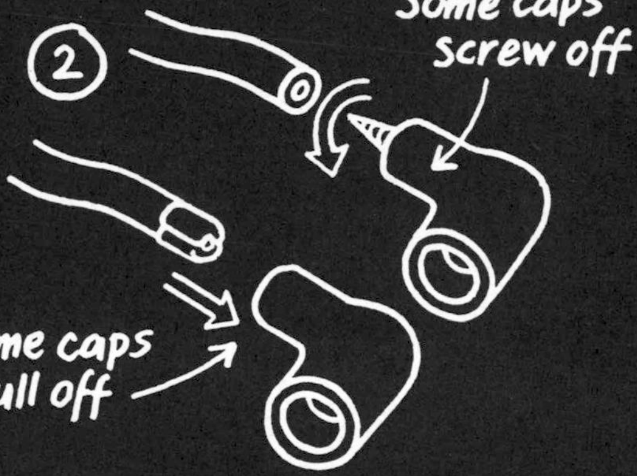

Some caps screw off

Some caps pull off

... hold end of lead near suitable earth (with rubber gloves or insulated pliers) and operate starter...

③

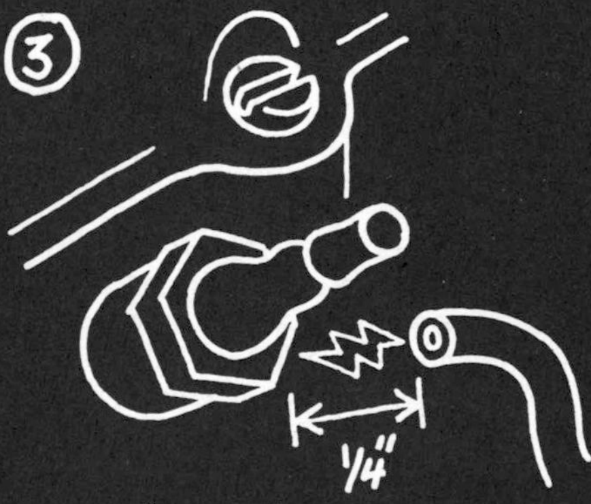

¼"

... good spark should jump gap.

④

Finally, remove plug, re-attach lead, and lay plug on cylinder head to earth plug casing...

...operate starter. Good spark should jump plug gap.

ignition system from the case. Then proceed to examine the plugs.

Plugs.

For plug examination you'll naturally need a plug spanner, which is one of those essential tools for even the most self-doubting roadside mechanic. The most practical type to get, though not the cheapest, is the T-bar type with a rubber insert which we described in the previous chapter. Having removed one plug — and ensuring as far as possible that there are no large lumps of grit hovering around the plug-hole ready to fall into the bore — you place it on the cylinder head somewhere so that the threaded part or the hexagonal section are in good electrical contact with the engine (which again might mean a bit of judicious muck-removing from a head-stud or whatever is most convenient to perch the plug on.) You then connect the plug to its respective lead and turn the engine over with the ignition on as before. The old-time mechanic's favourite 'fat' spark — a crisp, bluish-white crack — should now jump between the central electrode and the outer electrode (see Diagram 4). If this doesn't happen but the spark from the lead was all right, then the plug may be carboned or oiled up, the gap between the electrodes may be too wide or too narrow, the electrodes may be burned through overheating, or the china insulator may be cracked. Champion's invaluable boy scout's tool for plug maintenance (see p. 94) can then be used to clean any accumulated gunge off the plug tips and the gap should be reset. There's a golden rule of plug servicing, which is that you don't bend or in any way apply force to the centre electrode (the pin that runs vertically through the plug). Attacking this is a surefire way to break the insulation. Also, be careful how you get plugs in and out of the engine — if you're using a rudimentary plug or box spanner, make sure it's upright on the plug and firmly engaged before you start heaving. If you forget the former you'll break the insulator, and if you forget the latter you might mangle the metal parts of the plug and possibly damage the spanner as well. When you put everything back, plugs don't need to be overtight, by all means put a certain amount of effort into the last turn but don't treat the unfortunate plug as if it were a wheel nut. Many modern spark plugs have taper seats. Very great care must be taken not to overtighten these, as removal could prove impossible. Stripping the threads in a cylinder head is no joke to get fixed, and aluminium heads are naturally more than usually sensitive in this respect. Repeat the process with all plugs.

If the spark at our plug leads and plug points was satisfactory we can now assume that a shortage of fuel rather than electricity is the cause of the trouble, or that the engine has developed some more complicated mechanical fault. Although they might all have sounded a bit elaborate, these tests can be performed in a few minutes. It's not a bad idea to try them out first on a car in good working order so that you can alternatively (a) foul it up and find out what a breakdown actually feels like, or (b) get some kind of yardstick against which to compare a car that isn't doing what it's supposed to do.

If the spark was non-existent, then we need to be able to discover whether it's dead or merely hiding. So the next test, which basically checks the operation of the low-voltage circuit and the coil, is to see if a spark appears between the supply lead from the coil and the metalwork of the engine. As we saw in the opening chapter, this lead arrives at the centre of the distributor cover, from where the rotor transfers the current to the plug leads. On modern distributors, the coil lead can generally be simply pulled from the cover; on some older ones a tiny, spear-like screw on the inside of the cover retains it. Long before you actually get lumbered with a breakdown, find out if this is the sort of distributor you have. And if it is, make sure you carry a small enough electrical screwdriver in the car to be able to undo the screw. Knives, thumbnails and keys never seem to do much more than just add to the frustration.

Once you've got the coil lead out of the distributor cap, hold it or secure it a quarter of an inch from the clean metalwork again and crank the engine as before (see p.107). If a good spark appears this time, then we've proved that the low voltage supply and the induction coil are doing their job and the spark is vanishing somewhere between the supply lead and the plugs. Let's assume to start with that this is what happens, and that the trouble we're looking for has got to be somewhere in the distributor cover, the rotor, the plug leads or plug caps.

Distributor Cap.

Unclip this and examine it carefully in a good light. If the weather is damp or muggy there may be a film of condensation both inside and outside, which can easily act as a leakage path for the spark and divert it from its true purpose in life. Dirt and grease all over the outside don't help either, and can have the same effect. Clean and dry the cap with a soft cloth if any of these misfortunes appear to have befallen it. Some distributors are unhelpfully positioned just where they can catch a gremlin-producing spray of water and road dirt from other vehicles, and in these cases the whole device really needs to be protected with a suitably tailored rubber or plastic cover. Damp is generally the mortal enemy of good ignition, so make sure the plug leads and covers are dry and clean as well. If the weather is foggy or damp, dry everything with a cloth that has preferably been warmed somehow. Aerosols are on the market which will dry the ignition system and protect it with a wax coating.

Check each of the metal segments inside the distributor cover — if they're corroded and burned, clean them back to bright metal, though if the burning has gone so far that a deep gouge has been sliced out of each segment where the rotor passes it, scrap the cap and get another. Check the central carbon brush where the coil lead enters the cap — if the spring is weak or the brush worn down or even fallen out, there may be no contact at all between the coil lead input and the rotor. Check the cover and the rotor for cracks in the plastic — cracks in the cover may allow the spark to short from one metal segment to another so that it arrives in the wrong cylinder, cracks in the rotor may allow it to short to earth via the metal distributor spindle. Cracking in the rotor can be checked by holding the coil lead close to the brass electrode of the rotor and cranking the engine as in the earlier test — an extremely faint and noiseless spark may occasionally jump the gap but if a strong one does then the rotor is definitely past it, since it will be allowing the feed from the coil to shoot straight down the spindle instead of passing to the plug leads.

Tracking.

This odd phenomenon might reveal itself by a bit of scrutiny of the distributor cap before you clean the inside of it. With all the sparks hurtling about inside the distributor when the engine is working normally, ionization of the air causes the formation of ozone, exactly as it does in a thunderstorm. This leads to the deposition of nitrous powder between the electrodes, forming a thin black line which you might easily mistake for a crack until you come to clean it — the spark will jump between electrodes along this track. Washing with water will dissolve it, but make sure the cover is properly dry afterwards. Tracking shouldn't happen if you look the ignition system over on a Sunday morning every now and again. In fact a lot of things shouldn't happen if you do that.

Plug leads and caps are generally neglected by the home-maintenance person as a source of ignition trouble; and it's probably true that they're a much more likely contributory factor to rough running or misfiring than to total immobility of the car. Nevertheless, a spare ignition lead comes in handy as a testing device, this can be substituted for a suspect plug lead and the loose end held to the metalwork of the engine as usual to compare the spark obtained in this way with the original. Cheap and poor quality plug covers, especially some of those incorporating a radio interference suppressor can occasionally turn out to be an elusive source of weak sparking — easily checked by testing for a spark with a good plug and the suspect cover, and then the ignition cable alone. If you're going to replace all the leads, car accessory shops now sidestep the chore of cutting and clipping leads by providing ready-made suppressed leads with all the fittings ready and waiting. If you rewire a distributor cap, of course, it's sensible to paint each plug number on its respective socket in the cap with something

delicate like a photographer's retouching brush (if the manufacturer hasn't already provided a stamping to that effect). There's nothing more irritating than replacing all the leads to cure a misfire and winding up with a worse misfire than you started with because the leads are in the wrong order. If you're inexperienced, it's sometimes the last thing you think of and you convince yourself that you've done something disastrous to the engine.

Low-voltage Circuit.

But suppose we've performed our spark test and the lead from the coil is either dead, intermittently working, or provides a feeble spark. (Sometimes you might find as the engine cranks around that there will be a series of weedy sparks, mixed with the odd snappy one — this is an indication of a general decline in the efficiency of the low-voltage circuit, and possibly of the coil itself.)

Take a close look at the contact breaker points first, located on the baseplate of the distributor as we saw on p. 26. Familiarize yourself with what the points do and how — the projecting lobes on the central distributor spindle lever the points open and shut as the spindle revolves. So we need to make sure that this is actually happening. Put the car in top gear, let the handbrake off and slowly push it until the fibre or plastic heel on the moveable contact breaker is resting on the apex of one of the cam lobes. At this stage there ought to be a gap about the thickness of your thumbnail between the contacts, which should close if you push the car slightly further so that the heel moves on to a 'flat' portion of the spindle. If there's no gap whatever position the cam is in, or the gap appears excessively wide, then the points are in need of readjustment.

Check out about contact points again in Ch. 1. For the purposes of explaining what contact points do, we described them as consisting of a fixed contact and a moveable contact — in other words, the latter was the one that flicked backwards and forwards on the cam spindle, the former just sat tight. In fact the fixed contact is the one that can be loosened when the points are adjusted, with a screw passing through it to the baseplate.

(N.B. if you car is a bit long in the tooth, you generally find that a great many applications of the wrong-sized screwdrivers have reduced this screw to pulp. Once again, a preparatory inspection will have revealed this and it's well worth replacing it with a decent screw before you find yourself having to wrestle with it in an emergency.)

Once the screw is loosened, you'll find that the contact it passed through can be slipped slightly from side to side, which has the effect of opening and closing the gap between the points. So if you set the engine (by the top-gear pushing technique) into a position where the moving contact ought to be at its fullest opening point on the cam lobe, you can

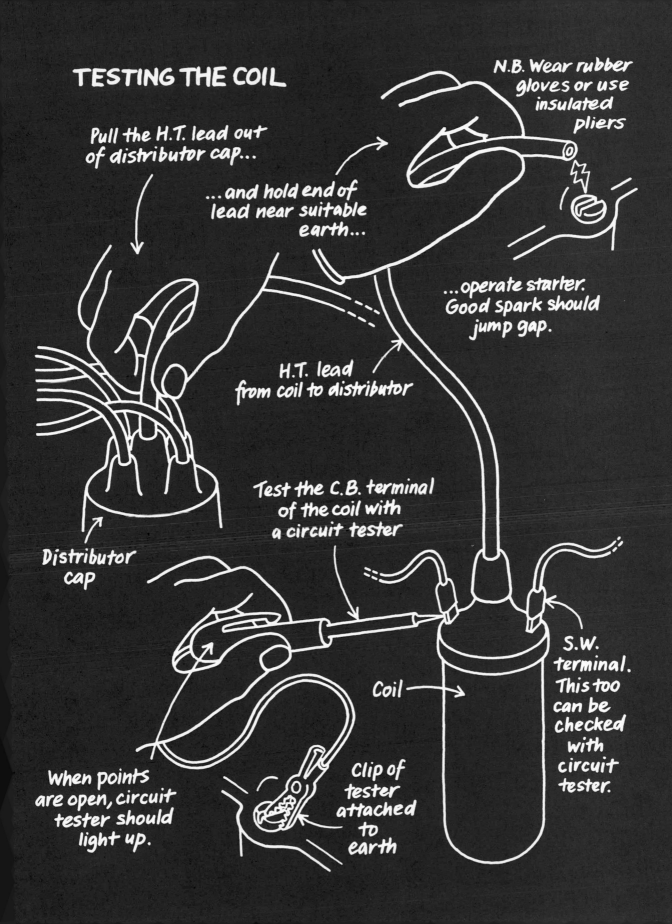

then move the other contact until the gap is correct, and then tighten it up. Naturally you need a better way than guesswork to tell when the gap's right — and the gadget to use is a device called a feeler gauge (see p. 94), which is simply a collection of steel strips of various thicknesses. You select the one that's specified for the job — and in the case of contact points it might be anything between 14 and 25 thousandths of an inch — slide the gauge in between the points and adjust the position of the contact so that the gauge feels nipped but not too tight. You then retighten the fixing screw. Some contact sets have special arrangements for accurately positioning the points gap: by incorporating a notch into which you can insert a screwdriver to lever the mechanism back and forth, or occasionally there's a special screw with a tiny cam attached that will move the points apart as you turn it.

If the points are more or less correctly gapped but dirty, greasy or burned, you can get away with tearing the striker from a matchbox and folding it to make an emergency file. Slip this between the points and gently rub them with the abrasive, cleaning up any dust afterwards with as grease-free a rag as you can lay hands on.

Once we've established that the points actually open and close and the gap is close enough to its correct specification not to be causing our total breakdown, there is then a corresponding checklist to be gone into for the low-voltage circuit.

Firstly you'll find there's a thin wire travelling from a terminal at the side of the distributor to a terminal on the ignition coil (this wire may have its centre section incorporated in a part of the wiring loom) — this terminal will be marked with a plus or a minus sign, or the legend C.B. (for 'contact breaker') depending on the vintage of the coil. Make sure that both this terminal and the one from the ignition switch on the other side of the coil top (marked S.W. for 'switch') aren't loose or dirty. Straightforward push-on connectors rarely give trouble, but the ones that are secured with a nut and a washer are sometimes a different story.

Now open the points by pushing the car in top gear until they separate, or by slipping a piece of card between them. Turn the ignition on and touch the coil C.B. terminal with the circuit tester, which should light up and indicate that the terminal is alive; with the points open, it should be.

If nothing happens on this test, check the S.W. terminal on the other side of the coil top — again you can do this with the circuit tester and if there's no life this time, the supply from the battery via the control box and ignition switch has failed. This is a pretty remote possibility but the ignition fuse may have blown; if this turns out to be the case, you can get home by attaching a length of wire direct from the live terminal of the battery to the S.W. coil terminal, or from the A terminal

of the regulator if the battery isn't easy to get at. It would be most unusual to find an ignition system incorporating a fuse. If, however, the switch has failed (which is common on Fords) the same procedure may be used.

If the S.W. terminal turns out to be live, then the most likely possibility is that the low-tension windings of the coil have shorted out and a new coil is the only answer.

If the C.B. terminal is live, then we've isolated the trouble to the contact breaker and condenser, or the high-tension circuit of the coil. Contact breaker or points trouble is the most likely fault of the lot — in fact it accounts for so many problems of bad starting and failure on the road that many manufacturers are busily devising sophisticated electronic devices to do the same job, with no crude moving parts to get dirty or out of adjustment.

Checking The Contact Breaker.
On the side of the distributor body (the lower, metal part of the instrument) you may find a terminal where the wire from the C.B. coil connection arrives at the distributor. Most modern units feed the wire in through a rubber grommet and connect inside the case.

Probe this with the circuit tester and make sure the points are closed (ignition on). Open them with your thumb and the test lamp should light, and be immediately extinguished when you let them close again. If the lamp doesn't go out, or if it glows dimly when the points are closed, then they're dirty or pitted and need cleaning up. If the lamp doesn't light, or appears feeble when the points are opened, then recheck with the test lamp at the C.B. coil terminal, and if necessary go right back to the ignition switch, if you can reach the back of it without dislocating half the wiring behind the dashboard or more probably dislocating your spine.

(As we remarked in the last chapter about using test lamps, you need to ensure that the blade is making good electrical contact with whatever you're trying to test, otherwise you might jump to the conclusion that there's an electrical failure simply because you haven't put the probe in the right place, or the terminal is covered with highly non-conductive muck. This may seem to be a fairly unnecessary reminder, but once the proper test procedure has been learned you don't forget it and it can save a great deal of lost time and temper.)

So what have we discovered by now in our examination of the low-voltage circuit with the tester? We should now have discovered whether the points are opening and closing correctly, whether the gap is acceptable, and a failure of the test lamp to be completely extinguished with the points shut will have proved that the points are dirty or burned and consequently have deteriorated in their ability to conduct current. If this turns out to be the case — and it's certainly one of the most familiar causes of bad starting, particularly when other contributary factors such as cold or wet weather reduce the effectiveness of the battery and starter — then we can generally get away in the short run with cleaning up the contacts with our torn-up matchbox, or better still the miniature file that comes with an ignition servicing tool. You don't need to take the points to bits to do this in an emergency — it's a thing to be avoided under such circumstances since points are inclined to be secured with all manner of tiny nuts and plastic washers, which impatience, cold and irritation tend to rapidly despatch into the bowels of the engine. Just rub the abrasive back and forth between the points, check the gap again and clean up around the baseplate.

If the test lamp doesn't light with the points open but the low tension supply is all as it should be, then there may be a short-circuit in the condenser so that the current is escaping to earth through it.

Condensers don't generally pass out without creating a certain amount of disturbance first, often in the form of a misfire or poor acceleration. Faulty condensers also remove the protection that prevents the points from burning, so they soon get blackened and pitted. If you flip the points open with your thumb a couple of times in reasonably shaded light, there should be a spark between them but a fairly feeble one. If it's a fat white spark, it suggests that the condenser has given up; you can get a second opinion for this diagnosis by disconnecting the lead between the condenser and the terminal post of the points, then try the spark test again. If there's no difference, it means an internal short in the condenser. If there isn't a spark in the first place, but a fat one when you disconnect the condenser lead, then the condenser is shorting to the distributor baseplate — its cylindrical casing has somehow become live. Either way, replacement is the only remedy — complete failure of the condenser will make the spark so feeble that the engine will probably not run at all. Condensers are usually fastened to the baseplate or body with a single screw and you have to reconnect the wire at the points terminal.

Though it's hardly likely you'll be able to remember how we got into all this, I'll remind you; a rudimentary test on the plugs and on the coil high-tension lead revealed the absence of a spark. But suppose the ignition system was OK, and the plugs appeared to fire normally as the engine was cranked over? The only option is to look at the engine's other 'source of supply', the fuel system.

Fuel System

The first move is to disconnect the feed line to the carburettor at the float chamber inlet — the works manual will reveal how this is secured. There will either be a hollow brass bolt which will have to be undone with a suitable spanner, taking care not to lose the fibre washers fitted to it, or a jubilee clip clamping the hose to the carburettor inlet pipe. This is another of those little details that you'd be wise to have investigated beforehand — the clips often use small Phillips cross-headed screws, which don't take kindly to being assaulted with ordinary screwdrivers.

So, with the fuel line disconnected, direct it into a jam jar or any other appropriate receptacle. You ought also to know by now whether your car has a mechanical or electrical fuel pump; if it's the former, turn the starter key and crank the engine over a few times, if the latter just turn on the ignition. Either way, a strong and regular spurt of petrol should come from the pipe. If this happens, you can reckon on it being a fairly safe bet that deficiencies in the fuel supply aren't preventing the engine from actually starting. Inefficient fuel pumps will sometimes prevent it from reaching its proper performance at high revs, but testing pumps to the required degree of sensitivity demands instruments of the sort we'll be looking at in the next section.

A good fuel supply suggests that the carburettor is the problem, and if this is the case then there are limits to what can be done at the roadside, particularly now that many modern carburettors have become such sophisticated instruments. Start by checking the carburettor controls, since this is just a matter of observation, once you've familiarized yourself with the layout that applies to your particular automobile. Check that the choke cable actually does what it's supposed to do, either closing a butterfly flap across the air intake of the carburettor, operating the starting carburettor, or lowering the jet assembly (S.U.s). You might find that the choke cable has slipped from its fastening in the choke actuating lever.

(Remember, once again, that you can only have the slightest clue about what you're looking at in these checks if you already have a reasonable inkling of how your particular carburettor works, which is something you should have already checked out from the workshop manual. Trying to learn the whole thing from scratch just when you get a breakdown is like trying to prepare for an exam ten minutes before the doors open.)

If the car has an automatic choke, make sure you know how this is supposed to work. The correct procedure for setting up the automatic choke before starting the engine is to depress the throttle pedal to the floor *once,* and then leave it alone. Then you operate the starter until the engine fires. The choke flap is then held shut by a spring, which is controlled by a device sensitive either to the water temperature of the engine, an electric sensor, or to hot air from the exhaust manifold. As the engine warms up, the heat expands the spring and the flap gradually opens to allow more air through the intake and progressively weaken the mixture.

Automatic chokes don't generally fail to enrich the mixture, but will sometimes fail to cut out when the engine is hot; this might well cause the engine to stop because the mixture is too rich at normal temperatures. If this is happening, refer to carburettor maintenance in Ch. 5, and to the illustrations of your particular carburettor in the wokshop manual. Automatic chokes failing to operate at all so that the engine won't start from cold are more unusual, though the S.U. starting carburettor fitted to more sophisticated conveyances using S.U. carbs can sometimes fail totally. This is an electrical device, controlled either by a thermostat in the water jacket, or on older types by a manual switch on the dashboard. The gadget is brought into operation by a disc valve, and if the solenoid that manipulates the disc valve develops a fault, then the engine won't start. To check it, remove the lead from the solenoid terminal on the carburettor, switch on the choke and check the presence of current at the lead with the circuit tester. If the lead is live, then the supply is all right and the solenoid itself must be damaged; no overhaul is possible, you have to get a new unit. This procedure is *dangerous* — sparks and petrol do not mix.

Though the comparative simplicity of the S.U. carburettor spares it from fuel blockage problems, you ought to familiarize yourself with the whereabouts of the fuel filters both at the carburettor float chamber and at the fuel pump. Some cars only have one or the other, some a filter installed in the fuel supply line to the pump; whichever is the case, running on dirty fuel or with a corroded fuel tank may send large quantities of muck up to the carburettor if the fuel level is allowed to fall very low. Gradually this will block the filters until the flow becomes severely restricted or cut off altogether. If disconnecting the supply pipe to the carburettor shows you that nothing's coming up, there may be a blockage in the line from the tank to the pump rather than a failure of the pump itself. You can soon check this out by disconnecting the pipe at the pump inlet and trying to blow down it. You — or an assistant — should hear bubbling in the fuel tank, and you shouldn't need to give yourself apoplexy to get this result. If the blockage is clearing, blowing through the pipe will get progressively easier.

If you should suspect an S.U. carburettor of a blockage in the jet itself — there'll be no neat petrol collecting around the base of the piston assembly even after repeated cranking of the engine — then it can often be cleared by turning the engine over while you keep the palm of your hand pressed over the air intake to create a high degree of suction

If on the other hand there's a great deal too much petrol around, possibly with leaks from the float chamber and the jet, you can suspect trouble in the float mechanism itself which is allowing the fuel level to rise excessively. The float may have punctured, which you can check by taking it out and shaking it — if there's a hole, you'll hear petrol slopping about inside. There may be dirt in the needle valve assembly. Some carburettors turn out to be prone to having their floats stick in the closed position, preventing fresh fuel from maintaining the proper level.

One last consideration in dealing with troublesome S.U.s. Being sidedraught carburettors (see p. 34) the air cleaner box will either be mounted directly on to the carburettor air intake flange, or above the carburettor (Leyland transverse engines) on a curved tube at the rear of the engine. You can't do much effective examination of your carburettor with either the cleaner or the adapter in place, so you'll need to get these out of the way first. The air cleaner box is generally only fastened with wing-nuts, the adapter tube by a pair of bolts.

With downdraught carburettors of the Solex, Zenith and Weber types, the air cleaner is a kind of 'pancake' assembly fastened over the mouth of the air intake, and you simply unbolt this and remove any fume-recirculating tubes there might be scattered around. With downdraught carburettors you need to be especially careful not to drop any nuts, washers or other impedimenta down the choke tube. If you don't realize you've done so, you may well hear an extremely upsetting rattling noise from the engine when you get it started again.

On a great many fixed-jet carburettors of modern design, an acceleration pump is fitted that is responsive to the throttle movement, and this enables you to conduct a quick check on the fuel supply to the carburettor without disconnecting the inlet pipe. Peer down into the choke tube and snap the throttle open a couple of times — a regular squirt of petrol should appear from the pump jet. Bad starting or lack of power that's directly attributable to carburettor problems in a fixed-jet instrument is nearly always due to partial or total jet blockages. Carburettor jets after all are metering devices, and some of them barely exceed the shank of a pin in diameter, so it isn't surprising that unless the fuel is kept perfectly clean, mishaps can occur. The only thorough way to service a carburettor is to remove it and blow through the passages with compressed air, likewise with the jet assemblies. A garage may do this for you, or you can take the instrument to one of the specialist carburettor servicing agencies who will if required rebuild the whole thing with new parts. *Don't* push bits of wire or pins through the jets, because if you enlarge the size of the holes, you'll simply upset the operation of the carburettor and probably knock quite a hole in your fuel consumption figures as well.

The workshop manual will explain the position of the jets on your particular carburettor, and normally you remove them with a screwdriver — make sure the tool is a good fit in the slot of the jet because they're made of brass and easily damaged. Take out jets one at a time and clean them, or else label their position clearly or make a note of the aperture size stamped on the top — sometimes carburettor jets look identical but the holes are of different sizes and you want to avoid putting them back the wrong way round.

If you experience a general loss of performance and you don't suspect the ignition system or mechanical faults inside the engine itself, then all that remains is to knuckle down to thoroughly servicing your carburettor as explained on p. 146, or possibly replacing the instrument altogether. Bad starting on the other hand is often due to a minor and temporary fault, and here's a shortlist of clues and remedies that might establish what the fault is:

If the engine starts well from cold with the choke out, but accelerates badly, is difficult to start hot and has an unsteady idle, suspect blockages in the idling jet and the passages inside the carburettor body. If it's difficult to start from cold but runs well once warmed up and the choke doesn't help one way or the other, then the starter carburettor or starter jet may be obstructed. Problems with hot starting, a tendency to stall, and a strong smell of petrol under the bonnet suggest carburettor flooding; the float may be jammed or pierced, or the needle valve stuck or dirty.

If the problem turns out to be in the fuel supply itself, there's a limit to what can be done in a hurry. A pump that has ruptured its diaphragm can't be temporarily rescued, though sometimes the valves can be freed if they're stuck or dirty. This depends on whether the pump design allows it to be dismantled — some mechanical pumps are sealed units. Electric fuel pumps occasionally fail simply through a dirty or loose electrical connection — thumping a reluctant S.U. electric pump will sometimes restart it for long enough to get you home, and if it starts working again, you'll hear a regular tick from it with the ignition on, which will eventually stop once the float chamber has been filled. Lastly, don't forget that a pump can't draw fluid from a container if air pressure can't push from the other side; fuel tanks or filler caps always have a vent for this reason, and if it gets blocked the fuel supply will simply stop.

Faults On The Road.

Though the problem that the average owner dreads encountering on the road is the total and inexpli-

cable engine failure, there are a number of more likely hazards that can crop up to make the journey irritating but not quite a write-off. These include:
Punctures.
Electrical and lighting faults.
Broken fanbelts.
Broken windscreens.
Overheating.
Blown exhaust or broken clamps.

Punctures.
You can't generally be in much doubt about acquiring a puncture, the car feels as if it's running over cobblestones. Usually the tyre will have gone flat while the car's been standing and you notice it as soon as you drive away. Don't drive on a flat tyre for any distance at all, or you'll quickly reduce the tyre to tatters. The instruction book that comes with your car will explain the jacking procedure for your particular model — most modern cars incorporate square 'jacking points' somewhere along the sills under the doors, and you fit the peg of the jack into one of these and then turn the jack-handle or spin the nut at the top of the jack with the wheelbrace. Don't forget to remove the hubcaps and slightly loosen the wheelnuts *before* you jack the car up, so that the wheels don't spin when you throw your weight against the nuts, and make absolutely certain that the car is on level ground. Remember also that wheelnuts have often been pulled up extremely tightly by previous owners or garage mechanics and that if the wheelbrace supplied only has a short handle you might find yourself struggling if you can't add some sort of extension to it.

Fit the spare wheel, and lower the car to the ground. Retighten the nuts exerting a reasonable effort but without going purple in the face; if the wheelnuts are convex at one end so that they fit into dished holes on the wheel, make sure you get them the right way round. Finally, check the tyre pressure. If your spare is in any way doubtful (it shouldn't be, but spare tyres are notoriously neglected) then drive carefully until you get to a garage that can repair the damaged tyre or replace it.

Electrical Faults.
Lamp bulbs blow from time to time, and you need to carry one spare for each type of bulb on the car. Lamp housings are generally held on by plain or Phillips screws, though some front sidelamp assemblies simply twist off as if you were removing a household light bulb. Headlamp bulbs can sometimes be reached from inside the car, when the bulb and carrier can be twisted off in one assembly; or the conventional Lucas headlamp fitted to a multitude of British cars has to be pressed forward and then twisted sharply to free it from its three alignment screws. Instruction books always explain these procedures.

Fuses occasionally blow, either as a by-product of bulb failure or simply old age; there's not usually much doubt about this, because several components serviced by the fuse will fail at once. Locate the fuse-box and replace the fuse that appears to be scorched with a spare of the correct rating.

More elusive electrical faults, such as those caused by broken switches, shorted wiring or dirty earth connections can sometimes be difficult to track down at the roadside. The electrical circuit tester is a big help, and the instruction book will carry the car's wiring diagram — but prior acquaintance with this would be advisable. Ch. 5 on the electrical system, goes into this subject in more detail.

Fanbelts.

The first news you usually get about broken fan-belts is a clattering noise from the engine and the ignition warning light coming on. Since the same belt often runs the water pump too, the car will soon start overheating. If you're somewhere near civi-lization, then you can drive very slowly to a garage once you've fished all the broken bits of belt out so that the pulleys can run freely. On many cars, fitting a new belt is simply a matter of slackening off the bolts that hold the dynamo, pushing the component forward so that the belt can be slipped over the crankshaft, water pump and dynamo pulleys, then levering back the dynamo until the belt is reasonably taut and retightening the nuts. Some cars with multi-bladed fans and cramped engine compartments are much harder. Stretch emergency fanbelts are available from stores these days and you would be wise to carry one in the car. If you have to drive the car with the belt missing, make sure that all unnecessary electrical components are turned off, since the battery will be discharging fast.

Windscreens.

In the early days of the M4, drivers must have seriously considered going back to flying helmets and goggles and doing without windscreens; road chippings were knocking them out like ninepins. Modern windscreens don't splinter but either crack or craze into blunt crystals, and if this happens when you're travelling fast you need to rapidly punch a hole in it to get your bearings. Stop as soon as you can and remove the rest of the bits. It's a comfort to fit one of the temporary plastic screens the accessory shops sell nowadays until you can get a replacement fitted.

Overheating.

Short of some reasonable excuse, such as a holiday traffic jam on a scorching day, overheating has become a much less frequent hazard to motorists than it used to be. Sometimes it may simply be caused by the fanbelt stretching or fraying so that

it slips on the water-pump pulley; retightening may help temporarily though usually it means a replacement belt. The radiator may be choked, though this would normally have suggested itself through earlier overheating troubles. The brakes may be binding, which you can check by jacking up each wheel in turn, or the engine may be trying to tell you that something about it is seizing up. If the radiator boils, stop the car and let it cool — don't take the cap off without protecting your hand and keeping your head out of the way or you may get scalded as the steam makes its exit. And don't pour cold water into a hot engine, or the shock may crack something expensive.

Sometimes the water will boil because the thermostat has stuck in the closed position. A temporary remedy is to consult the manufacturer's instructions for removing the thermostat altogether; this will make the car very slow to warm up, but will keep you going until you can get a replacement.

Burst hoses and loss of cooling water are rather more of a problem though most forecourts and accessory shops carry spares for all the popular makes. You might be able to arrange a short-term bodge by lagging the pipe with rag or a chamois leather and fastening it at either end of the split with copper wire.

Exhausts.

You shouldn't get caught out by rusty exhausts if you're keeping a regular watch on such things, but if you blow a hole in the silencer box the car is unlikely to be so noisy (if you drive carefully) as to force you off the road. A split between the downpipe from the engine and the silencer is likely to make rather more of a racket and a temporary repair can be made with a silencer bandage of the type obtainable from most accessory shops; you simply moisten this slightly, wind it several times around the hole and keep it in place with twisted wire until it hardens. Broken mounting straps can be sidestepped by temporarily wiring up the exhaust; you can see the advantage of carrying that coil of wire in the car at all times.

Troubleshooting Guides.

These are merely a rough indication of the possible causes of breakdown in things you can't normally fix at the roadside. The variation in types of trans-mission, braking and steering systems is so enormous — both from one manufacturer to another and within one company — that we can do no more here than suggest general faults and refer you to the works manual. This will tell you whether the fault is going to be within your powers and the capacities of your equipment, or whether you'd be better off simply removing the faulty unit from the car and taking it to the agent for repair or exchange.

Engine Won't Turn Over On Starter.

SYMPTOM.	PROBLEM.	CURE.
Driving lights dim.	Flat or damaged battery.	Charge, replace or boost with jump-leads from a serviceable battery Push-start the car.
	Loose battery terminals.	Clean and retighten terminals. Check the earth strap (if fitted) between engine and chassis. (Usually located somewhere on the clutch housing).
Driving lights bright — unaffected by operating starter.	Faulty starter solenoid or disconnection in battery leads to the starter.	Operate the solenoid manually if possible, or push-start car.
Lights bright — severely dimmed by operating starter.	Jammed starter pinion.	Place car in gear and rock it, or turn starter armature with spanner.
	Burned-out or shorted starter.	Push-start car. Replace or service starter as soon as possible.
	Seized engine.	Bribe bank manager.

Engine Spins On Starter But Will Not Fire.

SYMPTOM.	PROBLEM.	CURE.
Perform spark-plug test. If no spark . . .	Ignition shorting through condensation or damp.	Thoroughly dry ignition harness and inside of distributor cap.
	Distributor rotor cracked.	Perform test as described in text. Scrap rotor if faulty.
	Ignition leads perished or plugs fouled.	Clean or replace.
Perform spark-test with lead from coil. If no spark . . .	Faulty ignition switch (no supply to coil).	Bypass switch with wire until you get home.
	Shorting or broken low tension wires. Check circuit with tester.	Remake or replace.
	Dirty, wrongly gapped or pitted contact breaker points.	Clean, file up and reset. Replace points later if badly deteriorated.
	Faulty condenser. (Excessive sparking across points when flipped open with thumb.)	Replace.
	Faulty coil — indicated by test on low-tension terminals, or if coil produces no spark when remainder of ignition system is cleared.	Replace. Remember a coil may fail when hot but mend itself when cooled down. This suggests impending failure of the ballast resistor.

CONTINUED ON NEXT PAGE.

Perform spark-test with lead from coil. If no spark . . . (continued)	Some part of contact breaker moving arm earthed or broken.	Check contact breaker for shorts, or missing insulation between moving arm and baseplate. Replace points if spring is broken or weak.
Spark OK but no fuel at carburettor jet/ float chamber.	No petrol.	Curse yourself and set off on long trudge in blizzard with petrol can.
	Faulty fuel pump.	Check contact points on S.U. electric pumps. Check, overhaul or replace mechanical pumps.
	Inoperative float chamber needle valve.	Remove and clean.
	Filters blocked.	Remove and clean.
	Carb jets blocked.	Remove and clean.
	Vapour lock (only in very hot weather or high altitudes).	Douse fuel lines with wet rags.
Petrol flooding.	Overuse of choke.	Remove plugs and dry them out, or operate starter on wide throttle.
	Float or needle valve damaged or sticking.	Remove float chamber cover, examine and clean as necessary.
	Float chamber level wrong.	Adjust position of float on operating arm as specified by manufacturer.

Engine Conks Out & Will Not Restart.

SYMPTOM.	PROBLEM.	CURE.
No spark at plugs.	Ignition failure through short, disconnection, broken wire, water splashing over ignition system.	Check ignition system through as described. Dry out if necessary.
	Ignition failure preceded by rough running.	Check points and condenser.
No fuel at carb jets.	Run out of petrol.	Obvious.
	Jet blockage/filter blockage.	Examine jets and blow through.
	Water in fuel.	Drain tank, blow out fuel lines and refill.
	Petrol tank breather obstructed.	Remove obstruction.
	Fuel pump faulty.	Check contact points on S.U. electric pumps. Check, overhaul or replace mechanical pumps.

Cooling System Trouble.

SYMPTOM.	POSSIBLE FAULT.	CURE.
Overheating — normal weather conditions.	Radiator short of water or leaking.	Top up or repair leak.
	Fan belt slack.	Tighten or replace if frayed.
	Faulty thermostat.	Remove and check for action in hot water — replace if necessary.
	Clogged radiator.	Flush out or overhaul.
	Faulty water pump.	Remove and check — overhaul or replace.
	Retarded ignition.	Check with timing light. Retime if necessary.
	Weak fuel mixture.	Check and adjust.
	Lubrication trouble or seizing engine.	Check oil pressure/piston & crankshaft condition.
	Binding brakes.	Readjust or overhaul.
Overheating — very cold weather.	Radiator frozen — possibly low down in the bottom tank.	Allow to thaw, and add antifreeze.
	Sheared water pump — blades frozen up.	Replace, and add antifreeze.
Overcooling — normal weather conditions.	Faulty thermostat.	Check.
	Faulty temperature gauge.	Check.
	Sometimes a design failure of cars built for hot climates.	Drive South.
Overcooling — very cold weather.	Faulty thermostat.	Check.
	Too large a cooling area.	Partially blank off radiator.
Water loss.	Leaks at pipe joints.	Check and retighten or replace split pipe.
	Radiator overfilled and discharging through overflow.	Reduce level.
	Local boiling in cylinder head due to choked water passages or poor tune.	Flush out waterways with a radiator cleanser. Retune engine.
	Leaky radiator — may be barely detectible visually.	Remove radiator for specialist attention.
	Leaky head gasket.	Replace — surface grind head if necessary.

Clutch Trouble.

Clutch remedies generally require extensive dismantling.

SYMPTOM.	POSSIBLE FAULT.	CURE.
Clutch slip — engine races on acceleration but car doesn't.	No free movement in first inch or so of pedal travel.	Adjust clutch as per handbook.
	Oil on friction faces.	Dismantle clutch and replace as necessary.
	Faulty release mechanism.	
	Weak springs or diaphragm.	
Clutch snatches — difficult to let in gently.	Oil on friction faces.	Dismantle, examine and replace as necessary.
	Worn friction faces	
	Distorted or broken pressure plate.	
	Splines sticking on gearbox shaft.	
	Bent gearbox shaft.	
Clutch judders on take-off.	Linings out of alignment.	Dismantle, examine and replace damaged components. Have flywheel alignment checked with dial-gauge if necessary. Check condition of engine and gearbox mountings — also stabilizer bars.
	Pressure plate and flywheel misaligned.	
	Distorted friction plate.	
	Bent gearbox shaft.	
Clutch drags — difficult to engage gears.	Adjustment wrong — too much free movement of pedal and thus insufficient withdrawal movement.	Readjust. Check clutch master cylinder reservoir for loss of fluid.
	Oil on friction faces.	Dismantle, examine and replace as necessary.
	Gearbox shaft misaligned.	
	Pressure plate distorted.	
	Friction plate sticking on splines.	
	Friction plate distorted.	
	Release bearing worn.	
Clutch is noisy — rattles.	Worn release bearing or broken anti-rattle springs if noise disappears when pedal is slightly depressed.	Dismantle and replace.
	If no improvement, friction plate or gearbox shaft are worn.	Replace.

116

Tinkling noise at idle — disappears when pedal is depressed.	Worn thrust bearing if of the ball race type.	Replace or lubricate as per handbook.
	Ball thrust race unlubricated.	
Knocking at idle.	Friction plate splines worn.	Dismantle and replace.
	Gearbox shaft or its bearing in flywheel worn.	

Transmission Trouble.

Transmission troubles are hard to distinguish from one another. Localizing noises into one component helps.

SYMPTOM.	POSSIBLE FAULT.	CURE.
Vibration on front-engined, rear wheel drive cars. Run car up to point of max. vibration, then slip into neutral.	If the vibration immediately disappears, the noise lies in the engine and clutch.	Check for poor engine tune or mechanical faults/clutch wear.
	If it continues, trouble may be worn propeller shaft joints, worn splines on sliding shaft, or bent prop-shaft.	Wheel balance — check this first. Examine and replace as per handbook.
Knocking or clicking when cornering on front-wheel drive cars.	Loose U-bolts on inner drive-shaft joints (Leyland transverse engines especially).	Tighten or replace rubber couplings.
	Worn outer constant-velocity joints.	Replace.
Knocking when abruptly removing foot from throttle e.g. downhill in top.	Worn drive-shaft or prop-shaft couplings (especially with independent rear suspension).	Replace couplings or shaft assembly.
	Gearbox or rear axle faults.	Check and replace as necessary.
Whine or hum from rear axle on front-engine, rear-drive cars.	Worn differential gears.	Replacement normally necessary.
	Incorrect meshing between crown wheel and pinion.	Consult transmission specialist.
	Lack of oil.	Top up.
No drive transmitted to wheels.	Clutch or gearbox broken.	Check and replace as necessary.
	Fractured differential parts.	
	Stripped or broken halfshafts.	

Gearbox Trouble.

Same goes for gearboxes as for clutches — repairs involve removal of the box from car. Virtually all gearbox faults involve extensive and complicated dismantling. Visiting a transmission specialist and/or exchanging the box is usually preferable to tackling it yourself.

SYMPTOM.	POSSIBLE FAULT.	CURE.
Gearbox noisy with car stationary.	Worn constant mesh gears.	Dismantle, inspect and replace as necessary.
	Worn front ball bearings.	
Gearbox whines, knocks or sounds rough in all gears.	Worn ball-races.	Dismantle, inspect and replace as necessary.
	Worn thrust-washers permitting gear cluster to move endwise.	
	Broken components dropped into box.	
Gearbox noisy on one ratio only.	Chipped gear tooth.	Dismantle, inspect and replace as necessary.
Gear action stiff.	Binding at one or more joints in linkage.	Check. This can often be done without extensive dismantling. Replace linkage mechanism as necessary.
	Gearbox cover loose.	
	Linkage bent or misaligned.	
	Sliding hubs or synchromesh damaged or breaking up.	Strip box.
Difficulty engaging all gears.	Clutch drag (see previous section).	See previous chart.
	Worn or broken selector.	Dismantle, inspect and replace as necessary.
	Jammed synchro hubs.	
Engagement of two gears at once.	Broken selector.	Remove gearbox cover and check. Sometimes possible in situ.
Gears jump out.	Weak selector springs.	Replace parts as per workshop manual.
	Worn selector rods and locking plungers.	
	Worn gears.	Exchange box.
Gears jam in mesh.	Jammed or broken synchro hubs.	Always examine selector mechanism before stripping gearbox.
	Selector mechanism stuck.	
No drive to road-wheels.	Usually clutch, prop-shaft or differential trouble.	Examine, dismantle and replace as necessary.
	Stripped gears or dog clutches.	Dismantle and replace as necessary.
Oil leaks.	Worn seals.	Dismantle, inspect and replace as necessary.
	Worn ball-races.	

Brake Trouble.

SYMPTOM.	POSSIBLE FAULT.	CURE.
Poor braking.	Brake shoes worn or maladjusted.	Replace or adjust.
	Oil on linings.	Replace linings.
	Linings not to manufacturer's specification.	
	Scored drum or discs.	Have drums/discs machined or replace.
	Shoes incorrectly aligned.	Check and reposition.
Brakes need 'pumping'.	Master cylinder rubber seals worn or damaged.	Replace and bleed system.
Brake pedal springy.	Air in system.	Bleed.
	New linings bedding in.	Fault should cure itself.
	Brake drums distorting.	Have drums machined or replace.
Unbalanced braking.	Brakes need adjustment.	Adjust as per manual.
	Linings unevenly worn.	Check and replace as necessary.
	Oil on one or more linings.	
	Dirt in drums.	Blow out brake gear.
	Scored or distorted drums or discs.	Have drums/discs machined or replace.
	Springs loose.	Replace.
	Brake backplate loose.	Retighten.
	Linings not all of the same type. Poor maintenance.	Check and replace as necessary.
Brakes binding. Check adjustment first, then check for seized wheel cylinders – replace if seized.	Swollen rubber parts in master or wheel cylinders.	Strip and replace.
	Kinked pipelines.	Replace.
	Poor adjustment.	Readjust.
Brake squeak.	Dust or grease on linings.	Dust out or replace linings.
	Linings misaligned or requiring 'chamfering' to bed in (see text).	Check alignment, bed in linings to manufacturer's instructions.
	Linings worn down to rivets or metal backing (disc pads).	Replace.

Brake Servo Trouble.

Check with manual to discover whether your brakes are servo assisted.

SYMPTOM.	POSSIBLE FAULT.	CURE.
Servo fails — braking becomes more strenuous. Depress brake with engine off, then start it — necessary foot pressure should be markedly less. If not . . .	A collapsed vacuum hose is the most common fault	Refer to manual.
	Vacuum pipe unions leaky.	
	Air leak at cylinder.	
	Faulty valve or air leaks at reservoir (if fitted).	

Suspension & Damper Trouble.

SYMPTOM.	POSSIBLE FAULT.	CURE.
Road shocks and bumps severe — older suspension systems.	Rusty springs. Rubber mounting bushes on springs may have collapsed or hardened.	Lubricate with penetrating oil except where spring leaves lined with rubber.
	Worn or flattened springs.	Replace or have reset by specialist.
	Seized shackle plate.	Dismantle and free off.
	Faulty shock absorbers.	Replace.
Coil spring system.	Jammed suspension arms.	Dismantle and replace bushes.
	Faulty shock absorbers.	Dismantle and replace.
Hydro-pneumatic systems.	Pressure too high. Puncture in hydro-lastic system, or time height set too low.	Visit specialist.
	Valves damaged.	
Car sags at one side.	Weak or broken spring.	Replace or have reset.
	Loss of pressure on pneumatic systems.	Check for leaks. Refer to manual.
Springing bouncy — insufficient damping.	Faulty valve in shock absorber.	Test for action with bottom shock absorber link disconnected. Replace if necessary.
	Leaking shock absorber.	Replace.
	Worn shock absorber mounting bushes.	Replace bushes.
Damping excessive — springing too stiff (check by bouncing car at its corners).	Seized shock absorber.	Replace.

Steering Trouble.

Consult works manual for adjustments and overhaul to steering mechanism.

SYMPTOM.	POSSIBLE FAULT.	CURE.
Steering vague — free movement at the steering wheel before wheels seen to move in straight-ahead position.	Worn steering swivels or wheel bearings. Worn suspension dampers.	Check by rocking wheels with car jacked up.
	Worn steering balljoints. Worn suspension dampers.	Replace.
	Steering gearbox loose on mountings.	Retighten.
	Worn steering gearbox.	Overhaul or exchange.
Car wanders.	Tyre pressures wrong.	Inflate/deflate as necessary.
	Car badly loaded (or driver badly loaded).	Adjust load.
	Worn suspension dampers.	Check and adjust.
	Binding in steering mechanism.	
	Axles loose on springs.	Check and re-tighten.
Wheel wobble at any speed over 20 mph.	Wheels need balancing.	Specialist check.
	Wheel buckled.	
	Steering gear worn.	Check and replace as necessary.
	Steering track needs adjustment. These are not probable, but a general check of the steering geometry, camber, castor and kpi may prove more rewarding.	Consult manual.
	Tyre pressures wrong.	Check and inflate/deflate as necessary.
	Another possible fault is cheap remould tyres.	
Wheel wobble at low speed.	As above.	As above.
	Wheels inclined at wrong angle ('castor angle') due to suspension wear or damage.	Specialist check.
Car slews to one side — normal progress.	Tyre pressures wrong.	Adjust pressure.
	Steering track wrong.	Specialist check.
	Loose suspension parts.	Check/replace as necessary.
	'Camber' incorrectly set.	Specialist check.

CONTINUED ON NEXT PAGE.

Car slews to one side when braking.	Badly adjusted brakes.	Re-adjust.
	Oil on brake linings.	Replace linings. Trace oil leak.
	One seized brake mechanism (needn't necessarily be a front one).	Locate seizure; replace components as necessary.
Steering heavy.	May be a characteristic of the car.	Buy can of Spinach.
	Lack of lubrication to swivels.	Lubricate.
	Bent chassis.	Specialist check.
	Lack of lubrication in steering box.	Lubricate.
	Bent or maladjusted steering mechanism.	Check and replace as necessary.

Power Steering Trouble.

Refer to manual. Specialist attention usually necessary.

SYMPTOM.	POSSIBLE FAULT.	CURE.
Loss of efficiency.	No oil.	Replace. Check for leaks.
	Air in system.	Bleed system.
	Pump drive belt broken.	Visit power steering specialist.
	Pulley slack.	
	Pump valves stuck.	
	Pump worn.	
	Power cylinder worn.	

Wheel & Hub Trouble.

SYMPTOM.	POSSIBLE FAULT.	CURE.
Wheel wobble — jack up car and see if wheel can be rocked vertically. If there's noticeable play . . .	Wheel bearings are worn.	Replace.
	Wheel bearings are out of adjustment.	Adjust.
	Loose securing nut.	Retighten to manufacturer's recommendation.
If no play — spin wheel and check for true running with a piece of chalk held steady against the tyre rim. (See text) If inaccurate . . .	Wheel buckled.	Replace.
	Tyre bulged or badly fitted.	Remove for attention by specialist.
	Bent axle shaft on a driving wheel.	
Try the suspect wheel on another hub. If the fault disappears . . .	Original hub flange was buckled, maybe through accident damage.	Scrap wheel and replace.
General vibration, often at 60-70 m.p.h. range.	Wheels and tyres out of balance.	Have tested on a garage electronic balancer.
Loose wheel.	Worn or insecure hub bearing.	Check.
	Wheel-nut holes worn or elongated.	Scrap wheel.
	Dirt between nuts and wheel.	Remove, clean and replace.

Tyre Trouble.

SYMPTOM.	POSSIBLE FAULT.	CURE.
Wear at sides of tread — centre OK.	Pressure too low.	Inflate to correct pressure.
	Tyre overloaded.	Check loading of vehicle.
Wear on one side of tread.	Suspection out of adjustment (possibly accident damage).	Specialist check by garage.
Wear at tread centre. Ridged wear marks.	Pressure too high.	Deflate to correct pressure.
	Buckled wheel.	Replace.
	Unbalanced wheel and tyre.	Specialized check by garage.
	Snatching brakes.	Check, adjust or replace brakes.

Steady pressure loss.	Tyre badly fitted.	Check and refit tyre.
	Slow puncture.	Repair or replace tyre.
	Faulty valve.	Replace valve or tyre as necessary.
	Leaky repair.	Replace tyre.
Gouges, fractures and bulges – pressure low.	Under-inflation. Walls flexing.	Replace tyre.
	Overheating of cover through excessive flexing.	
Fractures, gouges, etc. – pressure high.	High pressure blowing out already existing weak spot.	Replace tyre.
Fractures, gouges, etc. – pressure correct.	Kerb collision.	Replace tyre.
	Damage from sharp object or suspension fault allowing tyre to be cut by bodywork.	

Chapter Five

Keeping Your Car Healthy.

People have started skipping servicing these days, according to the motoring organizations, because the cost of even routine work at £10-12 an hour is getting to seem like a luxury. The theory appears to be: if it's working, why mess with it? So you save the odd thirty or forty quid here and there, the car goes on starting and stopping, your driving subconsciously adapts itself to the inevitable deterioration and you just keep trucking on until something drops off. It's a dangerous economy, but understandable.

When they're working well, motor cars put a pretty bland face on the hammering that they have to put up with, but the idea of regular preventive maintenance is to keep on correcting the ravages of hard use so that you can expect to get the life out of the machine that the maker intended for it. Statistics don't indicate much, but the workload of an engine is staggering: in a 10,000 mile period of driving, each piston might travel 7,000 miles up and down its cylinder, each sparking plug might fire and each valve open and close 18 million times and the ignition system provide 70 million sparks. That kind of performance can't be maintained at a peak without a modicum of care and attention.

The Crypton Company, a firm that specializes in tuning equipment for the motor trade, refers to a survey that showed that two out of three cars on the roads in the U.K. had incorrectly adjusted engines. Naturally, it's good for the Crypton Company's business, but several of the faults don't need their equipment to correct them, merely adequate maintenance. Between 10% and 20% of the engines had faulty sparking plugs and retarded ignition timing. Between 20% and 42% had over-advanced ignition and out-of-tune carburettors. 77% had faulty contact points.

Cars should be serviced at fixed intervals determined by mileage, usually a minimum of 3,000 miles, nowadays more frequently double that. How much of this work you can take care of yourself depends on your enthusiasm and your equipment. Don't leave a job out of the service because you haven't got the tool it requires; get the tool or take the car to a garage. The servicing schedules are listed in the owner's handbook and the workshop manual; for these basic jobs you might well find that the straight-forward instruction book provided with the car will give you all the information you need for servicing, though some recent books are fond of implying that pretty well everything except polishing the car ought to be left to their agents. In a case like this, get hold of the workshop manual, which ought to be more forthcoming. (When a *workshop* manual says lay off such-and-such a component, it's usually sensible to believe it.) It's impossible to generalize about what jobs are necessary at what intervals, but this chapter concentrates on dealing with the typical ones.

Every Week.

1. *Check the fluid levels in the battery, radiator, engine sump, brake and clutch hydraulic fluid reservoirs, and the windscreen washer bottle.*
2. *Check the tyre pressures.*
3. *Check the operation of the lights and horn.*
4. *Check the efficiency of the windscreen wipers and washers.*

Battery.

Of course, you won't be able to feel a glow of pride about announcing to people at parties that you do these things to your car all by yourself, but everybody has to start somewhere. Because they're simple jobs, it's easy to get sloppy about them and there are generally more diverting things you can find to do with your weekends; then one day Nemesis calls in the shape of a dud battery or a clutch that doesn't clutch, or perhaps the attentions of the local constabulary. If your mileage is very high or you make a lot of long fast journeys, then make these checks every morning.

They're all self-explanatory, but we'll explain them anyway. First the battery. Not that you can confuse it with anything else on the car, wherever it is it's going to look something like the illustration.

Most cars have their batteries stowed under the bonnet these days, but some are in the boot, some even under the back seat. Check with the handbook.

Servicing the battery merely involves keeping the acid level from falling below the battery plates — something that's more likely to happen in summer than winter, unless the battery case has sprung a leak. In the case of older batteries, you unscrew the plastic plugs from each cell and shine a light inside to check the level. If the plates are uncovered, top up with distilled water, preferably from a proper dispenser so that you can control the flow. Don't use ordinary tap water. In the more modern battery on the right, you simply prise off the plastic strips that cover all the cells.

Don't peer into your battery with the aid of a lighted match or any other naked flame, or you'll lose your eyebrows, and maybe more besides. The fumes are highly explosive.

More Regular Battery Maintenance.

Though motorists expend a great deal of nervous energy on phobias about worn big ends and the like, the battery ought by rights to absorb a great deal of that attention. It's one of the most vital components of the motor car, and one of the most neglected. So, in addition to the weekly attention to the electrolyte level, there are a number of other battery jobs that you should carry out more regularly than the 3,000 mile service, preferably once a month.

Look for cracks in the battery casing, particularly if the electrolyte needs a lot of topping up. Any serious leaks are usually the death knell for the battery, even if it's in otherwise good condition electrically. Check the tightness of the terminals and periodically remove them for cleaning with emery cloth. Smear the clamps and the terminal posts with Vaseline and retighten them. Clamps secured with a pinch bolt (as shown in the illustration) are more reliable and less prone to working loose than the cup type with self-tapping screw, and you might find it a good idea to buy an earth strap and a live terminal of the pinch-bolt type to replace your old ones. The earth strap simply bolts into place on the bodywork, though you should clean up the connection point to bright metal before you tighten it up. The live terminal is easily fitted by cutting off the original clamp, baring an inch or so of the lead, passing it into the new clamp and tightening the grub screws.

Check the state of charge once a month with the hydrometer (see p. 94). Put the battery on an external charger if the readings are below 'Half Charge' but disconnect the battery from the car's wiring first if you have an alternator rather than a dynamo.

Brake and Clutch Reservoirs.

You won't have a clutch reservoir at all if your clutch is operated by a mechanical linkage rather than hydraulically, but you'll certainly have one for the brakes: the handbook will tell you where to find them both.

Older cars use metal reservoirs though the modern tendency is to employ transparent plastic ones, which makes checking the fluid level a lot easier. There may be a marker on the reservoir but in any case you should make sure that it's at least three quarters full. Keep the reservoir clean so that muck doesn't drop in when you take the cap off, and keep a tin of whatever hydraulic fluid is recommended for your car, with the lid tightly screwed down so that moisture doesn't get in and lower the boiling point. Never top up with dirty fluid that has previously been drained off either your car or somebody else's, and don't get the stuff on the paintwork or you'll need to start mugging up on your respraying as well. And if you find that the level is persistently going down, (disc brake systems do this naturally as they self adjust), then have the braking system checked for leaks by a garage or check it yourself according to the procedure established by the workshop manual. If the loss is on account of a perished or scored rubber seal in either the master cylinder (operated by the footpedal) or the wheel cylinders (operating the brake-shoes or pads) then it might finally give up altogether when you brake sharply — and unless your car is of a modern design with a fail-safe braking system then a big fluid leak at one point will mean total loss of stopping power all round. This is not an experience to be recommended, even for those who don't like a quiet life, so regard all fluid loss from the reservoir with suspicion.

Radiator.

Check the radiator water level with the engine cold. Cooling systems come in two varieties; the more modern version includes an expansion tank connected by hosing to the radiator itself, to catch any overflow as the water heats up. When it cools down again, the partial vacuum in the radiator sucks the excess out of the expansion tank and restores the level to normal. Check with the handbook to find out which type of cooling system you have; the sealed type with the expansion tank shouldn't need topping up unless water's escaping from somewhere, but the conventional cooling system should get regular examination, particularly in the summer months. (If your engine is air-cooled of course, you can ignore all this.)

Don't forget that on either type of system, you can get yourself scalded when you remove the filler cap if the engine's hot — and don't crane your neck over the radiator while uncorking it either, or you might find yourself being attacked by an unexpected geyser if the water is already close to boiling point. This is because keeping the water under pressure raises its boiling point, and releasing that pressure may allow it to boil

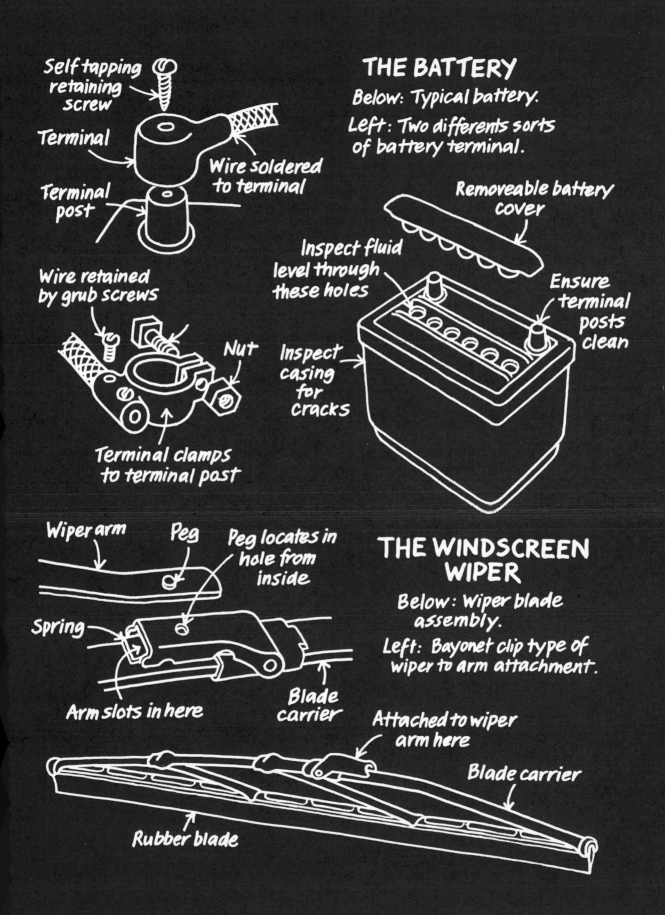

THE BATTERY

Below: Typical battery.

Left: Two differents sorts of battery terminal.

Self tapping retaining screw

Terminal

Terminal post

Wire soldered to terminal

Removeable battery cover

Inspect fluid level through these holes

Ensure terminal posts clean

Wire retained by grub screws

Nut

Inspect casing for cracks

Terminal clamps to terminal post

THE WINDSCREEN WIPER

Below: Wiper blade assembly.

Left: Bayonet clip type of wiper to arm attachment.

Wiper arm

Peg

Peg locates in hole from inside

Spring

Arm slots in here

Blade carrier

Attached to wiper arm here

Blade carrier

Rubber blade

suddenly. Top up with a mixture of tap water and anti-freeze in the same proportions as the solution already in the engine.

Engine Sump.
The level of the engine oil is marked on a dipstick, which you simply pull out, clean off with a rag, replace, and then remove again to take the reading. Do this on level ground or the oil may swill to one side of the sump and give you a misleading impression. Often there will be two marks on the dipstick, specifying maximum and minimum levels. The filler cap is usually on top of the rocker cover; but don't recheck the oil level immediately you've poured more oil in, it generally takes a minute or two to drain down to the sump and level off. Don't over-fill the sump, you'll simply raise the oil consumption.

If you should unaccountably find your oil level going *up*, this isn't the act of magnanimity on your car's part that it might appear to be. The only other fluid that could contribute to what's in the sump is water of course, and water most assuredly shouldn't be in there. If this should ever happen to you, get the engine compressions checked to see whether the head gasket is leaking. The problem may equally be a crack in the head or the block. Make sure though, before you start flapping about, that the car is parked on the level.

Screenwasher and Wipers.
Keep the screenwasher bottle full, and add a detergent to it that will help clean the windscreen and also lower the freezing point. Don't put engine anti-freeze in it because it won't do your paintwork much good. Prevent the spray jets from clogging up by keeping wax polish away from them; but if they do block, take them out, soak them in detergent and blow through them with a tyre pump. A bit of judicious poking about with a piece of fuse wire might help too, but be careful not to enlarge the holes. Failure of electric washers is usually due to a straightforward bad connection. Check the power supply by connecting the circuit tester lamp to earth and probing the terminals at the motor and at the dashboard switch.

Check the action of the wipers; if you suspect any trouble with the wiper motor itself, get it examined by an auto electrician or follow the manual's guidance. If the action of the wipers looks normal but the screen still appears to be coated in brown windsor soup, then the blades may be worn. The edges of wiper blades should be good and sharp; replace them if they're worn down or if the rubber has actually torn.

If you don't want to be let in for a lot of fiddling about, then buy a complete blade assembly rather than just the rubber insert. The blade may be attached to the arm with a bayonet clip or with a spring-loaded slot as shown in the illustration.

In the first case simply push the arm against the spring clip until the peg is below the level of the hole, and then pull the arm clear. In the second, press the blade and arm together to disengage the locking post and then turn the blade upwards to pull it free. Replacing a rubber is easy enough as long as you're sure you're getting exactly the same spare from the accessory shop (take one of the old blades along to be on the safe side). The rubbers have two strips of stiffening metal slotted in either side, so be careful that these don't fall out; then lever the locking tabs on the blade carrier outwards with a pair of pliers (don't bend them backwards and forwards more than you can help or they might break off), get the blade properly located and bend them back to retain it. Like many jobs on the car, making a careful note of the original set-up before you dismantle it is the best way to ensure that you don't wind up scratching your head in bewilderment.

Every 3,000 Miles.

Engine.
1. *Change the oil at this mileage if the manufacturer recommends it.*
2. *If the carburettor is equipped with a piston damper (S.U. or Stromberg C.D.), top it up to the handbook's recommended level with engine oil.*
3. *Check the fanbelt for correct tension and any fraying or deterioration.*

Ignition.
4. *Clean the plugs and reset the electrode gap.*
5. *Check the contact points, clean and regap if necessary.*

Clutch.
6. *Check the clutch release clearance according to the handbook and adjust if necessary.*

Steering and Suspension.
7. *Check the tightness of nuts and bolts in the suspension, check for worn swivels or bushes, and for fluid leakage from shock absorbers (see p. 136).*
8. *Check the tightness of nuts and bolts in the steering mechanism, attend to any lubrication points with the grease gun.*
9. *Check the condition of any rubber gaiters or seals enclosing the steering gear, drive shaft couplings, etc. If they're torn or leaking oil, replace them.*

Brakes.
10. *Check the brake linings and/or pad thicknesses, and the condition of all hoses and pipes.*

General.
11. *Check all fluid levels as per weekly service.*
12. *Take the oilcan to door locks, hinges and the carburettor linkage.*

TOPPING UP S.U. + STROMBERG CARBURETTORS

Right: S.U. carburettor
Below: Stromberg C.D. carburettor

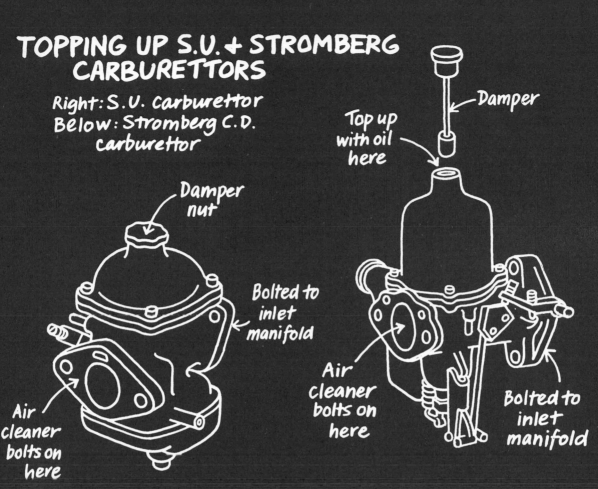

Damper nut

Damper

Top up with oil here

Bolted to inlet manifold

Air cleaner bolts on here

Air cleaner bolts on here

Bolted to inlet manifold

ADJUSTING THE FANBELT

Fan

Fan pulley

Fan belt

Crankshaft pulley

Dynamo

Adjusting bolt

Pivot bolt

When pivot and adjuster bolts are slackened off, dynamo can be pivoted to adjust play in fanbelt

Lubrication.

Attend to the car's lubrication at the intervals the manufacturer recommends. He built the machine, and he knows what's good for it. 3,000 mile oil changes are less common than they were, but are still recommended for cars whose engines and transmissions draw on the same oil, or if a lot of short-haul driving is done. As we saw in the first chapter, oil doesn't retain its robustness for ever in the torture chamber of the crankcase — as the engine runs, it's continually contaminating the oil with excess petrol, water and the corrosive acids that are formed as exhaust gases dissolve. Some oil manufacturers are now claiming greatly extended 'lives' for their products, but go by the recommended procedure for the car rather than the publicity for the oil, at least until the car builder endorses the idea as well. If the engine bearings and the gearbox and differential run in the same oil reservoir, then the intervals between changes are unlikely to be longer than 3,000 miles, with a change of filter every 6,000.

It's best to drain the oil off after a fairly substantial run, so that all the muck is floating in the lubricant rather than hiding in nooks and crannies of the engine. Get underneath the car and look for the sump drain plug. It may look like a conventional bolt-head, in which case you always use a ring spanner or preferably a socket to loosen it; an open-ended spanner could well cause damage on a fitting that may be large, tight and awkwardly placed. But it may not come undone with spanners or sockets but require a large Allen key or a specially shaped plug wrench obtainable from the car's agents (particularly with continental cars); if you've taken any account of all that tedious 'Be Prepared' advice in the Workshop Practice section, you'll have thought about providing for these eventualities before donning the overalls.

Whichever way you have to get the plug out, leave the sump to drain for a while to expel the last dregs of the oil. Get a big enough pan to catch all of it, or you'll find yourself desperately trying to get the drain plug back in when the pan starts overflowing all over the garage floor or maybe all over the street, which won't improve your popularity with the Town Hall. Servicing the car on ramps, axle stands or over a pit is the best course of action. Don't do oil changes by crawling under the car while it's simply supported on a jack; lying under a precariously supported deadweight is bad enough, but yanking away at obstinate nuts with wrenches in this position is asking for trouble.

Some drain plugs have a magnet attached to them to catch bits of floating metal. Clean the plug up before you put it back, and be careful when you do refit it that you get the thread in straight — the plug should easily turn by hand if the threads are undamaged and clean. The handbook may specify a torque reading for the sump plug or you may simply

have to rely on intelligent guesswork — but normally the shaft of the appropriate ring spanner will be of such a length that you only need to lean on it with a modicum of effort to get the plug tight. Replace the copper washer on the sump plug if it's badly distorted or squeezed flat.

Carburettors.

On the S.U. and Stromberg C.D. carburettors, the jet size varies with the air flow through the instrument and that air flow causes a piston or air valve to rise and fall in the choke tube (see Ch. 1 p. 36). If it rises too fast though (when you put your foot hard down) then the combustion chambers are momentarily starved of rich mixture for acceleration, so the movement of the piston is oil damped, rather as if it were a small shock absorber. Unscrew the nut on the top of the suction chamber and pull out the damper; top up with oil to the recommended level, push the damper back and screw it up. You'll feel some resistance from the oil as you do this, but any excess will be expelled through a little hole in the top of the damper.

If the carburettors require topping up more often than this, then the dampers are probably worn; you can get replacements from the agents for the particular instrument. (Going to the car's agents isn't a good idea, they'll probably try to flog you a new carburettor.) Don't forget to specify exactly what sort of carburettor it is, and the year and make of the vehicle it's fitted to.

Topping up is a simple enough operation on S.U.s, slightly complicated in the case of Stromberg C.D.s. The latter recommend the use of their own oil and in the case of some of their instruments there is a collar on the damper that has to be properly located in the guide rod. You need the air cleaner off for this, so that you can lift up the air valve to meet the damper when the latter has been screwed down.

Fan Belt.

Start by rotating the belt completely so that you can examine the whole length of it for fraying or deterioration. You'll have to put the car in top gear and push it with the ignition off to get the crankshaft pulley to turn the belt. Then check the tension: you shouldn't be able to depress the belt by more than a ½ inch at the middle of its longest run. If it's much slacker than this, adjustment is usually effected by loosening the generator pivot bolts and levering the generator outwards until the belt is properly tensioned. Then you retighten the pivot bolts. Don't get the fan belt too tight or it will strain the bearings of the generator and water pump.

Ignition.

Pull off the plug covers and leads, making sure you can establish later on which one goes where. Remove

ADJUSTING THE SPARK PLUG GAP

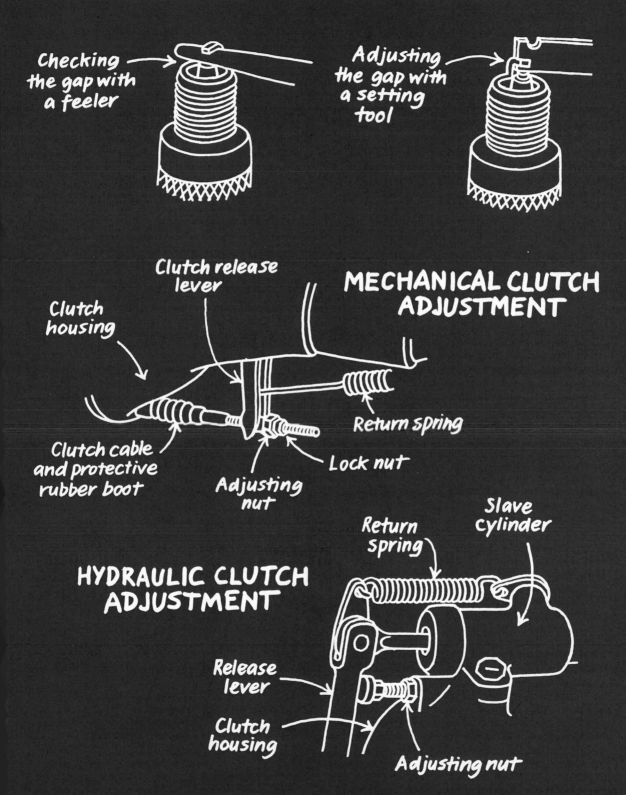

Checking the gap with a feeler

Adjusting the gap with a setting tool

MECHANICAL CLUTCH ADJUSTMENT

Clutch release lever

Clutch housing

Return spring

Clutch cable and protective rubber boot

Adjusting nut

Lock nut

HYDRAULIC CLUTCH ADJUSTMENT

Return spring

Slave cylinder

Release lever

Clutch housing

Adjusting nut

the sparking plugs with the plug socket and tommy-bar, box spanner or plug wrench (see p. 88). Clean the electrodes with a thin file (a metal nail file would do). Check the proper electrode gap with the handbook, and bend the outer electrode gently until the appropriate feeler gauge just slides in. If the plugs are being regularly serviced and replaced at 12,000 mile intervals then they shouldn't be badly burned or worn, but replace any that look as if they've seen better days. Plugs are always a good rough indication of the state of tune and wear of the engine, so examine them before you clean them and refer to p. 176 of the 'Tune-up' section.

Contact Points.

Although the owner-driver's manual usually says something like 'check distributor contact points, clean and adjust if necessary', it's a good idea to take the points off altogether since it's never very convenient either to examine or clean them in place and some distributors are so awkwardly situated as to make it virtually impossible. Once again, the handbook will normally provide an exploded diagram of exactly how the points are assembled, but in any case make a note of the position of any insulating washers which keep the current from escaping to places it isn't meant to visit. Oddly, when you don't understand how the ignition circuit actually works, it's very easy to replace points so that the insulation is in the wrong place and they short out. Once you do grasp the principle, which Ch. 1 should give you a hand with, then it's an almost impossible mistake to make again except out of sheer carelessness. *Remember that the moving contact on the spring blade must be isolated from the pivot pin of the fixed contact* – a plastic or fibre bush will run down the pivot to separate them. And the terminal where the leads from the coil and condenser are connected to the moving contact must likewise be isolated from the pivot – the plastic bush is likely to serve the same purpose, and a fibre washer will normally lie between the bottom edge of the moving contact and the fixed contact on the baseplate.

To get a breather from all that, take a look at the illustration.

After the points have been cleaned or changed, replace them on the baseplate and loosely fasten the retaining screw. Remember that whether you're replacing the points with the modern 'one-piece' type or the version in which the fixed and movable contacts come separately, you will have to double the contact breaker springblade back on itself so that the contact heel can slide over the pivot post, then set the gap as detailed on p. 106 and in the owner's handbook. Turn the engine by putting it in top and pushing the car until the heel of the moving arm is dead on the apex of one of the cam lobes. In this position move the fixed contact until the gap

between the points is at the manufacturer's specification as measured by the feeler gauge, and retighten the fixing screw. You generally find that the retightening part slightly alters the gap and you have to do it again until you get it right. With the points fully closed, make sure that the two contact faces are square with each other; any misalignment should be investigated properly and the cause rectified.

Some distributors provide a handy device for altering the gap without having to slide the contacts backwards and forwards by hand (which can have the same mesmeric effect as banging a golf ball from one side of the green to the other). This device is a tiny cam attached to a screw head, and you merely turn the screw slightly in either direction to produce the desired adjustment.

Clutch.

Though some modern cars are being fitted with self-adjusting clutches, most still require periodic clutch adjustment to compensate for wear on the centre-plate which makes the friction faces gradually 'thinner' (see Ch. 1. p. 43). On a mechanical clutch, in which the foot pedal is directly hooked to the release bearing by a chain or by levers, there will be an adjusting nut on the release mechanism underneath the car. With hydraulically operated clutches, in which the pedal action doesn't bear directly on any part of the withdrawal mechanism itself but makes its presence felt through 'remote control' – pushing fluid into a cylinder, forcing a little piston to slide that takes the clutch release with it – you merely have to maintain a recommended clearance in the linkage. The handbook will have the details. The clearance is usually measured with a feeler.

It's worth noting that if you do have a hydraulic clutch and the pedal suddenly goes to the floor without having any effect on the release, then look for the culprit in the hydraulics first, before you start tearing gearboxes out. The rubber piston cups occasionally give out and then of course no pressure can be built up in the system at all.

Steering and Suspension.

Start by checking the shock absorber action and the ride height. You do the former simply by pressing down hard on each wing of the car in turn and letting it go; it should bounce up once, and then settle. If it goes on bouncing, the shock absorbers are in trouble.

Measure the ride height on level ground by stretching a tape measure between the centre of the roadwheel and the centre of the wheel arch – compare the measurements on opposite sides of the car, and compare them with the manufacturer's recommended ride height. (If you can't get hold of

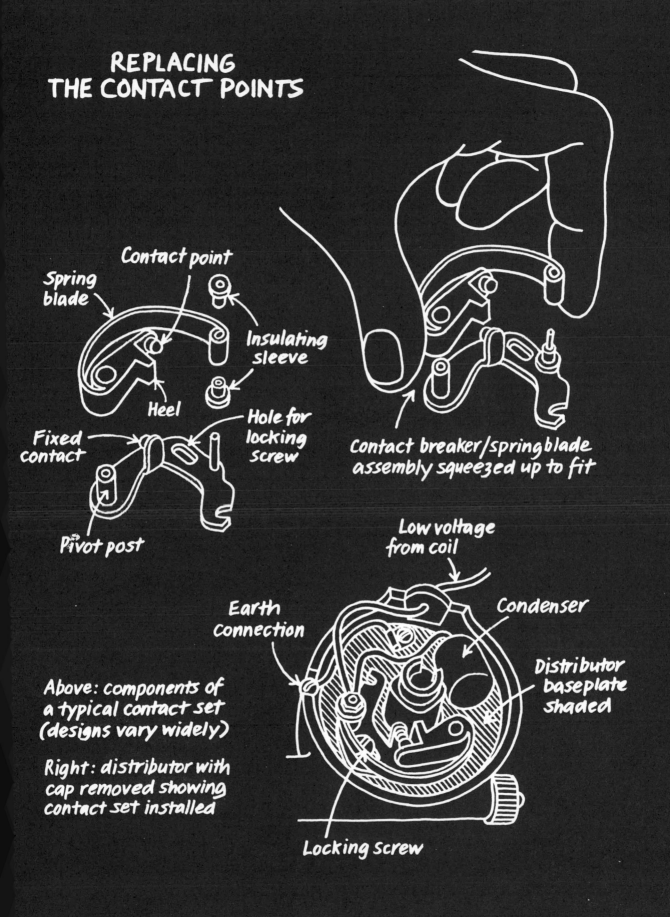

REPLACING THE CONTACT POINTS

Spring blade

Contact point

Insulating sleeve

Heel

Fixed contact

Hole for locking screw

Pivot post

Contact breaker/spring blade assembly squeezed up to fit

Low voltage from coil

Earth Connection

Condenser

Distributor baseplate shaded

Above: components of a typical contact set (designs vary widely)

Right: distributor with cap removed showing contact set installed

Locking Screw

this, you could always perform the same measurement in a car-park on a newer version of the same model. Be careful of possible restrictions to this innocent activity, such as the suspicious mind of the rightful owner.) Any imbalance between the two sides, or overall drop, is an indication of sagging suspension; older and heavier cars are particularly prone to it in time.

Checking for Wear or Damage.
If you take another look at the suspension section in on pps. 62 and 65 you can see that suspensions — despite great differences of design found on cars today — have certain features in common. The idea of suspension is simply that the wheels of the car should be free to move up and down over bumps while the bodywork keeps stable. So the paraphernalia holding the roadwheels has to be pivoted to the frame of the car and the action of the pivoting mechanism has to be both cushioned and induced to return to the position it was in before the bump. If the car has a solid axle, it might be bolted across cart-springs or leaf-springs. If it has independent suspension — in other words, the wheels on the offside and nearside can move to absorb shocks independently of each other — then they might be mounted on pivoting brackets or *suspension arms.* Both the shackle pins at each end of a leaf-spring and the pivot points of suspension arms are *bushed* where they join the chassis. In other words the swivelling action takes place at hardened steel bolts running in plastic or rubber bearings as shown in the illustration. It's in these bushes that wear takes place eventually. You can discover this by jacking the car off the ground, testing one wheel at a time and trying to establish whether there's any slack between a shackle or pivot pin and its bush. Make sure the car is thoroughly well supported when you attempt this, and remove the roadwheel as you test for wear at each hub in turn. Advanced wear in rubber bushes is pretty noticeable immediately — the bushes may swell up or tear, often through being attacked by petrol or oil. Test for slack by pushing a big screwdriver blade between each suspension arm and the mounting point and seeing whether you can discover any movement by levering at it.

Before you start checking your suspension system for wear, it helps to have some idea what you're looking at. It might be:

A MacPherson strut system. This is a straightforward coil-spring suspension in which the shock absorber is inside the spring; the whole unit is bolted to the frame at the top end, and has a ball-joint at the bottom where it's secured to the wheel. Check the mounting bolts at the top for tightness, and make sure that rust isn't developing around this spot on the inner wing — if it is, and you're not wise to it,

the whole suspension is apt to perform a spectacular collapse. There is also likely to be an anti-roll bar passing from one side of the car to the other, so check the mounting bolts on this as well. Lubricate the grease nipple on the lower ball-joint if there is one.

I should say that when it comes to checking the tightness of nuts, you don't need to go to such lengths with the spanner that you break out in a sweat just to produce another fraction of a turn. If the nut is secure, don't force it. Many suspension and steering nuts are locked with a split pin passing through the bolt (see p. 92); this type can't come undone, nor can you get a spanner on it. Just make sure the split pin is present, and not about to dislodge itself.

Double wishbone suspension. Check for wear in the inner bearings where the wishbones are pivoted to the chassis — levering between the wishbone and the frame shouldn't reveal any slack in the bushes at all. If it does, fit new bushes according to the instructions in the works manual. This often turns out to be a service station job, as do many suspension repairs if you don't have any means of compressing the coil springs.

Leaf-springs. Leaf-springs may be fitted at both ends of the axle or a single spring fitted across the width of a car (transverse leaf-springing). However they are fitted they all have rubber bushes mounted in spring eyes at the ends of the top leaf and are bolted to the axle or the underside of the body at the centre of the spring. Check the condition of the rubber bushes by levering them from side to side with a big screwdriver. They should be tight and the rubber should be springy and uncontaminated with oil. If they're perished or slack, it's time to fit new ones. Check the tightness of the mounting bolts at the centre. U-bolts are normally retained by two nuts on top of one another, the upper one preventing the other from loosening. You would normally have to tighten these by attending to the inner one first with an open-ended spanner and then pulling the locknut after it.

Lubrication of leaf-springs depends on their design. Some have rubber inserts between each leaf which are attacked by oil. Check the manual for the appropriate course of action.

Torsion bar suspension. The torsion bar is a metal rod that absorbs shocks by twisting along its length and then 'unravelling' to correct the ride. Once again, check all the rubber or plastic bushes by leverage against whatever pivots in them. Lubricate the grease points, check the nuts on the pivots and keep an eye on the ride height. If one side is dropping, you might be able to use the workshop manual's recommendations to correct it, since

SUSPENSION BUSHES

Position of bushes with independent suspension...

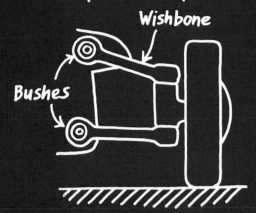

Wishbone

Bushes

Position of bushes with leaf spring suspension...

Bush

Spring shackle

Bushes

Section through wishbone suspension mounting (from above)...

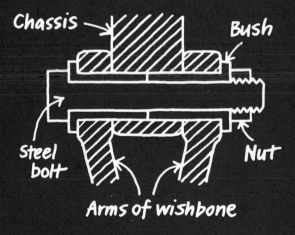

Chassis

Bush

Steel bolt

Nut

Arms of wishbone

Section through leaf-spring mounting (from end)...

Chassis

Bush

Steel bolt (shackle pin)

Nut

Spring shackle

The two halves of the bush butt together, and the bolt is a dead fit...

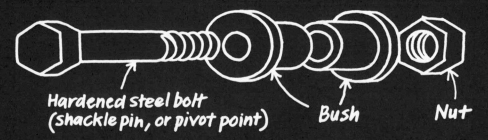

Hardened steel bolt (shackle pin, or pivot point)

Bush

Nut

torsion bars are adjustable; but some versions of this type of suspension are best left to the car's agents.

If your car is fitted with what's known as the De Dion tube type of suspension, you can't do any maintenance on this beyond topping it up with the oil recommended for the job.

Hydrolastic suspension. Look for fluid leaks anywhere around the pressure pipes or displacer units and check with the workshop manual about any other routine requirements appropriate to the type you have. Manuals certainly don't shy away from describing jobs you can do on hydrolastic suspensions, but before you launch into any of it you'd better make sure that your friendly local agent is happy to depressurize and repressurize the system for you. With the suspension 'down', you can just about drive the car, but only under 30 m.p.h. and over as short a distance as possible.

Shock Absorbers.
Shock absorbers are either of the lever type or the telescopic type (see page 66). Both of them 'damp' the action of the spring to stop it deflecting too far and oscillating too much after bumps. Shock absorber mounting bushes sometimes deteriorate. These are now an M.O.T. failure point, so it will pay you to make them part of your regular schedule. Damage to them will be pretty evident – either as slackness between the damper and its linkage to the spring, or as swelling or tearing of the rubber bushes. If you spot any fluid leaks on either type of damper, there's little to be done but replacement. Lever arm dampers have a provision for topping up, though you shouldn't ever have to make use of it unless there's something wrong with the device. If you do take the filler plug out, make sure you've scrupulously cleaned around it first; you'll do more harm than good if you let dirt drop into the reservoir.

Steering.
Like the brakes, steering is literally a matter of life and death, so if you've decided that garage bills have forever banished you from the portals of such places, remember that it's now only your judgement that's protecting your safety and that of your passengers. Your judgement should be perfectly up to it of course, since there's nothing mysterious about steering gear, but one of the natural but unfortunate features of home servicing is that the jobs that get done standing upright and in good light are often more thorough than those that require a lot of grovelling about underneath in road dirt and old oil. If you don't feel that you can comfortably take a good long look at the steering gear and brakes at the service intervals, then go to somebody who can. A very important consideration in all this is to be able

to get the car securely lifted and supported.

Having said all that, here's what you look for if you're able to work without discomfort or distractions. Start by looking at the rubber boots that protect the moving parts on rack-and-pinion steering systems, and also the constant velocity joints on cars with front-wheel drive. If the boot is torn and letting dirt in and oil out, it will have to be replaced; in the case of the steering rack, you'll need to split the outer steering ball-joint to slide off the boot (see p. 138). Check the tightness of the nuts and bolts that hold the steering mechanism to the bodywork or sub-frame.

Check the steering ball-joints for wear. Get a tight grip on the steering arm attached to the stub-axle, while somebody gently turns the steering wheel. If you see any movement in the steering rod before the arm you're holding makes any movement at all, then there's slack in the ball-joint and it will need renewing (see p. 138). If there's a grease nipple on the ball-joint, give it three shots with the gun. Don't overdo it, because ball-joints are protected with a rubber seal which will get uncomfortably swollen under excessive pressure.

Find out from the handbook how the steering column is linked to the steering box in your car. It may have a universal joint if the engine compartment is too cluttered for the column to be able to run straight from the cockpit to the steering gear. You should check this for slack by grasping either side of the joint and twisting it to uncover any lost motion. Somewhere in the steering column there may be a splined section and a clamp secured by a pinch bolt (e.g. where the column is secured to the steering rack). Make sure the pinch bolt hasn't loosened or you might find yourself doing a Keystone Cops routine in which the steering wheel has suddenly turned into an optional extra.

Check the steering ball-joints as before, by levering between the stub-axle and the joint with a large screwdriver with the car jacked up – if there's any up-and-down movement, the joint is worn out and needs replacing. This might be beyond you if you don't have any means of compressing the coil springs. Check the ball-joints on the steering arms as well.

Many cars with the worm-and-peg type of steering (see p. 60) are fitted with a steering idler on the opposite side of the car from the steering gearbox. Check both of these units to make sure their mounting bolts are secure, any slack in the bearings of either of the drop arms, or looseness at the joint between the drop arms and the steering and idler shafts should be looked into.

On all these tests, you can start by the well-tried method of jacking the front wheels off the ground and attempting to rock them vertically. Wear in the steering arm ball-joints will be revealed if you get somebody to hold the steering wheel tight on a

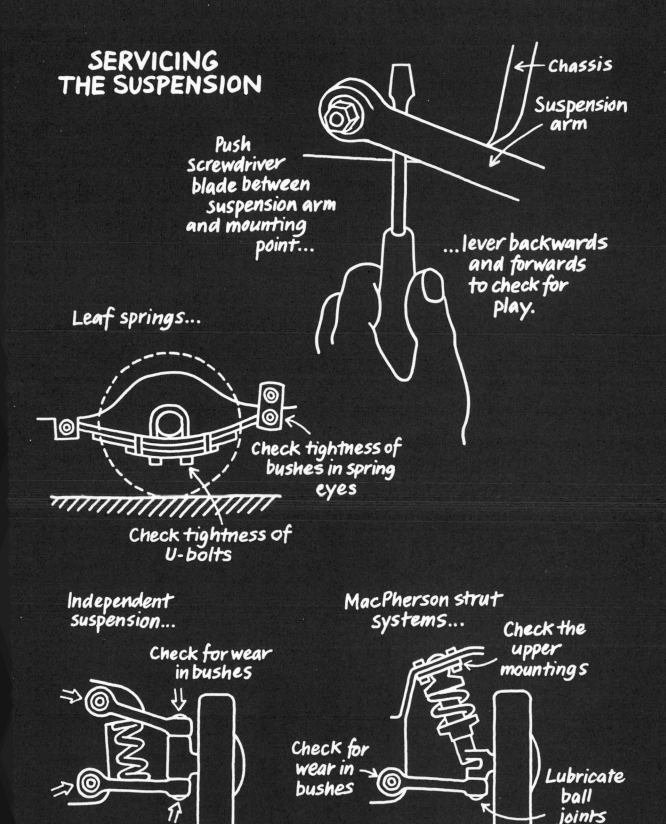

SERVICING THE SUSPENSION

Chassis

Suspension arm

Push screwdriver blade between suspension arm and mounting point...

...lever backwards and forwards to check for play.

Leaf springs...

Check tightness of bushes in spring eyes

Check tightness of U-bolts

Independent suspension...

Check for wear in bushes

MacPherson strut systems...

Check the upper mountings

Check for wear in bushes

Lubricate ball joints

rack-and-pinion system (hold the drop-arm on a worm-and-nut system) and then try to turn the road wheels from side to side. If there's any movement, it will be lost motion between the steering box and the hubs.

Replacing steering ball-joints is easy, and you should do it if you find any of them to be worn, suffering from up and down play, or with torn rubber grease seals. The only catch is that you need to have some means of breaking the tapered connections between the arm and the joint. The tool to use is (preferably) a ball-joint breaker of the type that forces the joint apart as you tighten a big draw-bolt; but cheaper wedged-types are available, which you simply bang into the joint to prise it apart. Slacken off the locknut on the steering arm, clean the thread, and mark it with white paint at the point that the ball-joint screwed up to. Then remove the self-locking nut from the taper, break it, separate the steering arm and unscrew the ball-joint. The paint will have left a 'tide-mark' which will tell you how far to screw the new joint on. You then push the taper back into its hole, secure it with a new locknut, and tighten the retaining nut on the steering up against the body of the joint. (N.B. Check the alignment afterwards, as the new ball-joint may differ, due to manufacturing tolerances.)

Steering gearboxes can often be adjusted for wear, as the manual will explain. Rack-and-pinion systems can't, and have to be scrapped — but their lifespan is probably a lot longer than that of the car.

Brakes.

A quick glance at Ch.1. (p. 62) will remind you that there are two types of braking system in common use today and sometimes a combination of these two: the drum brake and the disc brake. The former is operated by movement of the friction shoes or lining outwards against the inner face of a revolving drum bolted to the wheel hub, the latter by the grip of friction pads on a spinning disc similarly attached. Obviously the distance between these friction devices and the drum or disc when the brakes are 'off' is vital to the final efficiency when the brakes are actually applied; disc brakes adjust this distance of their own accord as the pads wear, but most drum brakes have to be adjusted periodically as part of the maintenance programme (though some types are self-adjusting).

At each service period in a drum system, check the brake system thoroughly for wear on the disc pads and wear on the shoes. Disc pads can easily be examined without any dismantling beyond removing the roadwheel; the shoes will require removal of the drums unless they're of the type that has inspection holes in the backplate; you can shine a torch through these and get some idea about how much lining thickness is left. The handbook will give figures for the minimum lining or pad thickness

before replacement is called for. To remove brake drums, simply undo whatever holds them to the hub, usually a couple of large Phillips screws. Then pull the drum towards you and generally it helps to rock it slightly from side to side to ease it off the shoes — if it's really reluctant, you may need to slacken the adjuster on the backplate to contract the shoes slightly. Don't manipulate the adjuster with anything with jaws that you happen to have around, you should use a proper adjusting tool which will have the right square or hexagonal hole in it. While you're at it, examine the wheel cylinders for leakage of fluid, the flexible hosepipes for perishing or chafing, and the metal brake lines for rusting. These are all M.O.T. failure points anyway, so it pays you to keep tabs on them.

Preventive maintenance on brakes as recommended by the manufacturers includes annual draining of the system and replacement of the brake fluid, and replacement of the wheel cylinders, the hoses and the master cylinder every 40,000 miles or three years.

Brake Testing.

Brake testing is normally done with the help of accurate instruments as it is on the M.O.T. test, but you can get a rough idea by testing the car on a flat road with no traffic and the opportunity to establish markers. A lot will depend on the road surface, the weather and the tyres, but in any case drive up to your marker at 30 m.p.h. and apply the brakes hard. Then measure the total stopping distance and if it's around 30 feet your brakes are excellent, if it's 50 feet they're not bad and if it's 100 feet you'd better get out and walk. If you strongly suspect the brakes of having developed some ailment, don't begin your testing with crash stops in case something gives out abruptly and sends you careering into somebody's hedge. Start at 15 m.p.h. or so and make sure that applying the brakes doesn't induce the car to slew or skid; uneven braking is an indication of poor adjustment, unequally worn shoes or pads, or oil on the linings.

Drum Brake Adjustment.

The drum brake works by the expansion of two curved 'shoes' against the inside of the spinning drum, thus slowing it down. When correctly adjusted, the friction linings of the shoes are almost rubbing against the drum, and are close enough to begin to have an effect on the motion of the car with even the lightest application of the pedal. As the linings wear down, this distance increases and the footbrake needs to be depressed further to get the same result. As you can see from the diagram, on the back brakes the shoes need to be levered outwards again at the end opposite to the wheel cylinder to put them back in the original relation to the drum. Eventually this becomes impossible be-

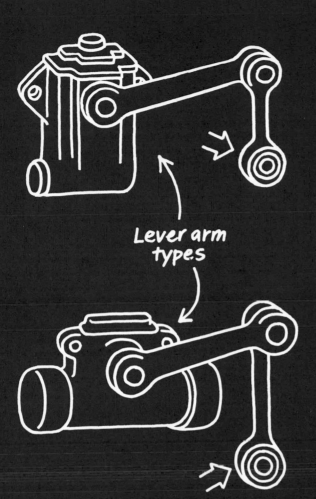

Lever arm types

Check the rubber bushes where indicated...

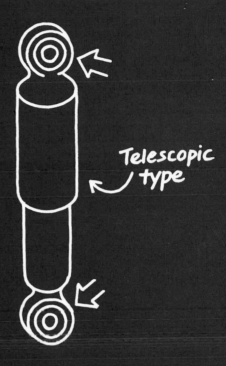

Telescopic type

CHECKING THE STEERING BALL JOINT

The drawing shows the brake drum & steering linkage viewed from behind. Watch the steering arm as the steering wheel is turned— any slack in the joint will show...

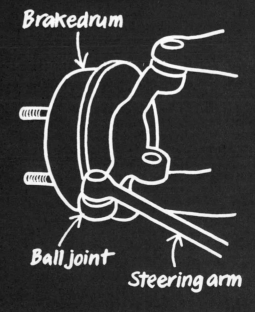

Brakedrum

Ball joint

Steering arm

cause the lining has become too thin; that's the moment to replace the shoes altogether.

Front brakes are normally of the 'two leading-shoe' type, with a hydraulic cylinder operating separately on each shoe; with this arrangement there are two adjusters and with the single cylinder leading and trailing type fitted at the back there's only one. Get the right type of adjusting spanner for your brakes, that way you won't butcher the profile of the adjuster until it becomes a shapeless lump. Adjusters sometimes turn in distinct 'clicks' and sometimes not, but begin by operating the foot pedal to centralize the shoes and then turn the adjuster until the brakes lock the drum solid. Then turn them back slightly until the drum is just free but you can feel a slight rubbing from the linings. Some brake adjusters are not on the backplate at all, but have to be reached through two holes in the drum itself; this type is generally slotted for a screwdriver blade, which you pass through the holes.

Many cars are now fitted with self-adjusting brakes and these need no maintenance except periodic inspection of the linings, and replacement when they get too thin.

Handbrake Adjustment.
This will be fully explained in the workshop manual, and since there are a good many variations of handbrake design there's no better place to look. Usually the rear shoe adjustment takes care of the handbrake mechanism at the same time, but the cables stretch eventually, to the point where the handbrake may not be fully applying the brakes even when the lever is pulled up as far as it will go. Make sure that the handbrake cables are able to move freely, and that their grease points are regularly attended to. Adjustment of the cable basically involves shortening it in some way. At the end of each cable is a fork called a clevis, which is pinned to a lever on the backplate that actually pulls the shoes. The cable has a threaded section at its ends, locked to the clevis by two nuts. You loosen these, pull the cable further into the clevis according to the recommended procedure, and then retighten the nuts. Handbrake adjustments are again performed with the handbrake off but the wheels locked solid by tightening the adjusters.

Replacement Brake Linings.
Replace the brake-shoes when the linings have worn down to $\frac{1}{16}''$ above the rivets, or $\frac{1}{16}''$ thickness if they've been bonded to the shoe. Brake-shoes are extremely cheap, particularly if you trade in your old ones. Use exactly the same kind of shoe as was fitted originally, and get it from the service agent for the car rather than trust extra-cheap alternatives.

Always slaken wheel nuts before jacking the vehicle. Jack up the car and remove the roadwheel and brake drum. If you have to take off the hub (see p. 63), then loosen the hub nut with the wheel

still on the ground if it's a really hefty one, such as you find on the back wheels of Beetles. Examine the drums first, for signs of wear and distortion. If they look dubious, get them checked at an engineering shop, and if necessary skimmed out on the lathe. Clean the inside of the drums and get rid of all dust and dirt. Asbestos dust – BEWARE.

If the shoes are clipped to their steady posts, remove the clips and springs with pliers. Then lever one of the shoes back from the wheel cylinder until it's clear of the slot on the piston and snaps back towards the centre of the brake under the pull of the return springs. At this stage you can lever out the trailing end of the shoe and remove both of them. Put an elastic band around the wheel cylinder to hold its piston in. Clean the backplate. Check which way round the pull-off springs are fitted to the shoes, and, if they're of different sizes, which one is at which end. Lay the new shoes and pull-off springs flat and carry them to the brake laid out as if they were assembled to the wheel. Slot one shoe into position and lever the other one over its wheel cylinder and adjuster with the screwdriver. Don't let the blade touch the rubber boot on the wheel cylinder or it might tear it. If the pull-off springs don't link one shoe to the other, but are hooked between each shoe and the backplate, then link the spring to the plate and to the shoe, and lever the latter backwards until it will slot into position on the wheel cylinder.

Discs.
The device that grips the spinning cast-iron disc in this increasingly popular type of brake is known as the *caliper* (see illustration).

The *fixed caliper* type of brake has two hydraulic cylinders facing each other on either side of the disc, which squeeze two friction pads against the disc when the brakes are applied. Sometimes there may be two pairs of cylinders on either side, to provide a back-up emergency brake if one of the hydraulic circuits should burst. The *swinging or sliding* caliper has only one of its pads actively pressurized by hydraulic fluid, the other one moving in response as the caliper itself pivots.

Pads need to be inspected every 6,000 miles, and $\frac{1}{8}''$ is about the minimum they should be permitted to wear to before replacement. Always replace them in pairs as you do for shoes, or you'll get uneven braking. Check the piston movement at the same time, by jacking the car up, removing the wheels and watching the brake action while somebody else depresses the pedal. Generally the pads will be rubbing slightly against the disc with the pressure off, and both pads should grip the disc evenly when they're activated. You can check this by slipping a fine feeler gauge between the pad and disc; if you've any reason to believe that one of the pistons is sticking, then check the manufacturer's

ADJUSTING REAR BRAKES

Section through rear brake assembly...

Brake adjuster

Brake shoe

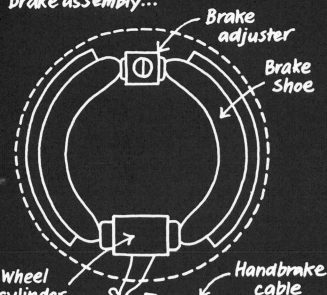

Section through rear brake adjuster. When wedge is screwed in, brake shoes are forced apart

Wheel cylinder

Handbrake cable

Handbrake may be adjusted here or at handbrake end of cable, depending on design

Rear brakes are normally adjusted from behind with a small spanner

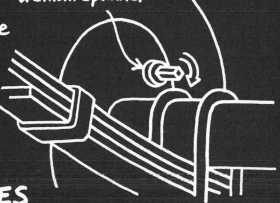

ADJUSTING FRONT BRAKES

Front brake adjusters normally work on cam principle. Sometimes front brakes are adjusted from behind (like rear brakes), sometimes from in front with a screwdriver

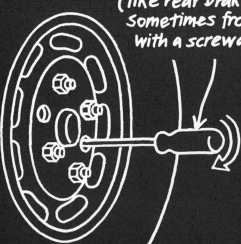

Section through front brake assembly...

Brake adjuster

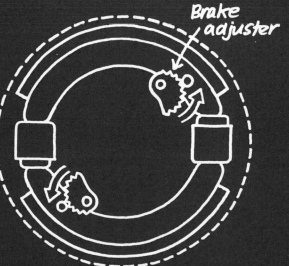

instructions for removing and overhauling the caliper.

Pad changing is simplicity itself, a great deal easier than changing shoes on drum brakes. Jack up the car, support it firmly and remove the road-wheel. Clean the caliper before dismantling it. Remove the pad-retaining split pins and any retaining springs. Grip the pad backing with pliers and pull it out as you turn the disc. Clean the pistons on Lockheed brakes with brake fluid, put back one of the old pads to hold one piston back while you move the other one — lever it with a screwdriver back into its cylinder, very lightly grease the new pad *backplate* and fit it with any shims (packing pieces) it might have accompanying it (whatever you do, don't grease the side of the pad that bears on the disc). Do the same with the other disc. You need to have the bleed screw open while you're doing all this so that you can move the pistons — any loss of fluid will mean that the reservoir must be topped up afterwards. Some disc brakes require the calipers to be taken right off the hub before you can change the pads; some feature dissimilar pads in each pair and you have to be sure you fit them to the right sides of the disc. Do not forget to pump the brake pedal to take up the extra clearance used for fitting — otherwise the first brake application could be your last!

Every 6,000 Miles.

Engine.

1. *Change the engine oil and the oil filter.*
2. *Check the valve clearances* (see Tune-Up Section, p. 182).
3. *Check the compressions if a gauge is available* (see Tune-Up Section, p. 176).
4. *Attend to the crankcase ventilation system if recommended.*

Ignition.

5. *Check, clean and regap the sparking plugs.*
6. *Check, clean and regap the contact breaker points and replace if necessary.*
7. *Put a faint smear of grease on the distributor cam.*
8. *Oil the distributor advance weights, pivot pin and spindle bearing according to recommendations. Stick to these, too much oil around the distributor is as bad as too little.*
9. *Examine the distributor cap, rotor, ignition leads and plug covers.*
10. *Check the ignition timing* (see Tune-Up Section, p. 180).

Fuel.

11. *Top up the carburettor dampers if fitted (S.U. and Stromberg C.D.).*
12. *Clean any fuel pump filters, line filters or float chamber filters.*

13. *Check carburettor idling and mixture adjustment* (see Tune-Up Section, p. 181).

Lubrication.

14. *Attend to all grease points as at 3,000 miles; check oil level in the gearbox and differential if there's any provision for this. Oil locks, hinges, carburettor linkages etc.*

Suspension and Steering.

15. *Check as for 3,000 miles. Get the toe-in and wheel balance checked at a service station.*

Brakes.

16. *Check pad and lining thicknesses as at 3,000. Adjust drum brakes if necessary, replace any worn pads or linings. Check hoses, pipes and hydraulic cylinders for leaks.*

Lights and Weather Equipment.

17. *Check the battery, the operation of all lights, the headlamp beam adjustment and the operation of the wipers, washers and horn.*

Cooling System.

18. *Check the water level and the condition of all pipes and hoses.*

Exhaust.

19. *Check the exhaust system for leaks, loose clamps, deteriorating mounting straps, etc.*

Lubrication and Oil Filter.

Get the engine hot and drain the oil off exactly as you did at the 3,000 mile service. While the sump is draining off, set about cleaning or replacement of the oil filter.

All engines have some sort of filtration system to catch foreign bodies floating around in the oil. Sometimes this system will be quite primitive, as it is on one of the most reliable engines in the world, the flat-four Volkswagen engine. It consists simply of a wire-mesh strainer at the oil pump pick-up pipe, and you have to unbolt a circular plate in the sump to remove it; servicing merely entails washing the filter with petrol and reinstalling it with new sealing gaskets. Most cars have this sort of simple filter in the sump, but augment it with a much more sophisticated type higher up on the pressure side of the lubrication system.

These external oil filters are normally replaced every other oil change (therefore usually at 6,000 mile intervals). The two most common types of filter currently in use are: the replaceable paper element type (which consists of a cartridge of material much like closely folded blotting paper, which is more or less what it is) and the disposable metal cartridge type.

In the case of the former, the element is usually housed in a metal cylinder secured with a long bolt passing through the base. You undo this bolt, withdraw the casing, remove the element and

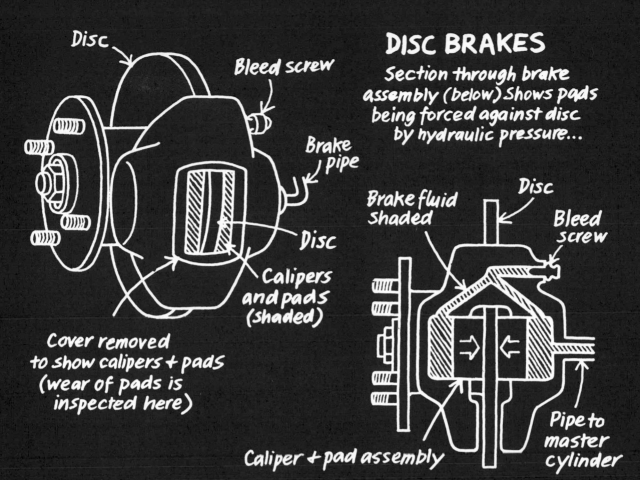

Disc

Bleed screw

Brake pipe

Disc

Calipers and pads (shaded)

Cover removed to show calipers + pads (wear of pads is inspected here)

DISC BRAKES
Section through brake assembly (below) shows pads being forced against disc by hydraulic pressure...

Brake fluid shaded

Disc

Bleed screw

Caliper + pad assembly

Pipe to master cylinder

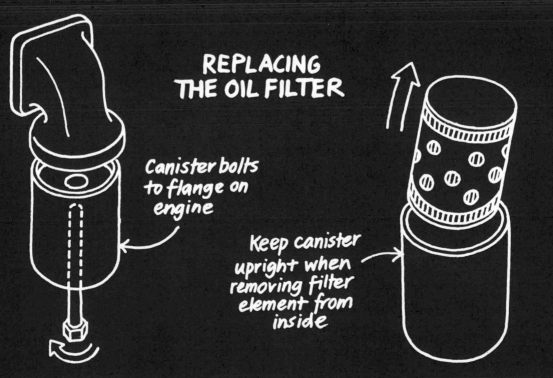

REPLACING THE OIL FILTER

Canister bolts to flange on engine

Keep canister upright when removing filter element from inside discard it. (Keep it upright as you do this, it'll still be full of dirty oil which you might quite easily inadvertently hurl over yourself.) Then you wash out the whole container in paraffin or petrol taking care not to lose any of the washers or springs attached to the retaining bolt, drop the replacement element into place, fit a new rubber sealing ring around the part of the filter housing bolted to the block (it will probably require a bit of poking about with a screwdriver blade or the like to get the old hardened one out) press the assembly back up against the upper housing and retighten the bolt. Then you run the engine and check for leaks. If there's a serious leak, then you might find that you haven't repositioned the canister dead square, or the new sealing ring is kinked, in which case you'll have to take it all to bits and start again. The latter point is often a tricky one to check, since you can only really see the lip of the housing if you're looking directly up at it from beneath the car in a good light.

The disposable metal cartridge is an altogether less fiddly proposition, and has been adopted on modern engines principally for its ease of servicing. You simply unscrew the whole canister, throw it away and screw another one in its place. The only snag is that the old filter will sometimes be too tight to unscrew by hand however hard you grip it; gadgets called strap wrenches are very handy at moments like this, but since you've no further use for the filter anyway, it's much simpler to hammer a large screwdriver through the case of the filter and use that to lever it free. Oil the sealing ring on the new filter and tighten it up by hand.

Valve Clearances and Engine Compression.
These items are fully covered under Tests 2 and 9 in the Engine Tune-Up section (pages 176 and 182).

Crankcase Ventilation System.
On modern engines, a ventilation system for the crankcase and valve gear is provided to prevent excessive condensation and sludge formation in the oil. Some are very simple, just a pipe in the side of the block. More sophisticated versions feed the fumes back into the inlet manifold or through the carburettor and fresh air is drawn in to replace them through a valve attached to the rocker box or some-times to the air filter. This 'anti-smog valve' is necessary to prevent too much air being drawn in and weakening the fuel mixture. Usually attention to this valve is required more frequently than at 12,000 mile intervals, but check it with the hand-book. If you take down the valve, refer to an exploded diagram on reassembly; wash the com-ponents with petrol.

Sparking Plugs.
Check the plugs as for 3,000 mile service.

Contact Breaker Points.
Check the contact breaker points as for 3,000 mile service.

The Distributor and Ignition Leads.
Distributors need lubrication like anything else with moving parts, but be sparing with it or the oil may get on to the points and start a misfire. A light smear of grease on the faces of the distributor cam, a couple of drops of engine oil into the centre of the spindle after pulling off the rotor arm, and a couple more through the hole in the baseplate are all that is necessary.

Check the distributor cover for the faults that we outlined under Troubleshooting (see p. 105). Look for burned or corroded terminals in the cover, black lines between them suggesting that 'tracking' has been taking place and the spark shorting out, and make sure that the carbon brush in the centre of the cover is present and able to move freely on its spring. If the distributor doesn't have this sort of arrangement for feeding the high tension supply to the rotor, then there will be a spring-blade in the centre of the rotor arm instead – you should check it for slackness, breakage or flattening.

Points ought to be replaced at 12,000 mile intervals in any case (see p. 132), when you also change the sparking plugs; and replacing the con-denser at the same mileage is not a bad idea either, since it's a cheap enough component and difficult to test for electrical failure. This ought to be the mileage when you perform a fully-fledged engine tune anyway (see Appendix) and all the compo-nents that affect the running of the engine will get a thorough going-over.

Ignition leads are often the most neglected part of the whole ignition harness. Chafed or split leads can allow the spark to jump to the metalwork of the engine without firing at the plug, or to jump from one lead to another so that the spark takes place in the wrong cylinder. Routine maintenance of the leads involves keeping them clean and free of grease, and replacement every 20,000 miles or two years is not a bad idea. Though you can buy ignition lead by the foot and make up the terminals your-self, it's simpler to go for the ready-made sets of leads that are available for four, six or eight cylinder cars, and you can simply pull the old leads from the distributor cap and press the new ones into place.

If your car has the earlier type of cap that held its ignition leads with tiny spiked grubscrews, then you just trim the brass contact from the end of the new lead, push it all the way into the hole in the cap and retighten the screw until it bites into the insulation and penetrates the central conductor. Establish which terminals on the cap supply which plugs and if necessary mark the cap or make a drawing – then you won't get confused over the order of the ignition leads.

Ignition Timing.

Ignition timing is covered under Test No. 7 in the Tune-Up section (p.180). If you're without the stroboscopic timing light, you can get an idea of the static timing of the engine simply by using the circuit tester.

Start by getting the hang of the timing marks for your engine; they might be on the crankshaft pulley at the front, in which case a notch in the pulley will usually line up with a pointer on the timing cover. There may be more than one pointer, indicating Top Dead Centre on number one cylinder, and various other crankshaft positions in advance of this; the handbook will clarify whatever system the manufacturer has used. Some Leyland transverse engined cars put their timing marks on the flywheel, and you have to remove an inspection plate on the clutch cover and use a mirror to see what they're doing.

Find out from the manual what the piston position should be for static timing, loosen the distributor clamp bolt, and attach the circuit tester between the distributor low-tension terminal and the metalwork of the engine. Turn the engine until the correct timing marks are lined up and the points should be just opening as indicated by the tester lighting up. Without disturbing the timing marks, turn the distributor body until it's in a position at which the points are just starting to open.

Stroboscopic ignition timing, as described in the Tune-Up section, is nevertheless the best way of doing the job, because you can check the full range of the ignition advance mechanism with the engine running.

Fuel.

Attend to the carburettor dampers as per 3,000 mile service.

Find out from the handbook where any fuel filters in the system are installed. The petrol pump will certainly have one, in the form of a gauze disc in the filter bowl in the case of a mechanical pump, and just under the inlet union in the case of an electric one.

If the handbook doesn't mention the fuel pump, then establish what servicing it needs from the workshop manual instead. There may also be a filter on the carburettor, usually at the inlet union on the float chamber, and sometimes one in the fuel line itself.

Blow through all filters, and make sure that any sealing washers or gaskets surrounding them are in perfect condition. This isn't just to obviate fuel leaks, but to prevent air getting in and upsetting the action of the petrol pump.

Carburettor Tuning.

Check the carburettor tuning according to Test 8 and p. 181, in the Tune-Up section. Dismantle and clean or repair if any faults are found.

Lubrication.

As for 3,000 mile service.

Suspension and Steering.

As for 3,000 mile service. Take the car to an establishment with electronic wheelbalancing and track-measuring instruments to get the steering geometry checked. Many tyre suppliers will offer this service.

Brakes.

As for 3,000 mile service.

Lights and Weather Equipment.

As for 3,000 mile service.

Cooling System.

As for regular weekly attention. Once a year, usually in the late autumn, flush the whole cooling system out and preferably backflush the radiator by removing the bottom hose and forcing water from a hosepipe up through the radiator. Refill the system with the recommended mixture of water and antifreeze and check for leaks. Antifreeze is notorious for unearthing leaks.

Check the action of the thermostat at the same time. This is a heat-operated valve, which prevents the water from circulating through the radiator when the engine's cold, and therefore enables it to warm up quickly (see Ch. 1 p. 41). It will be located on the cylinder head where the upper radiator hose joins the engine; you normally have to unbolt a casting that covers it and then you can lift it out. Drop the unit into a pan of water and bring it slowly to the boil — if the valve opens early (i.e. before the temperature indicated on it) while the water is still cool or if it doesn't open at all, change the thermostat. Renew it every two years, faulty or not.

Exhaust.

Check the whole system with the car on axle stands, ramps or over a pit. Take a good look at the rubber or asbestos mounting straps for fraying or weakening.

Every 12,000 Miles.

Carry out all the operations of the 6,000 mile service but replace the sparking plugs and the contact breaker and condenser, and the carburettor air filter element.

20. *Attend to any lubrication recommended for the dynamo.*

21. *Attend to any lubrication recommended for the water pump.*

22. *Change the gearbox oil if recommended in the handbook.*

23. *Change the rear axle oil if recommended in the handbook.*

24. Top up the steering gearbox oil if recommended.

25. Check the condition of the wheel bearings by jacking up the front of the car and attempting to rock the wheels vertically. If any slack can be traced to the wheel bearings rather than the steering swivels, adjust them according to the manufacturers' suggestions or replace them (see p. 162).

26. Remove the starter motor and check the condition of the commutator and brushes (see p. 169).

Periodic Maintenance.

Extra Attention to Carburettors.

24,000 miles is normally the recommended distance for a close look at the carburettor. It doesn't need a great deal of maintenance, but if you find that the appropriate tuning procedure for your instrument still doesn't result in satisfactory running, and you've eliminated the ignition system and the mechanical condition of the engine itself from the causes, then it's possible that the carburettor itself might have become worn.

Carburettors come in so many shapes and sizes these days and some of them have grown so sophisticated and temperamental about being touched by inexperienced hands that you should always refer to the workshop manual to discover what the foibles of your particular version are. Some of the thermostatically operated automatic chokes need the service station's attention over resetting and dismantling and you need to be careful about disturbing the choke and throttle connections when you take the instrument off the car. Remember that most carburettors are adjusted so that the throttle is opened slightly wider when the choke is in use, so that the idling speed is fast with the engine cold. If you put the thing back with this arrangement upset, then you might well find that the rich mixture stalls the engine and the warming-up period of driving becomes distinctly uncomfortable. The workshop manual will detail the resetting procedure.

At 24,000 miles, take the carburettor off the car, remove the float chamber cover and flush out the chamber with petrol to get rid of any sediment. Try to do this so that you tip the instrument away from any fuel passages in the base of the chamber and avoid swilling any muck into the emulsion block. Shake the float, and if you hear any petrol inside, replace it. An alternative test for a blown float is to submerge it in hot water and a trail of air bubbles will reveal a puncture. Replace the needle valve assembly in the float chamber cover; this is usually a simple matter of pushing out the pin on which the float or its operating lever pivots (the pin will usually only push in one direction), unscrewing the needle valve seat (for which you might need a very small socket or box spanner since there's rarely

room for the jaws of an ordinary spanner) and replacing it with a new one. Go to a carburettor specialist for your spares, and take the serial number of the instrument as well as quoting the make and year of the car.

If the workshop manual details a procedure for the setting of the float that actually determines the chamber level. This is an important job that's often neglected; but if you check back with the carburettor section on pps. 32 and 33 you'll find that it's the setting of the float level that actually determines the petrol level in the jets. If the level is too high, the carburettor may be flooding, causing bad idling and raising the fuel consumption. Symptoms are a 'hunting' exhaust note and black smoke regardless of alterations to the mixture control (see carburettor adjustment, p. 181).

Take out the jets and blow through them, preferably from a compressed air supply. Again, the works manual will show you where they are and which are which, and normally they'll be removable with a screwdriver. Make a careful note of which ones go where; on the Weber double choke carburettor, for instance, the idling and cruising jets are identical and side by side, but their apertures are actually of different sizes. If you are unlucky enough to muddle them up, the jet aperture size will usually be engraved on the top, and you can then refer to the technical specifications in the manual to find out which is which.

If you've noticed a flat spot during acceleration, the acceleration pump may be at fault; you can check its action while the carburettor is still on the engine by snapping open the throttle while you peer down the choke tube — you should see a little squirt of petrol injected as you do this. If there's a non-return ball valve in the pump that happens to be retained by the top cover of the carburettor, don't waggle the pump lever with the cover off, or the ball may fly into space. Get a new set of gaskets for the carburettor from the agent before you put it back together, air leaks are very bad for its health.

Periodic jet cleaning is more of a priority on fixed jet carburettors than variable jet types like the S.U. and Stromberg C.D. The jet on these instruments is much bigger and less prone to blockage; check the float setting and change the needle valve at 24,000 miles though. After a long period of use, you might consider overhauling the carburettor with a new jet and needle, piston damper and gaskets. All these spares are available from the carburettor agents but make absolutely sure that you've got the right parts because many carburettor bits look identical but are machined to fine tolerances that might actually be very different. If you take out the jet holder of an S.U., follow the workshop manual's instructions closely about re-centering it or the piston will stick.

Lastly, check the fit of the throttle spindle.

If it's worn, air leaks will make a slow idle impossible to obtain. There should be no slack in it, and you might be able to identify a worn spindle by smearing engine oil around the bearings while the engine is running; if it's drawn into the choke tube, you should get a puff of blue smoke at the exhaust as it burns. Air leaks will also reveal themselves if you're able to use the vacuum gauge (see p. 177).

Air Cleaners.
The air cleaner is bolted to the carburettor air intake, and when you dismantle the metal casing, you'll generally find a paper element inside which has to be replaced with a new one at 6,000 miles. Some air cleaners have an adjustable setting for summer and winter running, and the manual will tell you how to manipulate this.

Older cars often use an oil bath air cleaner, in which dust particles are trapped in an oil-wetted wire mesh. You swill this type in petrol to clean it at the recommended intervals, then re-oil it. Some filters are suspended in a well of oil, which is thrown away and changed at the service period.

Hydraulic Fluid.
Like any other kind of oil, hydraulic fluid doesn't have an unlimited life. It absorbs moisture from the atmosphere over time, which eventually lowers its boiling point and could cause brake fade in emergencies. For this reason, the manufacturers generally recommend a complete transfusion of brake fluid annually, and for this you'll need to bleed the brakes to get the air bubbles out. Jack up the car at the back and remove the rear wheels. Find the bleed screw on each brake backplate (as shown in your handbook) and clean it up to prevent grit getting into the circuit. For this job you should arm yourself with a length of rubber or plastic tube that will fit over the bleed screw (plastic is better, so that you can watch for air bubbles in it), a jam jar and a small spanner (preferably a ring spanner) that will fit the screw.

Fit the tube to the bleed screw, put enough fresh brake fluid in the jar to submerge the other end of the tube and undo the bleed screw half a turn. Now pump the brake pedal until the reservoir is almost empty. Fill the reservoir with fresh fluid.

Now get somebody to take care of the pumping for you while you watch the tube for air bubbles, and the arrival of the fresh fluid. Since releasing the pressure on the brake pedal will naturally tend to pull the fluid back into the braking system again, you will need to tighten the bleed screw after each depression of the pedal and while it's still being held to the floor; then release it, undo the screw half a turn again, make another pump, retighten the screw, and so on. Keep the reservoir topped up with fresh brake fluid so you don't draw air into the system at the top and waste all the effort, and when you see

the fresh fluid start to emerge at the wheel and there are no longer any bubbles in it, tighten the bleed screw and take the tubing off. Go round the car giving the same treatment to each wheel until all the old fluid has been expelled. In an all-drum braking system you should start at the brake farthest from the master cylinder and finish at the one nearest; in a mixed system you should start at the farthest disc brake and finish at the nearest drum brake.

A few points to remember. If you've got the wheels off the ground and the car on a jack, make sure it's properly supported before you get your assistant leaping about inside. And if you can't get an assistant, the accessory shops now sell all kinds of devices that enable brake bleeding to be done alone. The simplest provide a non-return ball valve in the plastic tube, so that the fluid can be ejected when you push the pedal down but is not drawn back when you release it. You can also buy a complete brake bleeding kit that doesn't require pedal-pumping at all; you simply fill up a canister with brake fluid, attach a feed tube to the master cylinder reservoir and your bleed tube to the backplate. Air is pushed through the canister by a hose attached to your spare tyre. You just open the bleed valve and settle down with a good book until clean or bubble-free fluid comes through, and repeat this at each wheel. Remember to use the right type of fluid for your braking system. If you do have to pump the brakes, Lockheed systems generally need a slow depression of the pedal and a quick return to get the air out, Girling aluminium bodied master cylinders require slow depression, three short pumps and a quick release (this is starting to sound like the script of a Carry On film) and Girling cast iron cylinders need you to go slowly both ways, pausing momentarily in between.

As well as bleeding the brakes simply to change the fluid, you'll also need to do it if you dismantle any part of the hydraulic system. If the brake action starts to feel 'spongy' or you need to pump the pedal to pull the car up, then air is getting in; and if the reservoir level is falling, then fluid is getting out. Either way, you would then need to make a close inspection of the master cylinder and wheel cylinders according to the instructions in the workshop manual, paying particular attention to the state of the rubber seals and any scoring or wear in the pistons or barrels of the cylinders. Seals are cheap to replace, but scored cylinders should be scrapped. When you replace seals, keep everything scrupulously clean, lubricate the new seals in brake fluid and make absolutely sure you put them in the right way round. Replace any flexible hosing that is chafed or perished, and any metal pipework that's corroded. If the pipes have been eaten away by rust, or the hoses cracked, then the first emergency stop could blow the fluid straight through them. Remember to fit new flexible hoses with a spanner firmly attached to their joints so that they can't strain or twist when you tighten the union nut on the adjoining metal pipe. New steel brake pipes can be made up on the premises of most accessory shops, but you would need to take down the section of pipe you've removed so that the new piece can be made to precisely the right length and curvature, and the right type of unions can be fitted.

The M.O.T. Test.

Every car over three years old is now required to have a test certificate issued by the Department of Transport, establishing that it is safe to use on the public roads. Once a car becomes eligible for testing, it must be re-examined every year. A few years ago the scope of the test was extended — in the early weeks of its introduction, 50% of the cars examined failed, an increase of 15% over the old failure rate. Since the requirements of the examination are quite specific, there's no reason for anybody to take his car into the testing station with obvious faults that will mean that the fee has to be paid twice over, plus the cost of whatever repair is necessary.

Not all garages are authorized to make the test, some specialize in it so that you can get the job done while you wait.

The test will consist of the examination of the 31 items as follows:

Lighting
(1) Obligatory front lamps.
(2) Obligatory rear lamps.
(3) Obligatory head lamps.
(4) Headlamp aim.
(5) Stop lamps.
(6) Rear reflectors.
(7) Direction indicators.

The obligatory front lights, rear lights, head lamps, stop lamps and reflectors must be examined to ensure they are in good working order and are fitted in the correct position to comply with the lighting Regulations. In the case of front obligatory lamps and rear obligatory lamps they must be visible for a reasonable distance. The aim of the head lamps must be checked to ensure when dipped they are deflected downwards and will not dazzle a person with eye level 1.1m, standing 7.7m away. Direction indicators must be in good working order and be of the correct colour.

Steering and Suspension
(8) Steering controls.
(9) Steering mechanism.
(10) Power steering.
(11) Transmission shafts (Front wheel drive only).
(12) Stub axle assemblies.
(13) Wheel bearings.
(14) Suspension.
(15) Shock absorbers.

All parts of the steering must be examined with the steering wheel being moved, so they can be examined under load, and then all parts should be examined for wear. The presence of nuts and bolts, their tightness, king pins, bushes and wheel bearings are included in the examination, as is excessive play in the steering. Where power steering is fitted it must be checked to ensure it is in good working order, without leaks. The transmission shafts of front wheel drive vehicles must be checked for wear and defects as must the suspension assemblies on all vehicles. Shock absorbers must be checked to ensure they are in good working order and without leaks.

Brakes
(16) Service brake condition.
(17) Parking brake condition.
(18) Service brake efficiency.
(19) Parking brake efficiency.
(20) Service brake balance.

All parts must be in good order, foot pedals and hand levers must have a reasonable amount of reserve travel when fully applied. Hand brake, or parking brake, must be such that they can be locked in the on position. The brake drums and hubs must be free from any visible evidence of oil leakage; there must not be any lack of balance in the brakes, and there must be no defect in the vehicle or its equipment likely to affect the brakes.

Tyres and Wheels
(21) Tyre type.
(22) Tyre condition.
(23) Road wheels.

The tyres fitted to all road wheels of the vehicle (the spare tyre is not included) must be checked to ensure:
(a) They are not recut.
(b) They are suitable with no mixing of type of tyre, i.e. radial ply with cross ply.
(c) There are no breaks or cuts in the tyre in excess of 25mm or 10% of the section width.
(d) There are no lumps or bulges, or exposure of ply or cord.
(e) The tread of the tyre shows for ¾ of the breadth all the way round the tyre. The depth of the tread must be at least 1 mm.

The road wheels must be checked to ensure they are in good condition, not excessively damaged, the right type for the tyres used and the stud holes are not excessively worn.

Seat Belts
(24) Security of mountings.
(25) Condition of belts.
(26) Operation of belts.

All vehicles which are required to be fitted with anchorage points and seat belts must be checked to ensure the belts are in good condition, operate correctly and are securely mounted.

General Items
(27) Windscreen washers.
(28) Windscreen wipers.
(29) Warning instruments.
(30) Condition of exhaust system.
(31) Effectiveness of silencer.

The windscreen washers and wipers must be in good condition and in working order, adequately able to give the driver a good field of vision to the front and on the front nearside. The horn or warning instrument must be in good working order, shall not consist of a bell, gong or siren for vehicles first used after 1st August 1973 and the sound emitted shall be continuous and uniform, not strident. The exhaust system shall be in good condition and effective enough to reduce the noise below the limits set by the Construction and Use Regulations.

In addition to the 31 points mentioned above the bodywork should be checked to ensure there is no excessive rust within 30 cm of the anchorage points of the steering or suspension.

All these items come under the regular maintenance schedules and you shouldn't be caught out by any of them; pay particular attention to the things that are hard to get at, like the suspension and steering gear.

Coachwork.

Strictly speaking, learning how to fix an engine counts as acquiring a craft, but somehow it never gets to feel like one. It always feels like exactly what it is: grappling with a lot of dirty and obstinate hardware, and concentrating on putting everything back together in precisely the same way that it came apart. Fixing bodywork, on the other hand, is not only proudly regarded as a craft by the people who practise it, it actually feels like one as well. After all, if you have good nerves, common sense, and most of the facilities, there's no logical reason why you couldn't strip down an E-type engine to the last nut and bolt and build it up again even if you'd never picked up a spanner before in your life; it would really depend on carrying out the workshop manual's instructions. You couldn't beat out a dent or respray a wing that way — this is the bit where experience makes all the difference between a professional job and the worst sort of Saturday morning bodgery.

This is not to put you off, but simply to say that there are limits. If you've got an old heap in your back garden that you might think about getting back on the road this year, sometime or never, then trial and error is not a problem and you could go on playing about with it in your leisure hours or until it started to turn out all right. With a car that you actually use for everyday transport this is all too much aggravation and delay and you'd soon

wish that you'd gone to the expert. On top of the problems of actually learning how it's done, extensive bodywork repairs need a lot of expensive gear — much of which you can admittedly hire these days — and various bits of handy inside information and short cuts that you can only find out the hard way or in the company of someone who's been at it a long time.

There is one further psychological obstacle; I found that the first faltering attempts looked terrific to me because there's a certain euphoria about trying one of these mystic arts out for the first time, and you're just glad to have got to the end of it with at least a marginal improvement; sometimes if you're glowing with pride about your new skill, even your best friends won't tell you that the repair looks like something their two-year-old could have knocked up with plasticine. Be satisfied with nothing less than a repair that's imperceptible from the original finish or when you come to sell the car prospective buyers will point derisory fingers at it and not be much concerned to spare your blushes. It may be a while before you get to this stage, but, like riding a bicycle, once you've got the hang of it you won't have to learn it twice.

Paintwork.

Cars are finished in a variety of ways. Older ones, and some contemporary hand-built models, are sprayed in synthetic cellulose enamel, and bodywork repairs are usually carried out using this material as well. It's a soft paint, and it isn't baked, so it's more prone to abrasion and other damage and needs a lot of looking after. Oven-dried finishes are now used almost universally at the factories and these will take a lot more hard use, though that dead flat, mirror-like quality that the early coachbuilders used to get with cellulose is getting rarer except on the kind of cars you'd need to sell your house to buy.

Cleaning paintwork is best done with a hose first of all, so that you don't rub grit into the paint, and if you can use a hose-brush with a detergent dispenser attached, so much the better, because the car can get a shampoo at the same time. If you're using a bucket and sponge, dissolve some detergent in the water and slosh large quantities of it all over the vehicle; don't sponge or brush it off until everything's good and wet. After shampooing, rinse the body down and dry it off with a chamois leather.

Polishing is a good idea at regular intervals. Get the car out of the direct sunlight, wash it and dry it off and make sure that you get all the road grime and grease off. If this won't budge with washing, then use a very mild liquid abrasive that the accessory shops sell for the purpose. (The whole car could benefit from a going-over with this stuff every few years, it makes a truly miraculous difference to the paintwork you might have thought had faded and dulled forever.) Then apply the wax polish with a pad of cloth and make sure you work it into joints and cracks to keep the rain out. Then polish it up with a clean soft cloth and keep refolding it so that when it clogs it doesn't smear the job. If you can finally buff it up with a lambswool mop on a power drill so much the better but go *very* lightly; if you bear down too hard and have the drill running too fast you can easily burn the paint.

You look after the brightwork and chrome in much the same way, cleaning off any tarnishing with a chrome cleaner and protecting it with wax polish. Once chrome has been badly attacked by corrosion though, there's not much to be done about it beyond getting another assembly from the manufacturer, getting one in better nick off a scrap-yard, or having the piece rechromed at an electroplaters. With the cost of such spares being what they are these days, it might be worth your while to get a quote from a plater before you buy the component to see whether you can restore it more cheaply than you could buy it. The snag is of course that the car would be without a bumper or door catch for the week or so that the plater would need to work with it, which in the case of the former would invite the attentions of the constabulary and in the latter the attentions of the underworld. If you do have anything rechromed, remember that deep pitting caused by rust can't be got rid of, and that the diecast parts sometimes used for catches and handles often react badly with the plater's acids.

Bodywork Repairs and Painting.

Repairing crash damage, except in very mild cases, is probably beyond most amateurs, but the kind of preventive maintenance that keeps the rust spots at bay and keeps you abreast of all the little cuts and abrasions that motor cars sustain on their perambulations is well worth learning. Accessory shops now stock pretty well everything you'd be likely to need in the way of filler, rust-killers, aerosols and so forth.

Rust is the bugbear of most motor cars, and owners of aluminium or fibreglass vehicles are mercifully spared its attentions. When dealing with it you have to be brutal, to the point where the surgery almost looks worse than the symptom at first. Make sure the rust hasn't gone right through the metal, which you discover by the simple expedient of stabbing it with a screwdriver; those relatively innocent looking eruptions of the paint around wing arches and door sills sometimes turn out to be gaping holes in the metalwork once you've set about them with blunt instruments. Once you've satisfied yourself that the rust is really only the superficial kind you get from flying stones or chippings, get hold of some 220 grade wet-and-dry paper and rub the damaged spot with this until the paintwork around the rust is 'feathered' — in other words you see the layers of primer and colour as if

you'd taken a slice off an onion and were looking straight down on to the rings. This is essential so that the contour between the good paintwork and the hole levels out gradually rather than in an abrupt dip that would require a lot of filling up. Wet-and-dry paper is easy enough to use, it's just a kind of waterproof glass paper. You tear bits off it rather than using it all of a piece, and keep dipping it into a bucket of warmish water with some washing up liquid squirted into it; the idea is to stop the paper from clogging and to lubricate the abrasion. When the paintwork is feathered off around the damage, use the abrasive paper to remove as much of the surface rust as you can and then thoroughly dry the whole area off. What will probably be left in the middle will be some pitting around the centre of the rust spot. Get a good proprietary rust killer from an accessory shop — such as Jenolite or Kurust — and use it according to the instructions. When it's ready for re-coating you'll find if you run your fingertips over the repair that you now have a cleaned-up area which nevertheless feels like a slight hollow in the paintwork. Gloss paint shows up every imperfection, particularly in an unflattering light, so you can't paint straight over this or the final finish would reveal a nasty looking 'puddle'. (Despite this, most amateurs *do* paint straight over their rust repairs.)

What you need now is a body-repairer's putty-knifing filler or stopper as it's variously called — and about the most practical kind to get is the one that's generally available from the suppliers of automotive refinishing materials to the trade, but rarely from the high street shops. This is called Bare Metal Stopper, and, as the name implies, it has the advantage of sticking both to old paint and to bare metal, though you have to make sure that the metalwork is clean, rust and grease free, well scuffed to give proper adhesion and that the paintwork all around is rubbed down to a matt finish. Stopper is a kind of putty with which you build up irregular surfaces, and you apply it with a 'stopper rubber', which is simply a square rubber pad with a sharp edge. Dig some of the stopper out of the tin, get it on the edge of the rubber and sweep it over the repair. Try to get it on flat the first go, because if you keep trying to smooth it out you'll pick up more stopper than you put down. After this you go off and amuse yourself for a couple of hours. Unlike fibreglass or any chemical filler, this stuff is air drying, so you can only apply it in one *thin* coat at a time or it will dry on the surface and forever stay gooey underneath. When this first coat seems reasonably hard, rub it down with the 220 wet-and-dry wrapped around a flat rubber block. Then run your finger over it and see if you can still detect any irregularity in the contour. If there is some, or there are still air bubbles or pinholes in the surface, give it another coat of stopper, let it dry, rub it down again and so on until the surface is perfect. Remember, paint has no filling power at all so the final result depends entirely on the quality of the preparation.

Once you're happy with it, you can start on the painting. First of all, you want to avoid getting paint in all sorts of unnecessary directions such as on the windows, the chromework, the tyres, the seats, yourself etc. If this is a small repair – say a couple of inches across by the time you've used the stopper on it – then cut a hole about twice the size in a piece of newspaper and tape it to the car with masking tape. Don't put masking tape around the edges of the hole you've cut and stick that down or you'll find that when you've sprayed the area and removed the paper you'll have a great ridge all around the sprayed bit that will be extremely awkward to smooth out. Leave the newspaper loose around the damage so that the hole restricts the spray area but allows the edges of the fan to spread out gradually. Now spray the damage with an aerosol of grey or white primer (white for pastels, grey for middling to dark colours) shaking the aerosol well, and applying it in short bursts so that you're virtually 'dry-spraying' it as they say in the trade. This isn't the coachbuilders' practice, since they'll apply paint from a spraygun really 'full' and wet, but they're expert enough to keep it just on the safe side of running and sagging, and if the solvent in the paint reacts with the undersurface, they know how to correct it. Really wet coats can sometimes cause what's called 'edge mapping' on repairs, where the outline of the stopper starts to show through the new paint and this is something you can avoid by spraying lightly and in very thin coats, allowing each one to dry out first.

When you've applied three or four coats of primer and it's *thoroughly* dry, rub it down with 400 grade wet-and-dry paper on the block, using plenty of water. Aim to feather the edges of the primed area into the surrounding paintwork so that they seem to 'flow' into each other. Once you've done this, you're about ready to finish the job off. Cut another mask of newspaper, leaving a hole bigger than the one you cut for the primer, and spray on the top colour. You can concentrate if you like on getting a high gloss by applying the paint heavily but remember to watch for runs – it's easier to get away with this on a horizontal surface but not so much fun on a vertical one. Make a smooth weaving 'pass' with the can, releasing the button when you get to the end, and depressing it again when you start the next sweep. Build the paint up lightly, then let it dry, preferably overnight. Most people are content to leave the job here, but if you want to be really professional there is a final sprucing up to be done. Rub the whole area, including the surrounding paintwork, with a very fine wet-and-dry paper, such as 800 grade, until it's all dead matt. Then bring

it up to a high gloss with an abrasive paste or polishing compound and a soft cloth, and you'll find that this blends the repair in with the original paint much more effectively than it did straight off the can, particularly for lighter colours.

You sometimes find that the aerosols supplied in the accessory shops aren't a perfect match. You can make sure that you don't simply buy the wrong one, of course, by checking the code number of the paint from a plaque that will be hidden somewhere on the car, or asking the car's agents what the colour is. If you're still in trouble, the most effective way out is unfortunately the most expensive way too, but it's not a bad idea if you ever intend to do any more elaborate spraying with a compressor. You find a local agent for one of the trade's paintmakers (such as Berger's, I.C.I., Glasso or Valentine's) buy a tin of the stock colour (usually a litre at the minimum, which is upwards of £7.00 these days) and have the supplier make some of it up into an aerosol can for you. That way you can keep going back with the same can for more aerosols when you need them.

A few points to bear in mind. Not all paint suppliers offer this service, so check them on the phone first. Make sure you give the can a good shake before you complain that the colour doesn't match and make sure too that you give the surrounding paintwork a really thorough compounding with liquid or abrasive paste before you spray on to it. The manufacturer's colour is unlikely to be much of a match with faded paintwork or road dirt.

All paint repairs follow much the same procedure as the one we've just run through. Really extensive rust damage that has completely penetrated the metal will have to be cut out with a grindstone in a power drill or even with tinsnips and make sure you remove *all* the damaged metal – then you'll have to make a patch with perforated metal, fibreglass matting and resin according to the instructions supplied with the material, sanding it off with a sanding disc back into rough shape once it's hard, and bringing up the contour of the job with cellulose stopper as before. A much better way is to make friends with a local coachbuilder and take the car round to him once you've cut the damage out so that he can braze in a new piece of metal and then you can go off and finish the rest of the repair yourself. Big bodyshops attached to motor agencies aren't amenable to this sort of communal 'Zen and the Art of Saving a Few Bob' procedure, but the one-man operation round the corner will sometimes do the trick given a bit of chatting up and crossing palms with silver. Fibreglass is nasty, smelly, pernicious stuff and it doesn't matter how much they say it's as good as the original, it still feels like mending a burst pipe by wrapping elastoplast around it.

One last thing about rust. Rust around wings, door bottoms, boot and bonnet edges, and around headlamps can all be cut out and repaired, and provided you're sure you've cut out all the tatty rust and chemically killed the rest, fibreglass will do a perfectly satisfactory job. But if you've got any weakening of the box sections, sills or the floor pan through corrosion, then go to an expert and get some advice because these are M.O.T. failure points and might cause a nasty accident anyway. Fibreglass is no use here, it's down to welding in new metal or nothing.

Dents.

Some dents are friendly, some aren't. There are times when you can just lean on the other side of the bulge and it pops back into shape. Mostly a lot of judicious banging about has got to be done to press dents back into the line of the bodywork, and panel beating is an art that you can neither learn from a book nor perform without an arsenal of hammers, pry spoons, anvils and other tackle. The expert who has developed his skill for an economic reason — he can get the job done faster by doing it properly — will beat the damage back to as near perfection as he can get so that the minimum of delay with filling and rubbing down is necessary. The amateur usually has to settle for something less elegant. You try to beat the damage back to as close to the original as you can get and build up the rest with lots of coats of stopper and lots of tedious rubbing down. There is a quick way, which is that you leave the dent exactly as it is, simply sand all the paint and rust back to bare metal with the power drill and a sanding disc, fill the whole thing up with plastic resin and sand it back to shape. Shortage of time sometimes demands this, and occasionally the dent is so awkwardly placed that there's no alternative, but it's an unsatisfactory kind of solution.

If you've got to buy panel beater's hammers to get the job done, then it's probably better to take it to a body shop. But a good many uncomplicated dents can be knocked out with an ordinary household ball pein hammer, the type that has one flat head and one domed. (Don't hit dents on curved surfaces from the inside with the flat face or you'll produce great weals on the surface and stretch it even further.) Knock the dent out from behind, keeping the hammer moving around so that you don't produce any 'pips' and when it's roughly back to shape move slowly and lightly over the outer surface with the flat face, levelling out any blisters and holding the hammer toward the end of the handle and letting it swing at the wrist under its own weight rather than flexing your biceps to operate it. To avoid knocking the dent straight back in again, you'll obviously need to support the job from the back, with something that more or less follows the line of the metalwork. If you're working on a flat surface a suitably doctored block of wood will do; if it's a curved or 'crowned' surface like a wing, then — apart from using a densely packed sandbag, preferably in a leather pouch — there is really no alternative but to buy a domed metal dolly or hand anvil from a coachbuilders' suppliers, and the most useful type is one with a short handle attached to it. Keep running your fingertips over the surface as you work and only stop once you're sure you can't get the metal any smoother. Bring it up to its proper contour with stopper.

You can get at the back of most dents by removing the interior trim, but modern cars are often 'double skinned' and professionals usually have to cut out a flap in the inner skin to get at the back of the dent, or pull it out from the outside with a slide-hammer, welding up the fitting hole afterwards. This is all a bit beyond the weekend coachbuilder, and resin filler is usually the only recourse.

Spraying.

Aerosols are invaluable in D.I.Y. body repairs and you wouldn't normally want to go beyond their use unless you needed to spray a really large area or even the whole car; if your intentions lie in this direction, then spray plant is available on hire. It's impossible to deal with spraying technique here, but there are one or two generalizations to watch.

Follow the paint supplier's advice as to which type of material is the right one for the job you're attempting. Make sure that you stir the paint really thoroughly, since pigments settle out in storage, particularly pastels, and you have to bring all the tints up from the bottom before the match will be perfect. Use a recommended thinners. Don't try to spray metallics, even the experts find them awkward. Mix your paint and thinners in roughly equal proportions, set your air pressure at around 40 lb./sq. in. if you're using a variable compressor, practise on some old bits of metal first and spray in smooth passes, releasing the trigger at the end of each pass and depressing it at the start of the next. Spray three or four coats of primer filler, let that dry and rub it down flat with 220 paper. Spray as many coats of top colour, but make the paint progressively thinner as you get to the last coats, finishing off with a mist coat of thinners only, which you'll use to 'wash the edge away' between the old and new paint if you're doing a partial repair. Make sure that any old paint you're blending into is completely free of grease, preferably washed down with a degreasant and then compounded with paste. Let the paint harden for a few days, then rub the whole surface down with 800 paper and compound it up, finishing off with the mop in the power drill.

Don't hang around too long in one spot or the paint will run and you'll have to let it completely dry before you can flatten it down. Do the job in a clean space and lay any dust on the floor with water so that it doesn't float around on to the job. Wear a mask or a respirator or you may faint, which is very unprofessional. Don't spray the wrong type of material on to a car that's already been repainted in a synthetic enamel (manufacturer's original synthetics are usually OK because the solvents have been baked out) or it will pickle up and you'll have to start all over again and maybe even strip the paint right off. If you want to spray cellulose over synthetic your paint supplier will be able to fix you up with a suitable sealer to spray on first.

Beyond Servicing.

Getting Your Head Examined.

Given proper maintenance and tuning, a modern engine will keep on coming up with its peak performance for many a mile, but eventually there is a noticeable power loss, an increase in fuel consumption and a tendency for the engine to 'pink' — that is, make a high-pitched metallic ticking noise — when the car is pulling hard. This might be expected to crop up at a mileage between 60,000 and 70,000 but it could be a great deal later than that — so much depends on the conditions under which the engine has been run. At any rate, this would be the sort of mileage at which you could anticipate performance problems being derived from wear and tear and the presence of undesirable foreign matter in the engine, rather than simply adjustment or tuning of the ignition or carburation.

It is impossible to make rules about the mileage when this will happen; a small, fussy engine will generally wear more rapidly than a big, lazy, slow-revving one; and whether the car was predominantly used for 'shopping' trips or long, fast runs will make quite a lot of difference too. A lot of short journeys and cold starting means persistent use of the rich mixture control — this washes oil from the cylinder walls and accelerates piston and ring wear. Cars don't react badly to being driven fairly strenuously, as long as they're not being actually hammered — because the most efficient working temperature is reached quickly and maintained for longer. It might seem unfair, but often a little old lady driving up and down to the shops at 25 m.p.h. with the choke half out is shortening the life of her engine more rapidly than the salesman who treats his car with indifference and spends half his life burning up and down motorways.

There is only one way to distinguish the need for attention to the cylinder head from more general engine wear, and that is by regular checks of the type we cover under Troubleshooting and Tuning or by going to a service station annually and getting the checks made there. The compression gauge is an invaluable guide.

The decoke or 'top overhaul' is comfortably within the scope of the home mechanic, and the procedure for head removal is always thoroughly investigated in the workshop manual. But as a word of warning, it's *definitely* not a good idea to approach this job, however much the spirit is willing, if your tool-kit is really rudimentary. A socket set of the right type for the car is desirable, since cylinder head nuts can often not be reached, still less shifted, with conventional spanners. Sometimes the generally undesirable open-ended spanner will earn its keep on jobs like this though, particularly if you're trying to undo the frequently inaccessible nuts that are perched between the carburettor body and the inlet manifold. The torque wrench — begged, borrowed, bought, hired or stolen — is essential for a top overhaul, since the head nuts have to be retightened to a precise and equal load.

You'll also need some clean rag and containers for the various nuts and bolts. Tobacco tins serve the purpose, though some people use egg-boxes and label the compartments according to which nuts and bolts came from where. Go to the agents for the car and buy a decoke gasket set, which will include a new cylinder head gasket, manifold joints and various other gaskets and washers, the applications of which will become obvious as you dismantle the engine. A set of valve springs is advisable, and a packet of rubber valve-stem oil seals if your particular design happens to make use of them (see owner's handbook). You may find that you need new valves as well, but if you're not in a violent hurry to finish the job (and if this is the first time you're doing it, you shouldn't be) leave purchasing a set of these expensive items until you've had a chance to examine the old ones. A very badly burned valve will have already made itself felt in the form of a misfire, and a compression test would reveal a severe drop on the cylinder affected. Slightly leaky valves can usually be ground back on to their seats in the combustion chamber, which is one of the purposes of carrying out the job. But for this job you should locate your friendly neighbourhood engine reconditioner; he runs an establishment rather different from a conventional garage, equipped with all manner of expensive machinery capable of restoring worn engines. He will also possess most of the gaskets, valves and other odds and ends that you will want for this job, so you may find it easier to do all your business in one place instead of going to the car manufacturer's agent. Even with a relatively simple job like a decoke, some of the work that might need to be done on the head is best entrusted to an engineering shop.

Dismantling.

Disconnecting the battery is your first move, since the quantity of spanners, disconnected cables and loose components that will soon be swilling around the engine compartment make short circuits uncomfortably likely. Then open the drain cocks and let the water out — there will normally be one outlet at the base of the radiator and one tap on the side of the block. In many cases the radiator drain takes the form of a hexagonal plug which is frequently in an inaccessible position and occasionally mangled by unsuitable instruments into the bargain, so be prepared for minor delays. (It's part of motoring lore that you can often do something mind-boggling like stripping a gear-box in less time than it might take you to undo one insignificant, inaccessible and mercilessly obstinate nut.)

The cylinder head has to be released from all its life support systems before you can get it off. Start with the water hoses, which will include the upper hose to the radiator, and possibly heater hoses too. Unscrew the jubilee clips retaining these and slightly twist the hoses until you break the scale that generally sticks them to the metalwork — then ease the hoses off the piping. Check with the workshop manual about any other hoses that might need to be released — Leyland transverse engines, for instance, have a tiny by-pass hose that joins the water pump to the underside of the head. This hose may need replacing and in any case doesn't take too kindly to the upheaval of head removal.

Disconnect the cables that operate the carburettor controls; generally the wire is pinched into the operating lever by a tiny screw and will often require a pair of very small open-ended spanners to budge it — a B.A. spanner set will most likely provide the necessaries. A small adjustable spanner and a pair of pliers might equally do the trick. Then slacken the little clamps holding the outer sleeves of the cables to the carburettor and pull the cables clear. Some throttle connections are a snap fit ball-joint — you have to prise off a clip holding the throttle rod to the operating lever on the carburettor and pull the two apart.

Once you've disconnected the petrol pipe from the float chamber you should now be able to unbolt the carburettor from the manifolding and put it somewhere safe, preferably where bits and pieces of grit and foreign bodies aren't likely to attack it. Don't turn the carburettor on its side so that the petrol in the float chamber swills sediment into the passageways in the carburettor body.

Now remove the manifolding, which may be a separate inlet and exhaust system or cast in one piece; either way, you'll usually find that you need the appropriate socket or ring spanner at the least to get the nuts out, because they're generally recessed awkwardly within the pipework. Manifold nuts usually have large retaining washers behind them so don't pull away the manifold until you've fiddled these out. Disconnect the exhaust downpipe and pull the manifolding clear of the head. (It might be necessary to loosen the front exhaust mounting and lower the downpipe before the manifold will clear it.)

Now the top end of the engine should be more or less cleared of impediments and you can work on getting the head off without too much difficulty; remove the rocker (or valve gear) cover, which you should really unfasten a little at a time at either end so that you don't distort it, if it's a pressed steel one. When you've got the rocker box off, you will see the valve operating gear — a line of rocker arms articulated on a shaft which is itself mounted on a series of pedestals. Then check with the workshop manual about the procedure for loosening the head stud nuts. On some engines you undo the retaining nuts or bolts that hold the pedestals to the head and lift all the rocker gear away, on others the head nuts hold the rocker gear down too and if you took them off first you would distort the head by allowing it to lift on one side while still fully tightened down on the other. The works manual will provide a diagram of the layout of the nuts from a bird's eye view of the cylinder head. Whichever arrangement is employed, when you get around to loosening the head nuts, unfasten them half a turn at a time in the order suggested by the manufacturer. In fact the diagram will most likely represent the *tightening* order, in which case you loosen the head in a reverse of this sequence. Keep running through the sequence until the nuts are no longer bearing directly on the casting, and then you can remove them completely.

Overhead camshaft engines naturally require a slightly different procedure, and once again this will be detailed in the manual. Usually the camshaft chain wheel has to be unbolted from the cam itself, but make sure you understand whatever timing marks are in use so that you know how to reassemble the valve gear and re-time it when you put everything back together. Remember, too, that once you've disconnected the cams from the drive chain, the pistons can move up and down if the engine should inadvertently be turned over but the valves will remain in whatever positions the now stationary cam or cams has left them in. In other words some of the valves will be open and might be hit by the rising pistons, causing all manner of expensive damage.

Once you've got the stud nuts removed, the head should lift fairly readily from the block, and nine times out of ten it will do just that. If it's a big engine, you may need help to lift the head off the studs squarely — if you get it coming up at an angle then it will bind before you've got it completely clear. If the head to block joint hasn't broken through the release of the pressure on the studs, then a bit of judicious tapping around the edge with a wooden or hide mallet should do the trick. A really obstinate cylinder head can sometimes be blown off by replacing the plugs and spinning the engine over on the starter; the resulting compression will usually break the joint. You don't, of course, do this on an overhead cam engine unless you've already removed the camshaft and let all the valves close completely, for the reasons we've already considered. Nor do you do it on what's known as wet-liner engines (see workshop manual), in which the cylinder bores

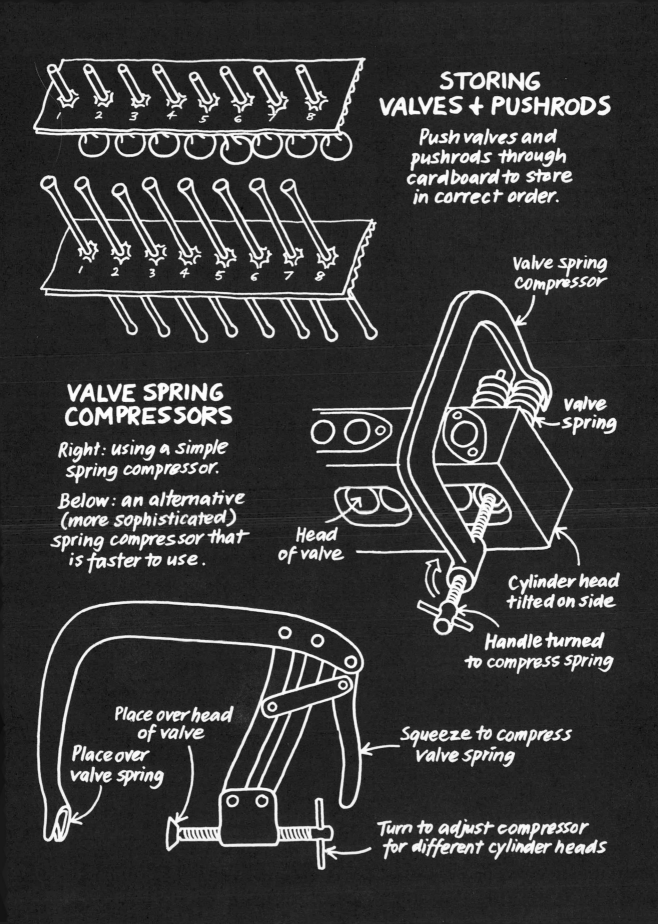

STORING VALVES + PUSHRODS

Push valves and pushrods through cardboard to store in correct order.

VALVE SPRING COMPRESSORS

Right: using a simple spring compressor.

Below: an alternative (more sophisticated) spring compressor that is faster to use.

Valve spring compressor

Valve spring

Head of valve

Cylinder head tilted on side

Handle turned to compress spring

Place over head of valve

Place over valve spring

Squeeze to compress valve spring

Turn to adjust compressor for different cylinder heads

are sleeves inserted into the water jacket of the crankcase — turning the engine over with the head loose in these cases may actually allow the liners to lift along with the head. Whatever method you use, avoid banging screwdrivers or similar implements in between the block and the head to split the joint — you'll almost certainly score the mating faces and possibly cause a gasket leak later.

Whether or not the rocker assembly was mounted on the head studs, it's a good idea to have removed it before you finally lift the head, so that you can take out the push rods as well and put them aside in the order in which they were fitted. The best way of taking care of this is to punch a series of numbered holes in a piece of cardboard and insert the rods into this, numbered from the front or radiator end of the head.

Once we've got the head on to the bench (all right, the kitchen table, then) the actual work involved in reconditioning it is thoroughly straight-forward. Scrape the combustion chambers clean, finish off if possible with a wire brush in the electric drill; scrape the piston crowns too, but use slivers of wood so that you don't scratch the soft aluminium pistons. When cleaning pistons, most mechanics leave a narrow ring of carbon around the circumference to act as an oil seal. Naturally, while you're performing this operation, a lot of chippings of carbon will be trying to get into the waterways, down the push rod guides and into the other cylinders — worse still, they may get into the tiny oil drilling that supplies oil to the rocker gear. So make sure that you've covered or plugged up with rag any holes you want to keep the dirt away from.

With the combustion chambers clean, the valves can be removed without any danger of all the scraping and scouring damaging the valve seats. For this you need a special gadget called a valve spring compressor; you can improvise around it in various ways, but such methods are likely to result in bits of metal propelling themselves past your ears in a generally alarming fashion, since the tension on the valve springs is quite considerable.

The valve spring compressor enables you to squeeze the spring so that its retaining collar can be removed, and then release it gently. The compressor is simply a metal jig shaped a bit like a woodworker's G-cramp; one end of it cups over the valve spring, the other bears against the valve itself from the combustion chamber side. Tightening a screw on the compressor effectively shortens the frame and pulls the spring down against the head.

When the spring is fully compressed you'll be able to remove whatever it is that fastens the spring to the valve stem. Often this fastener comprises two little crescent shaped bits of metal called 'collets'; they slot into a recess on the stem and you fish these out while the spring is tight and then unscrew the compressor. Some valve mechanisms

use a circular spring retainer instead with a small and a larger hole side by side; with the pressure of the spring relieved from this disc, you slide it to one side so that the larger hole lines up with the valve stem, and then you can withdraw it.

Keep the valves in the order they came from the head, as you did for the push rods (i.e. the punched card method). When the valves are out, clean the valve ports in the head as you did the combustion chambers, though this part of the decoke involves a lot more scraping and polishing into inaccessible corners. Carefully scrape the valves clean, and push pieces of rag soaked in petrol through the valve guides. Now is as good a time as any to find out if the guides themselves are going to need replacing, which you do by sliding each valve back into its guide and shaking the stem from side to side — any appreciable movement is a sign of a worn guide, and it's advisable to get these replaced at an engine reconditioner's and the valve seats recut at the same time.

If the guides seem OK, take a closer look at the condition of the valve seats in the head and around the corresponding edge on the valve face itself. You'll generally find that the inlet valves are in much better condition than the exhausts, and the inlets will act as a yardstick for the damage to the exhaust valves. The edge of the valve should still be fairly meaty, and the valve face perfectly circular; if the edge is worn very thin like an old copper coin, the face in any way misshapen, bits missing from the edge of the valve or the stem is bent, then throw it away and fit a new one. Really extensive damage to the valve should have been revealed by a compression test and by bad running in any case.

'Lapping' is an engineer's term that simply means rubbing two bits of metal together with grinding paste between so that the two mating faces gradually acquire precisely matching contours. Lapping or grinding in the valves is performed during a top overhaul to restore the gas-tightness between the valve and its seat when fully closed.

Some valves aren't meant to be ground in, having a special protective coating on the working surface which isn't to be rubbed away — the manual will tell you if this is the case. If it is, and the valves are pitted or damaged, all you can do is scrap them. New valves will require their seats in the head to be recut at the engineer's, if they're anything less than a perfect fit.

With conventional valves, grinding-in is a straightforward business. In addition to a tin of grinding paste (which will contain both a fine and a medium grade abrasive) you need a valve grinding tool, which is simply a stick with a suction pad on one end. With the head upside down on the bench-slide the valve you're going to lap into its guide with a little fine grinding paste smeared on to the face. Wet the suction cup and stick it to the valve. Holding the tool between the palms of the hands, rotate it back and forth, occasionally turning the valve around to redistribute the paste. Keep going at this operation until the valve face and the seating assume the appearance of an unbroken grey ring, free of pit marks. Check the evenness of the job by cleaning the excess paste off and making a series of soft pencil marks across the seat, like the divisions on a clock face. Then drop the valve back and rotate it through a quarter turn. The movement of the valve against the seat should have picked off the centre of each line, showing that the valve is in perfect contact all around its circumference. If any of the lines are still intact, go on grinding until things improve.

Checking the flatness of the head face is worth doing before putting back the valves — the engine reconditioner's can provide this service for you, and they can skim the head in a surface grinder if it appears to be distorted. Once you're happy about this, refit the valves, making sure that the ones to be used again are fitted to the guides that they originally came from. Slide new rubber oil seals on to each valve stem, slip a new valve spring into place with its retaining collar and use the valve spring compressor as before to squeeze the spring until you can slip the collet or other securing device back on to the valve stem. Collets are fiddly objects, and you may find that you have to move the compressed spring from side to side until you can install them; then slowly release the tool until the spring is fully expanded. Repeat this all the way along the head until all the valves are refitted. The head is now ready to be bolted back on the engine.

The new cylinder head gasket should be perfectly clean and eased gently down over the studs — make sure you've got it the right way round, and that it doesn't bind and damage itself passing over the studs. Then slide the cylinder head itself down the studs after it, taking a last check before you do this that there are no bits of grit or carbon left on the head face. Then run the nuts on to the studs until they're finger tight, and finally pull them up with the torque wrench half a turn at a time in the order shown in the manual. When the recommended torque is reached on all the nuts, the head is reinstalled.

(One minor aside, before we leave the subject of cylinder heads, and that's on account of the studs that locate the head on the block. It shouldn't normally be necessary to take these out, but sometimes removing one of the nuts will accidentally bring the stud along with it. Or you might find that for some reason one of the stud threads is damaged and the stud has to be replaced. A convenient way to remove and replace a stud is to run two nuts on top of each other on to the thread and use a spanner on the lower nut to loosen the stud. A Mole wrench or a Stillson on the unthreaded part will also shift it, though the tool will leave its teethmarks on the stud and any engineering purist would turn white at the sight.)

If all is well, replace the manifolding with a new gasket, and put back the valve gear and push rods if you haven't already had to do this before bolting the head down. Fill the radiator, check for leaks at the water hoses, and check the tappet clearances roughly with the engine cold. Then start it up and let it get warm; when it reaches its normal running temperature stop it again and recheck the torque readings on the head nuts, give the manifold nuts an extra fraction of a turn if they'll take it fairly willingly, and set the tappet clearances accurately. Since you should have done this overhaul at a mileage when a tune-up was also due, do it now according to as many of the tests detailed in the Appendix as you're equipped to carry out. The ignition timing and carburettor idling adjustments should be checked after a top overhaul in any case. Run the car for 200 miles and then check the head nut torque and the tappet clearances again.

Major Work.

Very little of the last job has much to do with replacement of worn parts, unless the valves have burned or the rocker gear is worn. More fundamental overhauls of the engine generally require it to be out of the car, and this is naturally something that puts most owners off, particularly if they don't have especially salubrious conditions to work in. It does no harm though, to have some idea as to what a full engine overhaul really entails — and the ways in which you can make it cheaper if you're willing to undertake at least part of the work yourself.

Roughly speaking, between 80–100,000 miles you could expect to find gradually increasing wear on the pistons and rings, the cylinder walls, the crankpins and bearing surfaces at the bottom end of the engine, the oil pump, and possibly the timing chain. Very little of this kind of wear actually brings the car to an abrupt halt the way an ignition or carburation breakdown does. The car simply gets noisier, consumes more oil and loses power; if the crankshaft bearings are getting slack the oil pressure will drop, a hammering noise will become more evident, and if you leave it indefinitely the vibration may eventually break the crankshaft or a connecting rod. Things definitely shouldn't slide that far, unless you only intend to throw the car on the scrap-heap when a major repair is necessary.

Tracing engine noises becomes easier with the aid of a stethoscope if you don't mind being ridiculed for crouching over a heap of jangling old iron looking like an extra from 'General Hospital'. You might hear a general knocking sound from somewhere high up on the block, and the trusty stethoscope might put your mind at rest by localizing the sound in the dynamo or the water pump rather than inside the engine itself. Be careful, by the way, that you don't catch your hand or the instrument in the fan blades while you're making this check, or you might end up needing the stethoscope yourself.

Worn big-end bearings clatter at the base of the block when the engine is under light load or no load; and if the clearances aren't excessive, the noise will disappear when the engine starts to pull hard. If you can hear the sound at idle, short out each plug in turn or pull off each plug cover and see if it quietens down when any particular cylinder is out of action; if it does, then the inference is that a connecting rod bearing is worn in that cylinder but the rest aren't bad. If there's a deeper rumbling or thumping from much the same region of the engine, and it gets worse when the car is pulling hard, then this might well be worn main bearings — in either case, the oil pressure will have dropped considerably by the time all this racket becomes apparent. With the engine hot, the oil warning light will be very likely to come on at idling speeds and will eventually be reluctant to go out even as the speed is increased. Knocking noises from the top end of the engine, particularly those of a much higher pitch, may indicate trouble in the little end bearings or the piston rings. A light metallic tapping that only appears with the engine cold is probably 'piston slap' — an effect set up by loose pistons and frequently disappearing as they expand once the engine gets warm. Some engines have a considerable amount of piston slap even in good condition but if the effect is accompanied by lost compression and high oil consumption, then there's probably more piston wear than there should be. A similar noise to piston slap that only appears when the engine is hot and pulling hard against a load is 'pinking', or detonation caused by a premature explosion of the fuel. This might be on account of excessive carbon build-up in the combustion chambers — a sign of an overdue decoke — the wrong grade of fuel, or over-advanced ignition timing or a stuck advance mechanism.

If a combination of the car's mileage and general decline has convinced you that a substantial improvement to the engine is inevitable, then the reconditioners are likely to be able to offer you some alternatives. If you feel brave, are equipped with the workshop manual and a comprehensive set of tools, you can remove the engine, strip it down completely and take the vital bits (crankshaft, cylinder block, con-rods etc.) to the engineers for measurement and machining back into shape. If you don't fancy this, the firm will very likely be able to offer you what's known as a 'short engine' in exchange for your own. This is simply an overhauled crankcase assembly; the wear in the cylinders has been got rid of by boring them out to a larger size and fitting bigger pistons; any ovality in the crank pins is trued up by grinding the pins to a slightly smaller diameter and fitting suitably undersized big-end and main-bearings, and also included

will be a new timing chain and a new oil pump. The major work of an engine overhaul is thus done for you, you don't have to flap about whether or not the big-end bolts are at the right torque or the piston rings assembled properly after you've put everything back together; you simply refit your original cylinder head and ancillaries and you have a reconditioned engine.

If you do rebuild your own engine, then make sure that you keep things clean, that you're equipped with a torque wrench for the big-end and the main-bearing bolts, that the piston rings are correctly fitted to the pistons with their respective gaps disposed at '12 o'clock', '4 o'clock' and '8 o'clock' around the circumference of the piston to prevent compression loss, and that you fit the pistons carefully to well lubricated bores with a proper piston ring clamp. If the pistons are of the 'split skirt' type, make sure they're the right way round as described in the manual. Oil the bearing shells before you bolt them up, (a mixture of engine oil and STP is a good initial lubricant) and use new tab washers, split pins or self-locking nuts on the bearing bolts. Use new gaskets throughout, replace the oil pump. Run the engine in carefully, not exceeding 40 m.p.h. in top for the first 200 miles, 45 for the next 200 and 50 m.p.h. for the first thousand. The engine reconditioners may have their own recommendations, and you should consult with them. It is suggested that the engine should be run with a maximum of $\frac{1}{3}$ throttle for the first 300 miles and then a maximum of $\frac{2}{3}$ throttle for the next 500 miles.

Transmissions.

Before we start getting down to the nuts and bolts of dealing with clutch overhauls, remind yourself of the functioning of a clutch by taking another look at p. 45. Wear on the clutch manifests itself in two ways. You might find that it's becoming increasingly difficult to engage gear smoothly, and that there's a considerable amount of slack at the start of the pedal travel before you feel spring pressure; this is due to wear in the release bearing or possibly lack of fluid in the clutch hydraulic line or wear in the linkage if it's a mechanically operated clutch. The alternative is 'clutch slip', in which the engine revs don't appear to have much effect on the roadwheels and which might eventually get so bad that the car will barely climb hills.

The components of the clutch that are most liable to wear are the friction faces of the centre-plate or driven-plate, the springs or diaphragm that keep the pressure plate squeezed against the driven-plate when the car is running in gear, and the release bearing that comes into contact with the release lever mechanism that compresses the springs and withdraws the clutch when you step on the pedal.

As the friction faces wear down, the centre-plate effectively becomes 'thinner'. The pressure-plate, pushed by the springs or diaphragm, has 'followed' it and moved automatically closer to the flywheel to compensate. Since the whole principle of the clutch release mechanism is that any movement of the perimeter of the pressure-plate in one direction is turned 'inside out' by the release levers, the pressure pad itself moves gradually rearwards as friction plate wear increases. The clearance between the release bearing and the pressure pad may eventually disappear so that the former is actually butting up against the latter — when this happens, the pressure-plate can't move any closer to the flywheel regardless of how much more the friction faces wear. At this point the 'squeezing' effect of the clutch is lost and the mechanism starts to slip.

Naturally, adjustment is possible to get rid of the early effects of this process. You simply move the release bearing back a bit to restore the clearance, and the driver's handbook and the works manual will both explain how this routine adjustment is effected, and the intervals at which it's to be carried out. Free movement at the clutch pedal is a good guide to the state of things — there should normally be about ¾" of slack at the top of the pedal before you start to feel the resistance of the springs. Keep maintaining the adjustment as the clutch wears. When there's no adjustment left, the centre-plate has worn to the limit and the clutch must be dismantled to replace it.

Clutch wear can also take other forms, such as drag or spin resulting in noisy gear engagement, and rough take-up or judder. Generally these are all associated with some kind of damage sustained by the centre-plate, or misalignment or wear of the gearbox primary shaft. Release bearing wear can also result in a condition where slack at the pedal means that you can put the clutch straight to the floor without the mechanism being fully withdrawn, and this will also cause a lot of trouble with gear selection. All these snags require surgery.

Access to the clutch and the necessary dismantling procedure is fully detailed in the workshop manual, and the gearbox always has to come out unless the engine needs an overhaul anyway and you elect to remove that instead. While clutch repair is actually no more difficult than, say, a brake overhaul, its snags are matters of inconvenience rather than expertise; the job is dirty, cramped, often obstinate and strenuous. Most modern cars with a conventional front-engine, rear-drive arrangement require their gearboxes to be withdrawn from underneath the car so you either have to be working over a pit or have the car really robustly supported on axle stands or ramps. Remove the ring of nuts and bolts holding the gearbox bell housing to the back of the block (some you'll be able to get at from underneath, some from the top), and, supporting its weight, take off the starter motor,

earthing strap, speedometer drive and reverse light cable. Release the gearshift mechanism from inside the car, disconnect the propellor shaft flange and mark the two edges with white paint so that you re-assemble them the same way round. Drain the gearbox oil, support the rear of the engine with a piece of timber on top of a jack to spread the load (preferably get this support just *behind* the sump rather than bearing on the sump itself), then remove the rear gearbox mountings and slide the unit back clear of the clutch.

Sounds easy, doesn't it? The first time you do it, particularly if you're alone and lying on your back under the car, is usually an alarming experience nevertheless. Not only is the gearbox heavy and extremely dirty, but you're trying to support its weight in an awkward position; and supporting its weight is very important, because it should never be allowed to rest on the primary shaft while the latter is still in the clutch, This can distort the clutch plate (not unduly serious if you're replacing it anyway) but more significantly it can bend the gearbox shaft itself and the resulting running troubles would be disconcerting at the least. You have to slide the gearbox clear of the clutch on as near to a level plane as the available space will permit, though toward the end of that movement you may find you have to tip it for the rear of the box to clear the chassis or the prop shaft. Check with a flashlight shone into the clutch mechanism that you're not putting any twisting or levering force on the clutch itself. The gearbox really has to have some sort of additional support other than your own flagging forearms, and a platform cobbled together out of bits of timber is not a bad idea; a simple jack is inclined to fall over as you lug the gearbox backwards.

What you see once the box is out is the clutch mechanism bolted to the flywheel face. To remove it, first, you've got to stop the engine from turning over; a screwdriver wedged between the starter ring teeth and the bell housing will usually suffice. Then undo the clutch cover bolts a little at a time and diagonally, so that you release the spring pressure evenly around the rim and don't distort the cover. The screwdriver will almost certainly drop out of the ring gear several times while you're doing this and the whole flywheel will then turn round, so stock up on a few choice curses while you're doing it; this is protection you'll need throughout the whole job actually.

With all the housing bolts removed, mark the cover and the flywheel face with a couple of drops of white paint so you can put it back in the same position. Some clutches will only go back one way in any case, but the insurance does no harm. Once the clutch cover and pressure-plate assembly is unbolted, the centre plate will drop out.

Replace the centre plate in any event — if you've thought it worth going this far because of clutch trouble encountered on the road, then this is the least you can do. If the clutch plate has worn down to its rivets, then the pressure-plate and flywheel may be scored; this doesn't happen often, fortunately, since severe clutch slip is usually encountered before things get that bad. If it has happened, the flywheel will have to be unbolted from the crankshaft and taken to the engine reconditioners' to be skimmed smooth, and the pressure-plate will have to be exchanged for a new one.

Clutch slip where the friction plate turns out to be not unduly worn can sometimes be due to oil getting on to the linings and burning to a glazed deposit on the surface that will impair the grip on the plate. This will be visible as a dark discolouration on the lining. Don't expect clutch linings to be rough or asbestos-like simply because they're meant to impart friction; after prolonged use, even linings in good condition acquire a very high polish, and this doesn't interfere with their ability to do their job. If oil has been getting on to the clutch, the most likely sources of a leak would be the rear main bearing of the crankshaft and the front bearing of the gearbox – a substantial oil leak will in any case be evident from a pool of oil in the bottom of the bell housing which will probably have descended on you as you pulled the gearbox free.

The pressure-plate you don't dismantle because its setting-up involves the use of accurate measuring instruments; if the centre-plate seems OK and you suspect weak springs or a weak diaphragm of causing the slip, have the unit checked by a service station and if necessary make use of the exchange scheme to get another. Last but not least, take a look at the release bearing which you'll find installed into a sort of wishbone device inside the gearbox bell housing. Sometimes these are steel bearings, and they tend to wear down the inner ends of the diaphragm faster than they wear themselves. The carbon ring type of bearing sometimes gets scored or worn unevenly, or may come loose in its housing – it's helpful to be able to compare one of these with a new one to assess the amount of wear on it.

So, having decided how much of the clutch it's necessary to replace, you then set about putting the whole lot back together. There are a few details to be attended to in fastening the clutch to the flywheel again. The first is that you get the centre-plate the right way round; the hub at the centre of it is usually longer on one side than the other and if you get it backwards then the clutch won't withdraw properly. There are sometimes markings on the hub that make this clear. Sandwich the centre-plate against the flywheel by pushing the pressure-plate assembly back on to the pegs provided for it on the flywheel, getting your identifying paint-marks lined up and then loosely screwing back the bolts.

You're almost ready now to pull the cover bolts tight, but naturally if the centre-plate isn't squeezed

up in an exactly central position, then the gearbox primary shaft will be out of line with it and you'll never be able to get the gearbox back. You can line it up by eye alone, but to get a level and steady look at the clutch if you're doing the job from underneath the car isn't a particularly comfortable or accurate operation. Accessory shops now sell a special aligning device (called a 'mandrel', which is not an East African rodent) which consists of a metal rod with a variety of different sized cylinders looking like cotton reels which you can push on to it and which will suit the clutches of most popular cars. You find the cylinder that's a snug fit in the splined hub of your particular centre-plate, and the smaller cylinder that fits into the centre bearing of the flywheel, run these on to the rod and push it into the centre of the clutch, if necessary juggling the plate around until the mandrel locates in the flywheel bearing. When you've managed this, the centre-plate will be positively located in exactly the right spot; you can then tighten up the housing bolts diagonally and a half turn at a time until the clutch cover is tight. Then remove the mandrel.

Gearboxes.

The phenomenal price of gearbox spares these days has made stripping down and rebuilding a box hardly a practical proposition. If you want to try, the average conventional unit can be dismantled in three quarters of an hour or so, using the workshop manual. It is not as terrifying as you might imagine. Doing things in the right order is always important but doubly so when it comes to gearboxes. The mainshaft is like the thread of a necklace with objects of all different shapes and sizes slipped on to it; the important thing is to make sure you don't muddle up the order they're suspended in, and the exploded diagram in the workshop manual, though it might look a bit mind boggling, is actually the best way to keep track of things. The only part of the job that actually does involve the prospect of flying springs is when you push the outer synchro-mesh sleeves (see p. 51) off the inner synchro hubs. There's normally a ring of three or four sprung ball bearings inside, so when you perform this operation, I suggest you simply put the whole lot into a plastic bag and separate them there. The golden rule is: *don't lay a spanner on a gearbox without the appropriate workshop manual to hand.*

Fortunately, really nasty mishaps to the gearbox aren't frequent and they don't usually come suddenly unless the box should for some reason jam in mesh. Most gearbox faults sneak up as irritating driving problems, such as jumping out of gear, noisy or difficult engagement, stiff action of the lever, general noise and whine. Difficult engagement may of course be a clutch fault, and you would need to be certain first of all that the friction plate is free to move on its splines, that there isn't some misalignment in the clutch and that the release bearing isn't worn out before you blamed the gearbox. Clutch trouble would of course mean that the problem would be present on all the gear ratios, whereas a faulty synchromesh might confine it to one. Since the box would have to come out in any case to attend to the clutch, you wouldn't be losing much time if it turned out to be the gearbox instead.

You might strip down a gearbox if you weren't pressed for time or if, for some unaccountable reason, you were simply interested in how it's put together. A much simpler solution for the more faint-hearted and realistic, is to simply exchange the damaged box. There are two ways you can go about this. You can go back to the agent for the car and exchange the gearbox there, and for many popular modern types you probably wouldn't see much change from £150. Or you can go to the gearbox specialist, who may be able to provide you with an 'exchange' unit. Few people other than the manufacturer offer 'reconditioned' units. Try to make sure that your gearbox is reasonably clean and of course that the oil is drained off before you trade it in. Don't forget to fill up the replacement with fresh oil to the recommended level before you take to the road again.

Not all gearbox troubles require replacement of the whole works. If you're not daunted by at least carrying out a cursory inspection of the unit with the top cover off, then it might at least be worth trying to establish what has failed, and how much the replacements would be in comparison with an exchange unit. You could argue, for instance, that a repair that might run out at £30 worth of spares would be a practical proposition, since a replacement unit will rarely be less than £70, if it were nearer £50 in spare parts, then you might as well part with the extra for the replacement for the sake of the guarantee and the avoidance of aggravation. Don't be tempted to buy scrapyard gearboxes unless they carry a guarantee too, because you can have no real idea of how undamaged they are until you install one in your car.

Jumping out of gear (a common enough fault) can often be cured simply by fitting new springs and balls in the selector mechanism, and possibly replacing the selector forks. Noisy engagement might simply require new baulk-rings or synchromesh rings. If the gearbox has locked solid, don't fear the worst, it might be something broken or slipped in the selectors which are located in the top cover of the box. If the unit has seized up, but removing the top cover enables you to lever the gear clusters in and out of mesh by hand, then clearly the seizure isn't in the box itself and must be associated with the selectors. Make sure, though, that the gear clusters will move *fully* in and out of mesh when you

do this. Seizure or partial seizure can sometimes come about through the sliding hubs themselves becoming damaged or distorted, usually through a mainshaft bearing having itself broken down and allowed the shaft to whip. When this happens, an exchange box is generally the cheapest way out.

Gearbox lubrication and maintenance is no problem, and nowadays some cars are designed to use the same lubricant for the life of the box. Where checks are possible, use the oil specified by the manufacturer and establish the level by whatever means is provided; some old cars use a dipstick, most modern ones have a plug on the side of the box (see owner's handbook). You squirt the oil into this from the squeegee bottle until it starts to overflow.

Refitting the gearbox can sometimes be a bit of a struggle. It's the sort of job where you're torn by the conviction that too much brutality will damage the clutch or the gearbox shaft, but too little will leave you wrestling with it all day. The idea is to slide the gearbox smoothly forward so that the splined primary shaft slots into the splined shaft of the clutch and then into the flywheel centre bearing; the likelihood of this happening first go is remote, though you might be blessed with beginner's luck. It helps, if the box doesn't seem to want to know, to put the cogs into top gear and turn the propellor shaft flange at the back as you push so that the splines can line up. Once it goes in, get the gearbox supported firmly underneath so that the shaft doesn't bend, wriggle out from under and get a few of the uppermost bell-housing bolts into place. Then replace all the other bell-housing bolts, the starter motor and earthing strap and everything else you had to disconnect. Refit the gearbox rear mountings and remove the jack and the wooden spreader from the rear of the engine. Reconnect the clutch operating mechanism and you should be ready to go. The clutch will of course need adjustment now, since the lining thickness has been abruptly altered.

Transverse Engines.

The gearbox can sometimes be removed from a transverse-engined car with the engine in place, but if it's mounted underneath the engine as it is on Leyland vehicles, then the whole lot has to come out. For both gearbox and clutch overhauls on these engines, you have to use a very large socket and a lot of muscle power to shift the retaining bolt in the middle of the flywheel, and then a special flywheel puller (which you can hire) to draw it back off the crankshaft. Then you unbolt the clutch housing to enable the gearbox and engine to be separated.

Whatever you do, don't forget to replace the rubber ring between the gearbox and crankcase of the Leyland engine where the oil pickup passageway traverses the two; if you leave the old one in and there's an air leak you won't get any oil pressure and you'll have to take the whole lot to bits again to replace it.

Prop shafts and Transmission Joints
In the conventional power distribution arrangement, with the engine at the front of the car and the driven wheels at the back, a propellor shaft carries the motion of the gearbox to the rear axle. The axle being mounted on springs, this means that its height is continually being varied as the car bounces, and it can also move slightly backwards and forwards. To accommodate this movement, the prop shaft is made in two sections that can telescope into each other and the joints and the gearbox and axle flanges enable it to move up and down and from side to side while it's spinning. These are universal joints (U.J.s).

Normally they consist of needle roller bearings, held in place by a spring clip. Modern prop shaft joints are usually sealed for life and don't require lubrication, but the older types are often provided with a grease nipple and you should check with your manual about routine attention to this. It's worth noting that lubrication of these parts is easy to ignore because they're almost more difficult to get at than the suspension, and you may in any case have to push the car in gear to bring the joint round into a suitable position to get the grease gun on to the nipple — this isn't very convenient if you've got the car raised, and it might be easier to lift the driven wheels entirely and turn them round by hand with the car in gear.

Broadly similar shafts and joints are fitted to cars with independent rear suspension systems, though in these cases the differential itself is bolted to the frame and the prop shafts replace the conventional axle shafts. In the case of front-driven cars, the same principle applies, though of course a very elaborate form of ball and socket joint is necessary at the outer ends, to enable the front wheels to be turned from lock to lock.

Wear in the drive or propellor shaft joints usually makes itself heard as a distinct 'clonk' when the drive is reversed; such as when you take your foot off the gas going downhill, or abruptly open the throttle after the car has been cruising in top. You can then check for wear by getting the car raised and securely supported, and grasping the transmission on either side of the suspect joint and trying to twist. Any slack between the two sections will be obvious.

Check with the workshop manual about over-hauling the transmission joints on your car. The older Hardy-Spicer shafts can be overhauled with kits available from the makers, but the more modern versions require the whole shaft to be replaced. If the forks of the joints have themselves worn, the holes that the bearing assemblies fit into will have elongated; then you have to replace the whole joint.

Front Wheel Drive C.V. Joints.
Constant velocity joints can be renewed by the home mechanic; warning of wear in them is given when the front wheels knock with the car driven round in a tight circle on either lock.

Follow the works manual closely; there may be a special procedure for lining up the telescoping shafts on reassembly, requiring you to have marked them before you took them apart. Pack the new joint with the grease supplied for the job, fit it with a new rubber cover, and secure the rubber with wire. Tighten any steering joints and hub nuts to the recommended torque. You need a hub puller for this job, which you can either hire or buy. As we've said elsewhere on the subject of hub removal, if yours is the kind of car that needs the hubs withdrawing just to check the brake linings, then it's worth your while to invest in a suitable puller.

Wheels, Hubs and Tyres.
Manufacturers specify intervals at which the bearings should be removed, checked for wear and pitting, regreased and refitted.

Most front hubs are simply removed by slackening the large retaining nut in the centre after removing the grease cap and the split pin. Some hub nuts are self-locking, or pegged by knocking over a thin metal lip on the top of the nut — these are simply loosened like an ordinary nut. Sometimes the hub will pull off without the use of an extractor, but if you should need one they can be obtained from tool hire shops or bought for fairly reasonable prices — but make sure you get one that's of the right dimensions for the job. Some cars have integral brake drums and hubs, which means you have to pull them every time you want to do a routine job on the brakes — in this case it would be daft not to invest in a hub puller, because you're going to be making quite a lot of use of it. Sometimes you can get away with re-fitting the roadwheel once the retaining nut is removed, and pulling on the rim of the wheel to draw the hub.

Don't forget that if the retaining nut is of the lipped type that has to be 'peened over' (an engineer's term for locking something by spreading it or flattening it out) then you throw the old ones away and replace them. The manual will give a torque figure for retightening them.

Wear in the front wheel bearings is usually evident from the amount of rocking motion you can get from grasping the roadwheel at the top and bottom with the car jacked up. This isn't an infallible guide because some hubs have a certain amount of built-in slack in any case, but the extremes will be unmistakeable. Refer to the workshop manual for the adjustment procedure if

UNIVERSAL JOINT

Forked ends of shafts pivot on 'spider'. Bearings reduce friction.

'Spider' links yokes at right angles to each other

Needle roller bearings

Retaining clip

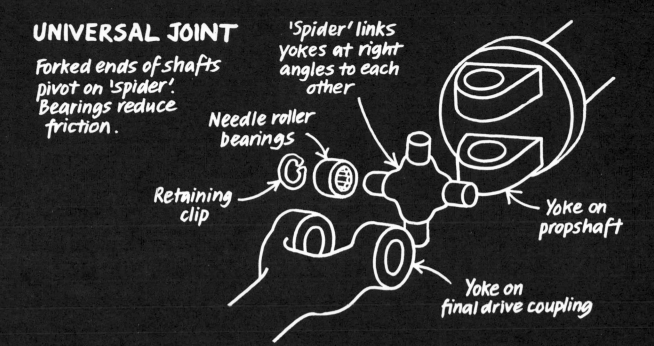

Yoke on propshaft

Yoke on final drive coupling

Output shaft to hub

Cage carrying steel balls (cut away)

Outer socket (cut away)

Inner socket

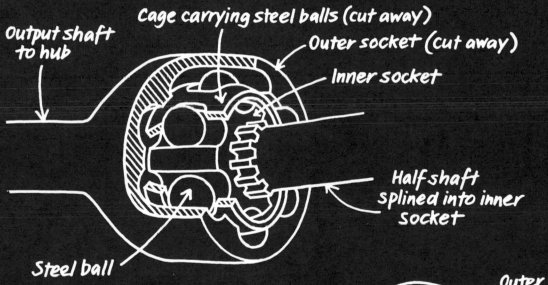

Half shaft splined into inner socket

Steel ball

CONSTANT VELOCITY JOINT

Normally used for drive shafts. Steel balls held in cage transmit drive from inner to outer socket.

Right: section through joint.

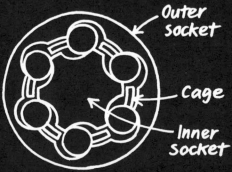

Outer socket

Cage

Inner socket

Wiring Diagram For Mini.

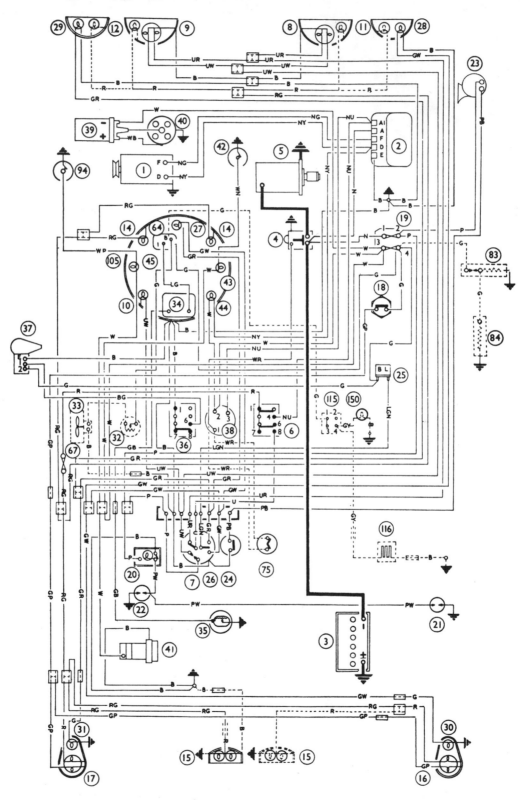

Key To Wiring Diagram.

1. Dynamo.
2. Control box.
3. 12-volt battery.
4. Starter solenoid.
5. Starter motor.
6. Lighting switch.
7. Headlamp dip switch.
8. Righthand headlamp.
9. Lefthand headlamp.
10. Main-beam warning lamp.
11. Righthand sidelamp.
12. Lefthand sidelamp.
14. Panel lamps.
15. Number-plate lamp (two for Van).
16. Righthand stop and tail lamp.
17. Lefthand stop and tail lamp.
18. Stop lamp switch.
19. Fuse unit.
20. Interior light.
21. Righthand door switch.
22. Lefthand door switch.
23. Horn.
24. Horn-push.
25. Flasher unit.
26. Direction indicator and headlamp flasher switch.
27. Direction indicator warning lamp.
28. Righthand front flasher lamp.
29. Lefthand front flasher lamp.
30. Righthand rear flasher lamp.
31. Lefthand rear flasher lamp.
32. Heater switch (when fitted).
33. Heater motor (when fitted).
34. Fuel gauge.
35. Fuel gauge tank unit.
36. Windscreen wiper switch.
37. Windscreen wiper motor.
38. Ignition/starter switch.
39. Ignition coil.
40. Distributor.
41. Fuel pump.
42. Oil pressure switch.
43. Oil pressure warning lamp.
44. Ignition warning lamp.
45. Speedometer.
64. Bi-metal instrument voltage stabilizer.
75. Automatic gearbox safety switch (when fitted).
76. Line fuse, 35-amp.
83. Induction heater and thermostat (when fitted).
84. Suction chamber heater (when fitted).
94. Oil filter switch.
105. Oil filter warning lamp.
115. Rear window demister switch (when fitted).
116. Rear window demister unit (when fitted).
150. Rear window demister warning light (when fitted).

Wiring Diagram Symbols.

Battery. Bulb. Coil. Capacitor. Transistor. Thermistor.

Resistor. Voltmeter. Diode. Brush contact. Earth. Contact points.

Ammeter. Switch. Zener diode. Switch (courtesy light door switch). Fuse. Variable resistance (rheostat).

Wiring Colour Codes, Sizes & Ratings.

CODE.	COLOURS.	SIZE.	RATING.	CIRCUITS.
N.	Brown.	44/·012	27·5 amps.	Battery and generator circuits.
Y.	Yellow.	14/·010	6 amps.	Overdrive circuits.
W.	White.	28/·012 14/·010	17·5 amps. 6 amps.	Ignition circuit and accessories protected by ignition switch but unfused (petrol pump etc.).
G. L.G.	Green. Light green.	14/·010	6 amps.	Auxiliary circuits fed through ignition switch and fuse 4 or A4.
P.	Purple.	14/·010	6 amps.	Auxiliary circuits fed through fuse 2 or A2.
U.	Blue.	28/·012 14/·010	17·5 amps. 6 amps.	Headlamp circuits fed from terminal S2 or H on lighting switch (blue to dipper switch, then blue/white for main beam and blue/red for dipped beam).
R.	Red.	14/·010	6 amps.	Lighting circuits including side, tail, and panel lamps.
B.	Black.	Various.	Various.	Earth return circuits.

Section Of Vauxhall Car Wiring Diagram.

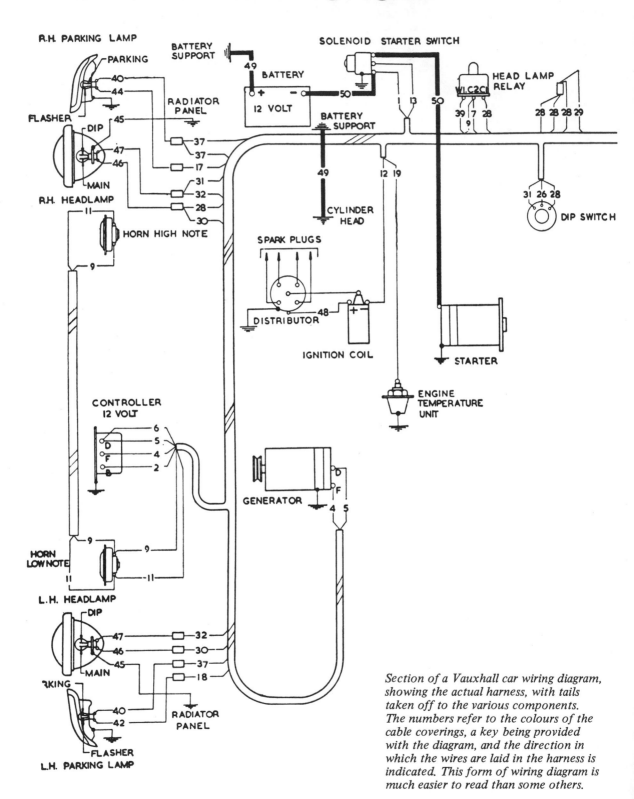

Section of a Vauxhall car wiring diagram, showing the actual harness, with tails taken off to the various components. The numbers refer to the colours of the cable coverings, a key being provided with the diagram, and the direction in which the wires are laid in the harness is indicated. This form of wiring diagram is much easier to read than some others.

there is one; it takes the form of tightening the hub nut until the lost motion is removed, but don't overdo it. The idea is that the nut should be tight enough to steady the wheel but not to stiffen its rotation.

Wash out all the old grease and dirt with petrol, examine the ball bearings for cracks and looseness in the cage. Slack may be evident between the inner ring of the bearing and the outer part. Replace any oil seals present when you remove wheel-bearings.

Maintenance of the rear hub bearings is usually necessary when oil or grease is getting on to the brake linings. A failed oil seal at the outer end of the axle shaft may often be due to a worn bearing allowing the half shaft to drift and distort the rubber seal. Use the manufacturer's recommendations as to fitting new seals. They're delicate articles, and ham-fisted assembly can leave you worse off than you were at the start.

Wheels and Tyres.

The setting-up of what's known as the 'steering geometry' and the balancing of tyres on the wheel rims is a scientific business, and since it's a service that wheel and tyre specialists offer pretty cheaply, you'd be wise to avail yourself of it once a year. Unbalanced wheels and badly adjusted track can cause uncomfortable vibration and maybe even steering wander at high speeds. If you've done anything naughty like clout the wheels against a kerb lately, get the check made then to make sure you haven't knocked anything out of true.

Since the tyres are what keeps you and your car sticking to the road, it's a good idea to make a regular reconnaissance of all of them, and remove embedded stones and any other objects that the tyres may have picked up. Regard any swelling or lumps on the tyre walls with great suspicion — if possible, immediately swap such a tyre for the spare wheel, and get the ailing one checked. Don't mix radials and cross plies on the same axle, and scrap any tyre with a tread depth of less than 1mm.

If the tyre is worn excessively on one side of the tread, then the wheel may be misaligned or the track wrongly set. If it's worn at the centre and not at the edges, then it's been running over-inflated.

Electrical Maintenance.

Wiring diagrams are horrible looking articles, by and large. As with a great many things that tend to make the mind go blank, the problem is that you're not necessarily looking for anything in particular on them, so there is only this fearful onslaught of undifferentiated information. Like getting on to Marble Arch roundabout in the rush hour, you should never tangle with a wiring diagram without knowing exactly where you're coming from and where you want to get to, or the experience is apt to produce a ringing in the ears.

Wiring diagrams aren't exactly drawn up by the devisers of conundrums. If an electrical gadget fails, the diagram can tell you where to find the cable that supplies it and where the possible failure points are — which are normally fuses, switches and earth connections. These days, car wiring diagrams are getting mercifully easier to follow, as you can see from the difference between the Mini example on p. 164 and the section from a Vauxhall system on p. 166 . Apart from being simply far more abstract in appearance, the Mini diagram uses two keys (an alphabetical one for the cable colours, and a numerical one for components) so its use involves a good deal more cross-referencing.

In both cases, each of the fine lines represents a wire, and each of the little boxes on the wires a snap connector which either joins two sections of cable together or enables one to branch out in several directions. Each wire has letters or numbers tagged to it somewhere along the run, which refer to a colour code and tell you what colour the particular wire is on the car. All you need to do now is to be able to follow each wire with a pencil point and you can use the diagrams.

Just as an example and a test of stamina, try figuring out the ramifications of the lighting circuit on the Mini diagram. No. 6 is the main switch, with a supply cable and a wire or wires leaving it to operate whatever devices are on the circuit. Three wires sprout from our No.6. One is marked NU (brown with a blue stripe) one R (red) one U (blue). If we follow the brown-and-blue wire with a pencil we can find that it runs up to the A1 terminal on the control box, so it's clearly the feed wire. If we follow the red wire, it passes through a fuse on the left-hand side of the diagram and then splits into three cables now marked RG (red with a green stripe). One of these goes to the two panel lamps so that the instruments are illuminated as soon as the sidelights are turned on. One goes downwards to the rear sidelights. One curls back across the centre of the diagram, makes a run up the right-hand side, and then splits at a snap connector (centre/top) to feed the front sidelights.

Still awake? The third wire leaving the light-switch (U or blue) travels down to the dipper switch on the steering column (No.7) and divides into an outlet marked UR (blue with a red stripe) or one marked UW (blue with a white stripe). So if the dipper switch is linking the blue wire to the blue/red outlet, the current will now travel to a snap connector at the front of the car which splits the cables between the two dip-beam filaments in the headlamps. If it's switched over to the UW (blue/white) outlet, then it will lead instead to the main-beam units, and one of the blue/white wires will also travel to the bulb 10 on the speedo to illuminate the mainbeam warning light.

To test a failure, we bring the faithful circuit

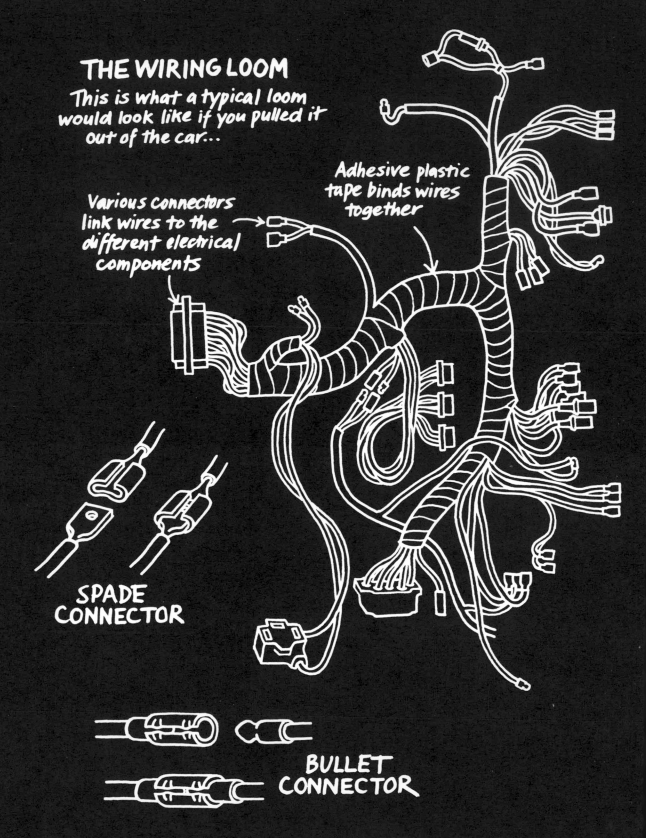

THE WIRING LOOM

This is what a typical loom would look like if you pulled it out of the car...

Adhesive plastic tape binds wires together

Various connectors link wires to the different electrical components

SPADE CONNECTOR

BULLET CONNECTOR

tester into the fray (see tools, p. 92), clipping it to the nearest convenient bit of unpainted and unrusty metalwork and then probing the terminals of the doubtful circuit. As a general principle you could say that you start checking a failed circuit at the end nearest the appliance that has packed up and work back through its switchgear to the power source, which may be either the car's regulator box or its fusebox. Somewhere along the line you're likely to find a dirty, loose or separated connection, a burned-out switch or a cable that may have chafed through its insulation and be shorting out to the bodywork. Where this is the case you'll sometimes flush it out when the circuit tester lights up at one end of what the diagram shows to be an uninterrupted cable run, but remains dead at the other end. The only inference is that the wire itself is broken (*an open circuit*) or grounding itself on the metalwork (*a short circuit*) and you should check the length of the wire and its insulation with the tester.

By far the most frequently encountered electrical fault on motor cars is simply dirty terminals, particularly in bits of the vehicle that are exposed to road dirt and rainwater. The earth connection symbol on a wiring diagram simply means that the wire is bolted to the bodywork at that point, and these are frequently spots where corrosion eventually breaks the circuit. If the tester reveals the feed wire to a dud lamp to be live, for instance, and the bulb isn't blown, you can earth the lamp to a clean bit of bodywork with a piece of wire. If this cures the fault, then unscrew the real earth connection, clean it up and refasten it. Always carry spare fuses on the car, and the diagram will tell you which ones protect which circuits. Repeated fuse blowing usually indicates a short. Non-standard fittings like extra lamps sometimes use line-fuses contained in a spring-loaded plastic cartridge; if the spring weakens or the terminals corrode, then the circuit may become unreliable.

Radio suppression.
Radios are frequently standard fittings on motor cars these days, but if you fit one of your own the instructions that come with the device cover most of the eventualities as long as you ensure that:

The *polarity* of the instrument (i.e. whether it's positively or negatively earthed) is the same polarity as the car or it will blow up (the radio, not the car).

Suppressors are fitted to the plugs, the coil and the generator, to limit the interference of the electrical activity in the ignition system. Interference can also come from electric clocks and windscreen wiper motors.

The Battery.
This is the heart of the electrical system. The only maintenance we've considered for it up to now is its cleanliness, the tightness of its connections and its state of charge as measured by the hydrometer.

Occasionally the battery may go so flat that you need to give it an external charge from a battery charger. You can get hold of one of these in any motor accessory shop, but make sure that if you own one of the increasingly rare cars fitted with a 6 volt battery, that the charger you use is suitable for it.

You may need to take the battery off the car to charge it, so make sure when you put it back that you get the terminals connected the right way round (the battery terminal posts are marked + and − and there should be a corresponding marking on the connectors) or else you're liable to do expensive damage to the alternator or the radio.

If the battery is running flat persistently, or is difficult to recharge on an external charger, then it may be past its useful life; get your local garage to put a high rate discharge tester on it. If it can't be saved and you have to replace it you might buy one from the service station and they'll probably fill it and give it the initial charge for you. If you buy a battery from an accessory shop it's likely to be *dry-charged*; the battery comes in a box with several bottles of battery acid. You have to break the seals on the acid bottles, taking a great deal of care not to hurl the stuff around. The battery can be used immediately after it's been filled, but the battery manufacturer is likely to recommend a short period on the charger to bring it up to full capacity.

If you're charging your battery on the car, don't run the engine at the same time, and disconnect the terminals if the car is fitted with an alternator. If the battery is going to be out of use for some time, fully charge it before storing it, and give it a freshening charge once a month.

Cut-out and voltage control units — which regulate the way that the battery is charged by the generator — are adjustable and their contacts can be cleaned, but maintenance of these devices is best left to an auto-electrician, to whom you should go if you suspect the charging system of failure. Workshop manuals generally describe the testing and adjustment of regulators in fairly chatty terms, but you really need both an accurate tachometer (rev. counter) and a voltmeter to do a proper job.

Generator.
Dynamos are being increasingly superseded by *alternators,* which are able to provide a charge to the battery at much lower engine speeds and can supply twice the current of an a.c. dynamo of similar size. Alternators are not amenable to home maintenance, and checking the fan belt tension regularly is all the servicing they need. If you need to replace an alternator, compare prices of exchange units with your local auto-electrician as well as with the agent for the motor car. You may well find that the former will get you a better deal.

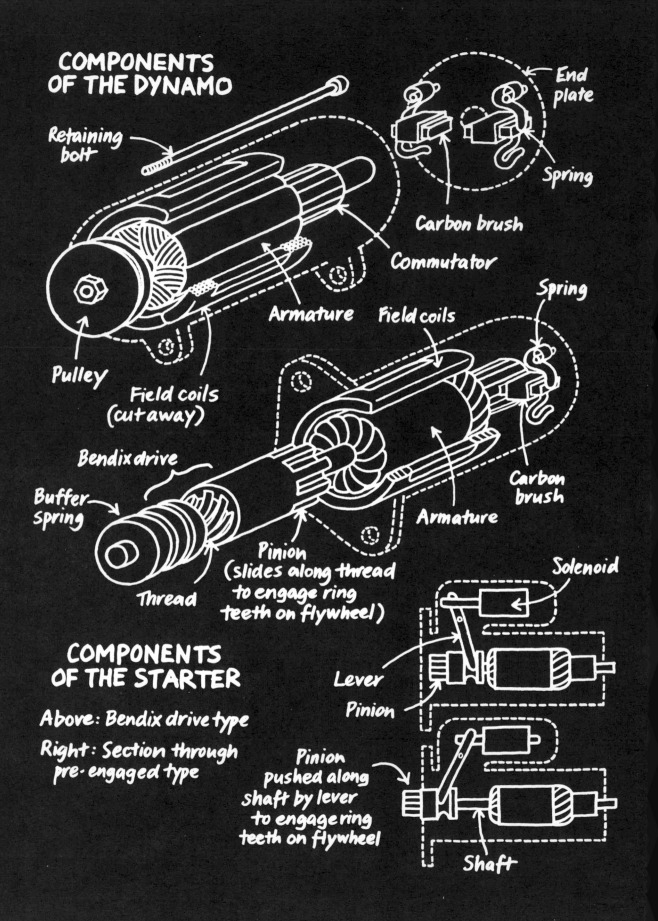

COMPONENTS OF THE DYNAMO

Retaining bolt

End plate

Spring

Carbon brush

Commutator

Armature

Field coils

Pulley

Field coils (cut away)

Spring

Bendix drive

Buffer spring

Carbon brush

Armature

Thread

Pinion
(slides along thread
to engage ring
teeth on flywheel)

COMPONENTS OF THE STARTER

Above: Bendix drive type

Right: Section through pre-engaged type

Solenoid

Lever

Pinion

Pinion pushed along shaft by lever to engage ring teeth on flywheel

Shaft

If the method of generating electricity on your car is by a *dynamo*, check it at 12,000 mile intervals, oiling the rear bearing through the oil-hole provided, and squinting through the rear end-plate slots while the engine is running at around 3,000 r.p.m. to check for excessive sparking. If the dynamo is putting on such a display, then take it off the car, undo the two long bolts passing from the front end-bracket of the device to the back, and remove the back bracket. This will come away complete with the brush gear. You can then clean the commutator, which is the copper ring at the rear of the armature, with a petrol soaked cloth. With a broken piece of hacksaw blade, scrape gently at the insulators between each commutator strip to ensure that they remain slightly below the level of the commutator surface. If the brushes are worn down to ¼" or so, replace them with new ones. Deal with one brush at a time, pulling back the spring clip with a screwdriver, undoing the terminal screw of the brush lead and lifting it out. Replace the brushes exactly as they were assembled. You'll find, when it comes to sliding the end bracket back on to the commutator, that the brushes will hit it and frustrate your efforts. The trick is to wedge the end of the spring against the side of each brush holder as you assemble the dynamo, then flip the springs back over the brushes with a small screwdriver when everything is back in place.

If you're fitting an exchange dynamo, and for popular units these are extremely cheap, you will have to polarize it according to the earthing arrangements on your car. Fit the dynamo to the engine and find the 'F' terminal on the regulator box. Disconnect the wire from this terminal and touch it momentarily on the 'A' or 'B' outlet of the control box — this will polarize the dynamo correctly.

Starters.

Starter motors are built pretty much like dynamos, but work in the opposite manner — that is, a current fed to the starter makes it spin round, whereas the dynamo is induced to spin round by the engine and the fan belt to actually *produce* a current. Sluggish operation of the starter (which may be too slow to permit the engine to fire), isn't a frequent fault on motor cars. It's almost always due to a bad connection at the battery, or the earth strap on the engine and rarely to an internal fault. If you're sticking to the routine of regularly cleaning the battery terminals, then you shouldn't be caught out this way, but occasionally the contacts in the starter solenoid switch may become troublesome. You can test this by shorting out the solenoid terminals; if the starter now spins normally, the solenoid was at fault.

If a bit of judicious circuit testing and cleaning of connections isolates the trouble in the starter motor itself, you'll need to remove it from the engine. It's normally secured by two or three bolts, passing through the clutch bell housing and you'll have to disconnect the main battery cable, and the wire that feeds the solenoid if this is mounted on the starter.

The engine's flywheel has a ring of teeth around it and the starter motor has a pinion threaded on to the armature shaft which engages with the flywheel teeth and cranks the engine round. But we don't want the starter to be hitched to the engine once the latter actually starts running or it will revolve so fast that it damages itself. The drive gear of the starter will be either of the inertia engaged type or the pre-engaged type. On the inertia-engaged starter, the pinion slides down on a screwed sleeve when the motor is operated, engages with the flywheel, and then slides back again once the engine is running faster than the starter. Pre-engaged starters are more positively located, a lever being moved by a solenoid on top of the motor, pushing the pinion into mesh with the flywheel and disengaging it as soon as the starter key is released.

If the pinion and sleeve are very dirty and this has been making the starter stick, clean them up with petrol but don't oil them or they'll go on sticking. If the teeth on the pinion are very mangled, replace the pinion; but the same effect is likely to have damaged the flywheel ring gear too and replacing this is a much more extensive dismantling job. Examine the commutator as you did for the dynamo — it should be clean and free of burning or pit-marks. Examine the bearings at both ends of the starter. If the armature shaft is sloppy in its bearings then the spinning part of the motor may be able to short on to the field coils inside the casing and make the motor turn slowly, or not at all. Bearings can be repaired by an auto-electrician, as can any other damage to the instrument. If you need to replace the brushes, you'll have to break out the soldering iron, since the pigtail leads of the brushes are connected direct to the field coils. On a starter with copper tags on the coils, simply unsolder the old brushes, clean up the tags and attach the new ones; you'll find multicore solder most convenient to use. If the starter has aluminium alloy strips to the field coils cut the old pigtails off but leave ½ inch or so still attached to them; solder the new brushes on to these, and wrap the joint with insulating tape so that it doesn't short on to the starter casing.

Lamps.

You don't have to do much about lamps except to ensure that the rubber seals are keeping rainwater from rusting the reflectors, and replace blown bulbs. The only catch is figuring out how to remove the lamp glass. If it's a headlamp, you generally only have to detach the chrome surround, which is usually secured by a single screw, and then turn the lamp slightly so that it frees itself from the spring-loaded retaining screws. Once you've withdrawn it from its housing, you turn and withdraw the backshell rather as if you were releasing an ordinary domestic lightbulb from its socket — the bulb will then slip out of the main light unit. Make sure that you replace it with one of an identical type. Side-lights and indicator lights may be removed by twisting and withdrawing the plastic lampglass or undoing the Phillips screws that hold it to the body of the lamp. Many modern headlamps don't have a replaceable bulb but are of the sealed beam type; the lamp is one big bulb, gas filled, with the elements inside. If it fails you have to replace the whole thing.

Headlamp Alignment.

One of the requirements of the M.O.T. test is that the headlamps should be correctly aligned. On full beam, the lamps are supposed to shine parallel to the road surface and straight ahead of the car. Garages use various jigs to check this, but you can get a reasonable idea from shining the lights at a wall. With the tyres at the proper pressure, and the car free of unusual loads that might alter its ride height, park on level ground 25 feet away from a wall; on main beam the centres of the bright spots of the illumination should be at the same heights as the centres of the headlamps from the ground and the same distance apart.

The headlamp will generally have three adjuster screws. You screw the top one in or out to vary the height of the beam, and the other two to swing it to the right or the left. They're accessible once the chrome surround is removed.

Indicators.

If the dashboard warning light of the indicator system fails but the lamps themselves keep working, then the warning light bulb has probably blown. If the timing of the flashes changes, or the lamps stay on continually and don't flash, then the flasher unit is almost certainly to blame; the only effective test is to substitute one you know to be in good condition.

Fitting Extra Lamps.

There are various regulations governing extra lights for cars. If two auxiliary fog lamps are used, they may be used instead of the headlamps. If one fog lamp is used, it may be used in addition to the headlamps. NOTE: It is illegal to connect rear fog lamps to operate in conjunction with the brake lamps. The main stipulation is that you should fit two of whatever kind of lamp you opt for — and both should be fitted at the same height off the ground, between 2 ft and 3½ ft. Get the lamps securely mounted, adjust their beam settings according to the instructions and make sure that the black earth lead is securely fastened to the body-work and the live cable to the switch is taken from a distribution point in the wiring harness rather than straight off the battery, which many owners are inclined to do. Use rubber grommets to protect any new leads where they pass through holes

in the bodywork, and use 14/.010 cable for new lighting circuits. Take the feed wire to the switch off the lighting circuit's existing fuse terminal, off the existing lighting switch itself, or plugged into the sidelamp circuit with a snap connector.

When you fit accessories, get an assortment of the necessary odds and ends before you start work: terminal tags, insulating sleeves, cable of the right thickness, grommets, insulating tape and some solder. Decide whether you want the accessory to be available when the ignition is turned off — which would be the case for clocks, interior lights, cigarette lighters, radios and so forth. Now you know how to read your car's wiring diagram it shouldn't be difficult to discover a variety of points in the wiring where you could attach feed wires for accessories. Sometimes the car manufacturer has left a spare terminal on the ignition switch or the lighting switch for extras, sometimes you have to use a bit of ingenuity. Use a circuit protected by a fuse where possible, or take the wire direct to the fusebox. Some of the fuseways will function only with the ignition on, others with it on or off. Check which is which with the wiring diagram. Don't forget to fit a dash-board indicator light with your new lamps, though this will often be part of the kit.

Connectors within the wiring loom are either spade terminals or bullet snap-connectors — you can generally crimp the bare wire into the spade connector with pliers, but you would need to solder it into the bullet connector. Always protect the joint with an insulating sleeve of rubber or plastic or it may touch the bodywork and short out.

Advanced Engine Testing.

Undoubtedly a careful owner can keep an engine in quite a reasonable state of tune without investing in all kinds of sophisticated testing equipment. It boils down to how much of a premium you put on your spare time. If you're a placid and patient tinkerer, happy to spend half a day trying to locate the fault that an instrument might have pinpointed within minutes, then maybe you'd want to leave things as they are. But there's no doubt that the use of instruments — particularly now that their availability and cheapness on the do-it-yourself market has changed out of all recognition within the past couple of years — not only brings accuracy and reliability to the job, it also fosters a different attitude on the part of the mechanic. Instruments give you confidence, all those neatly inscribed dials and flickering pointers foster the impression that you actually know what you're doing. I think that the reason is that it breaks the barrier between you and the machine. You stand there, scratching your head and feeling at a loss while the machine clacks and grumbles and shakes and puffs and somehow — unless you just naturally feel at home with machinery anyway — it seems to be living in a different and malevolent world and all that racket is its way of laughing at you. The instrument is a lifeline. Suddenly you can see all that clacking and grumbling reduced to a measurement or the behaviour of a needle. It's a great morale booster.

Experience tends to show that engine troubles rarely develop one at a time, particularly if the car hasn't been thoroughly serviced and maintained. In some cases only instruments can separate the causes and stop you from floundering about in the dark. Remember too, that, though you might be able to bring common sense, application and dexterity to the job, you're unlikely to be bringing experience to it or you wouldn't be reading this book. Instruments are not a substitute for experience but they can minimize the disadvantages of a shortage of it. A busy mechanic might be able to tell you that that misfire isn't the ignition trouble you've spent a weekend trying to fix, but uneven compression caused by a burning exhaust valve or a leaky head gasket; never having had to distinguish these problems

before, you might eventually conclude that the compression tester, which will reveal cylinder trouble in minutes, is the only sensible way out of the dilemma.

To get a real grip on the vagaries of the motor car and stop it from dictating to you, you need to have a systematic testing procedure which you *never* vary, and which you perform as often as you perform a major service (see p. 145). You should also adopt it when the engine develops an operating fault. It might all seem like a lot of fuss and bother for nothing, but unless the fault really is a blindingly obvious one — like a disconnected ignition lead, or a broken fuel line — it's as well to be sure that the trouble hasn't come mob-handed. Professionals in tuning stations, who have a reputation to protect, will never pass the car back to the customer just because a new set of plugs and ignition leads seems to have corrected a loss of performance. If the punter later discovers that the performance is improved but still leaves something to be desired, it's decidedly bad business for the tuner to finally discover that the ignition advance is stuck or the vacuum unit leaking. Late may be better than never, but it might well be too late to save that particular customer's business.

The other important bit of self-discipline is that you restrict yourself to a thorough reconnaissance before you start tinkering with the clockwork. If you readjust everything adjustable before you're sure what the fault is, you may only bury the problem deeper than ever. You wouldn't thank a doctor who amputated your leg for an ingrowing toenail, so make sure you collect as much information together about the existing state of tune of your engine, running badly or not, before you set about correcting it. List the tests on a piece of paper and mark your observations down, then you won't feel tempted to go through the whole lot again if you get distracted halfway through to watch the 3.30 at Chepstow, change the baby's nappy, or snatch that 'swift half'.

Firstly, to deal with the instruments that will provide you with all this useful information. Top of the list, because ignition timing and checking the behaviour of the advance and retard mechanism really can't be tackled without it, we put the *ignition timing light.* This is simply a neon bulb (neon bulbs don't explode if you put very high voltages through them) in a plastic handle which you wire in series with the Number One sparking plug; in other words, one of the instrument's leads slots into the spark-plug cover, the other clips on to the plug itself. The effect is that every time the plug fires, the lamp flashes — with the engine ticking over, these flashes will be so close to each other as to produce a stroboscopic effect. Remembering the ground we covered in Ch. 1 about how the distributor, crankshaft and valve gear were synchronized so that the spark would always turn up at the right point in the operating cycle, it's clear that the spark in our Number One cylinder and consequently the flash in our timing light is going to happen when the crankshaft is in exactly the same position every two revs of the engine. So if you made an identifying mark on something rotating with the crankshaft — such as the fan pulley at the front, or the flywheel at the back — and a corresponding mark on the carcase of the engine in this position, the two marks would line up every time the Number One cylinder fired. And as the ignition progressively advanced itself with an increase in engine speed, the two marks would move slightly apart from each other, since the spark would be occurring at a different relative position of the crankshaft.

Now, since at idling speed the crankshaft is still whizzing round at 800 r.p.m. or more, these marks wouldn't be a great deal of use for anything on their own. But if we could examine the relationship between the two pointers in a dim light, with a lamp that would only come on when the plug itself was firing and go out again while the other cylinders were going about their business, then the effect would be that we could only see the two pointers at the instant when they were supposed to be in line, and they'd be in the dark at all other positions of the crankshaft. This is a very slow motion way of considering it of course, but the stroboscopic effect of the timing light does exactly this; it makes the rapidly rotating crankshaft pulley or flywheel rim appear to be stationary because it only illuminates it at one precise instant in its travels. So we wire up the timing light to the Number One plug, run the engine at the manufacturer's recommended idling speed, shine the light on the timing marks and check that they line up. If they don't, we slacken the clamp bolt on the base of the distributor, and slightly turn it one way or the other until they do line up. The workshop manual will specify whether the timing marks are on the fan pulley of the engine, or on the flywheel rim; in the latter case, a small observation plate generally has to be moved aside on the clutch housing to get a look at the marks. Timing lights come in a cheap

version and a luxurious version. The latter is a Xenon tube which provides a much more intense flash so that you can even use it in broad daylight; but it's more of a service station instrument, and perfectly serviceable neon lights can be found in the accessory shops for a few pounds.

Next on the list of useful gadgets is an *electrical test-meter,* and these are now marketed in a handy combination form with several scales on one dial providing a variety of information about the ignition and electrical systems. You will find that many of these units will combine a voltmeter, revolution counter or tachometer, and a dwell meter — the last being an instrument that instantly tells you whether the contact breaker gap is correct or not without all that pushing and pulling the car in gear and waving feeler gauges around.

Then comes the *compression tester,* an invaluable device for providing you with advance warning about valve failure, and the state of wear in the top half of your engine generally. Compression testers that are best suited to the home mechanic working alone are unfortunately the most expensive ones, but you can get away with a cheaper model if you can enlist a bit of assistance while actually making the test. The principle on which the gauge works is straightforward enough, very similar to what happens when you take a pressure reading on your tyres. If one tyre is leaking, the pressure in it will be low. If your engine is suffering from loose pistons, broken piston rings, leaky valves, worn valve guides or a blowing cylinder-head gasket, the pressure produced in the combustion chamber while the piston is rising on the compression stroke will naturally be a lot less than it would be if the chamber were virtually airtight. The compression tester is simply an air pressure gauge that reads up to 200 lb./sq. in. or so, and you fit it to each plug hole in turn and crank the engine over on the starter with the ignition harness disconnected so that the car doesn't start. A tester that enables you to do the job all by yourself, such as the Hawk model, has a plug thread on the end of the air-line so that it can simply be screwed in place of the plug. Cheaper models simply have a rubber bung which you press into the plug hole, and then somebody else has to operate the starter while you keep the gauge from going into orbit in response to the pressure in the cylinder. Halford's sell a cheap combination tyre and compression gauge which gives a more approximate reading but is useful as a rough guide to engine condition. A last but important consideration about compression gauges is whether or not your engine is so awkwardly designed that the gauge you've bought can't be used on it. Some gauges are of a rigid construction, OK for conventional engine designs but difficult to use on something like a Volkswagen or a Porsche where the cylinder heads are low down and parallel with the wheels. The

174

compression tester with a flexible hose is vital on cars such as these.

The instruments we're considering up to now would certainly provide you with a thoroughly professional insight into your engine's metabolism, and unless you've found yourself to be especially hooked on the whole business you could easily halt the liquidity crisis at this point. Whether or not you add the *vacuum gauge* to your arsenal is really a matter of personal preference; I happen to be one of those converts who has found the thing indispensable having used it once. Once you've gone through the admittedly slightly laborious business of fitting one, you find that it's *instantly* sensitive to the condition of the engine and its state of tune; you can adjust carburettor mixture and ignition timing with it, you can spot air leaks, choked exhausts and air cleaners, broken valve springs, and pick up valuable clues about all kinds of mysterious faults that seem to defy detection.

The principle the vacuum gauge works on takes us back to all that stuff about the way that the fuel is sucked through the carburettor by the action of the reciprocating pistons. Take the condition of the idling engine, with the throttle plate almost shut. The idle is the lowest speed at which the engine will run smoothly having overcome the deadweight of its own moving parts, the friction in the bearings and the bores, and the compression resistance in the combustion chambers. All these factors combine to try and stop the internal combustion engine until it has worked up enough momentum to overpower them. We know that if we open the throttle further to admit more air, more fuel is pulled through the carburettor and the engine speed rises. We also know that the power developed by the engine – its capacity to overcome resistance and provide effective leverage or torque – is not at all the same thing as its speed. So to get the maximum power from the engine at idling speed, the fuel needs to be burned in the most efficient manner possible, which means accurate carburettor and ignition tuning. If the tuning's wrong the power is reduced, and instead of a nice smooth tickover the engine will give up under the strain of the friction and pumping losses, and stumble to a halt. To keep it running despite the bad state of tune, we'd need to open the throttle wider. This wouldn't increase the speed, the engine would simply need to be burning more fuel to handle the same job. If we could measure the amount of air in the induction manifold of the same engine under both these conditions – good tune and poor tune – we'd find that there'd be more of it for the same idling speed in the latter case than in the former.

Well, the vacuum gauge is our method of measuring that amount of air. Or rather, it's our method of measuring the degree of suction on the induction side of the engine, and it registers a result in inches of mercury on a dial. Supplied with every vacuum gauge is a full set of diagnoses suggested by different vacuum readings at various engine speeds. Considering the usefulness of the instrument in terms of providing a quick overall 'screening' of the condition of the engine and its running efficiency, the only obstacle to the use of the vacuum gauge (it certainly isn't price – gauges are simple instruments and fairly cheap) is the relative inconvenience of fitting it. Gauges are provided with an adaptor that's generally threaded to the 2 B.A. specification; the gauge has of course to be fitted to the inlet manifold, preferably somewhere centrally. This means removing the carburettor and inlet manifold from the engine, threading a hole in the manifold with 2 B.A. taper and plug taps and a suitably sized twist drill, then putting the whole lot back together to make the test. If you expect to keep your car for some time, then of course the effort expended on fitting the vacuum adapter will repay itself every time you do a tune-up. When the gauge isn't in use, you simply plug the hole in the manifold with a suitably shortened 2 B.A. screw. The vacuum gauge marketed by Smith's is intended for permanent fitting to the car's dashboard.

Vacuum gauges offer a subsidiary advantage into the bargain, because they invariably incorporate a pressure scale as well – a low one, running up to 6 or 8 lb./sq. in. This scale is used for measuring the output pressure of the car's fuel pump, and the gauge can be used to measure its suction as well. A combination of both sets of readings can keep you posted about impending valve or diaphragm trouble in the pump. This is useful news to have, since fuel pump failure isn't terribly amenable to those Old Indian Tricks that get you home in an emergency.

So that's more or less the works when it comes to tuning instruments; and compared to the costs of garage servicing and tuning at upwards of £7.00 an hour, you might find that they would fairly rapidly earn their keep if you expected to keep up the enthusiasm for home motor maintenance over a period of a few years. The Hawk accessories company market a boxed set including their compression tester, timing light and a combined vacuum and fuel pump gauge, and if you added an electrical test meter you'd be well set and not broke. (You could of course pool the instruments with other foolhardy locals of the same persuasion.) Quite apart from saving some hard-earned cash by doing your own tuning, the satisfaction of cracking a really elusive problem by a combination of native wit and good equipment is a genuine delight. And probably more so if your normal line of work lies in quite a different direction.

Testing Procedure.

Let's go back to where we came in, trying to establish a reliable and illuminating test procedure that will flush out even the most crafty and obstinate of engine ailments. Start by taking the car for a run – unless the power failure is so severe that you don't dare risk it in traffic. Don't dawdle too much, and get the engine up to its normal operating temperature, usually revealed by the temperature gauge needle settling in a central position.

Test 1.

Examination Of Plugs.

Remove all the plugs from the head and lay them out in the order you found them in. Check first of all that the plug type as inscribed on the insulator is one of the range specified by the manufacturer for your engine. Then make a note of the information provided by the state of the plug tips.

(a) If the side electrode is clean and dry but appears to be a bleached off white colour, the mixture provided by the carburettor may be too weak. This verdict would be supported if the engine was inclined to an unsteady or 'splashy' exhaust beat at idling speed.

(b) If the side electrode is clean and dry and shaded anything from a biscuity-fawn to grey or light brown, you can take this to be an indication of a reasonably accurate carburettor setting.

(c) If the side electrode is covered with a fluffy black soot, it's an indication that the carburettor setting is rich, this would be supported by a rhythmical misfire and black smoke from the exhaust at idle.

(d) If the plug is oiled up, it's no help to you as a guide to mixture setting. Oil is clearly getting into the combustion chamber somehow, either as a result of worn piston rings and bores, or worn valve guides or both.

(e) If one plug appears clean but a dull grey in colour while all the others look normal, it may be that this particular plug isn't firing at all. Often a dud plug will be wet with petrol.

While you're at it, inspect the plugs for general wear and damage. Hold them up to the light, and see if the inner surface of the side electrode is worn away where the spark jumps from the central conductor. If the electrodes are generally damaged or eroded it may be that the plugs have simply been in the engine for too long, or that something's over-heating in the cylinder head.

While the plugs are out, we can now go on to:

Test 2.

Compression.

Before you embark on this, read the instructions provided with your particular compression tester, and have a glance through all those unnerving facts and figures in the engine specification data of the works manual to see if there's a normal compression figure suggested by the manufacturer. If there isn't, you can estimate one by a bit of elementary maths. A figure that always will be quoted, even in the driver's instruction book, will be the compression ratio for the particular engine. Atmospheric pressure at sea level is around 14.7 lb./sq. in., and 14 or so at 1,000 feet above. You can get a good working compression figure by multiplying the compression ratio by 14 and adding another 14 to the result. Say the compression ratio was quoted as 8.1, then the normal compression would be: (14 x 8) + 14 which is 126 lb./sq. in.

Armed with this information, we then fit the compression gauge to the first plug hole. Make sure that you haven't spent so much time pondering on instruction books and compression ratios and figuring out which end of the tester is which that the engine has gone stone cold. Compression tests should only be made with the engine at normal operating temperature and all the metal parts fully expanded.

With the gauge fitted and the ignition dead (it's best to disconnect the coil CB terminal rather than risk damage to the coil by letting it swallow the spark that can't run to earth anywhere else) crank the engine over on the starter, ensuring that the throttle is propped wide open. With all the other plugs out, you'll hear a steady beat every time the tested cylinder hits its compression stroke, and you count eight of these and then stop the test. Make a note of the reading on the gauge, operate the valve to return the needle to zero, and go through the whole performance at each plug hole.

The results you've obtained from this series of tests are known as the 'dry compression' figures. You then run through it again with a tablespoon of oil squirted into each cylinder with the aid of a syringe, or a squeegee bottle or something similar. Don't add the oil to all cylinders at once but one at a time, followed by the compression test. Note the results alongside the first set.

Why all this rigmarole with oil? The answer is that a compression reading is always ambiguous as it stands. If the reading on a particular cylinder is a great deal lower than the normal figure suggests it ought to be, or a great deal lower than the other readings on the engine, then we know there's a compression leakage right enough – but is it the cylinders or the valves that are to blame?

Let's say there's a broken piston ring (see p. 11) in one of the cylinders. This would suggest itself by a dry compression reading that might be 20 or 30 lbs below the rest. We still wouldn't know for sure that the drop wasn't being caused by a leaky valve, so the addition of oil to the cylinder provides a temporary seal and briefly blocks the leakage past the ring. So when we performed our 'wet' tests, all the readings would appear to be back to normal. This would be pretty conclusive evidence of a damaged ring or bore.

But if the pistons were all right but a valve was on the blink, naturally the addition of oil wouldn't result in any improvement. In this case, there would be a low reading on one cylinder through both sets of tests.

Don't worry too much if the compression readings aren't spot on the manufacturer's specification or the rough figure you obtained from the formula. Differences of 10 lb./sq. in. or so are perfectly acceptable. Only differences of 20 lb./sq. in. or more are a strong indication of trouble, but check the tappet clearances before you fear the worst.

There are a few straggling details to be watched when you test an engine's compression, and generally the gauge manufacturer warns you of them in his instruction sheet. In the first place, if the engine design is such that the pistons aren't upright — such as in horizontally inclined engines like VWs, and some steeply canted Vee-engines — there's no point in performing the wet test at all because all the oil will slide to one side of the combustion chamber. The same applies to side-valve engines, not that there are many of them to be found these days. It's also worth noting that the compression reading with the throttle wide open will be higher than if it's left shut; Hawk recommend propping the throttle fully open with a piece of wood whilst testing with their instruments.

The tester may give you other kinds of results than the most familiar one of a single reading out of step with all the rest. The compressions may be generally low if the engine is old or has covered a high mileage, but you'd get other signs of that such as poor acceleration, high oil consumption and a smoky exhaust. Two low readings on adjacent cylinders would suggest that either two valves are on the way out, or that the cylinder head gasket is leaking between the two cylinders. Very low overall readings on a newish engine suggest valve timing that has slipped out of adjustment through damage or failure of the valve operating chain or belt. Overall low pressures would not be caused by gasket failure or warped head — those would show up on one or two cylinders only.

If you don't have a compression tester, you can't provide anything as comprehensive as this information in any other way, though it's possible to get some sort of a rough idea as to whether all the cylinders are pulling their weight. If the engine has a starting handle you're laughing; though this invaluable device has all but gone out of fashion on the sleek and sophisticated modern family car. With the starting handle, and replacing the sparking plug in each cylinder in turn, you should feel a definite resistance as you pull the engine against the compression. A very weak cylinder will feel decidedly slack.

The electrical test meter will provide some of the same information if it's fitted with an accurate low-reading rev counter with a range something like 0–1,500 r.p.m. You connect the instrument up

according to the instructions, set up a fast idle of something like 1,200 r.p.m., then disconnect each plug lead in turn with a rubber glove. The rev counter will show a definite drop as the engine starts running on three cylinders; the drop may well be something like 200 r.p.m. If it only drops fractionally, or not at all, then something is clearly amiss in the cylinder that isn't contributing much to the proceedings. It might of course be merely a dud plug or a faulty ignition lead or cap, and you'd need to establish that by substitution before you went on to blame the engine, but at least it would be a clue. If the car has an electric rev counter fitted as standard, you could get an assistant to check the behaviour of it while you short out the plugs, though it wouldn't be as accurate as a specialized instrument.

And if you don't have any of this tackle at all, you can of course simply use your ears. If the engine shows a definite drop in idling speed when you disconnect the leads on the good cylinders but less of a drop on one in particular, then that cylinder needs investigation — first for an ignition failure, and then for a mechanical fault. At this point you could always borrow a compression gauge, or run the car round to the garage for a second opinion.

If you don't have the compression gauge or the rev counter but you or a previous owner has fitted the engine with a vacuum gauge adapter, then you can perform exactly the same test. The only difference is that you're looking for an unequal drop in the vacuum reading when you short out the bad cylinder. Good cylinders will show a drop of 1½ – 2 inches of mercury for a four cylinder engine, ¾ – 1½ for a six, ¼ – ¾ for an eight. If the drop is minimal or there isn't one at all, check the spark in that cylinder and if it's OK, blame trouble in the valves or pistons, or possibly a very badly adjusted tappet clearance.

Test 3.
Vacuum Reading.

The vacuum test is slipped in at this point because we happen to have digressed on to the subject, but skip it if you don't feel like going to the trouble of fitting the instrument. (If it's the trauma of actually drilling holes in bits of your engine that holds you back, then you could always remove the inlet manifold and take it round to the local garage, or a light engineering firm, or a practical friend to get the threaded adapter fitted. The only thing you need to be careful about is using the right size twist drill for a 2 B.A. tap, and not letting it shake about so much that it drills an oversize or elongated hole.)

With the gauge fitted, you can then run through all the tests suggested by the instrument manufacturer's literature; they can all be worked through and the results noted in minutes. The vacuum reading at idling speed with the engine warm ought to be between 18 and 22 inches and the needle should be fairly steady. A few sporty engines with greatly overlapped valve timing (in other words with the inlet and exhaust valves spending a greater part of the cycle both open at the same time) will always give a lower vacuum reading, but it will never be lower than 15 if the engine is in good condition.

Don't attempt to tune the engine to alter the vacuum reading at this stage, merely note the results. Accelerate the engine smartly and hold it at around half its maximum revs. The reading should fall by 5 inches or more, then rise again. If it falls slowly, the air cleaner may be choked. Then accelerate the engine sharply to the same speed again, and snap the throttle shut. The needle should fall abruptly, then rise quickly again to the normal reading or above it. If the fall is slow on sharp acceleration, and the rise to normal is equally sluggish, the inference is a choked exhaust pipe setting up a lot of backpressure in the engine's breathing. Accelerate the engine hard up to near peak revs, then abruptly close the throttle again. If the reading falls rapidly to near zero, then climbs up to 3 to 7 inches above the normal reading momentarily, the engine is sound. If the needle falls OK, but returns to normal sluggishly, the inference is worn valves, rings or bores. A lot of fluttering of the needle at very high revs suggests faulty valve springs. Kicking of the needle at low revs indicates ignition trouble, and a weaving needle at a slightly low vacuum reading suggests faults in the carburation.

If you have a vacuum gauge, it's sensible to perform a cranking test at this stage — you simply close off the throttle butterfly completely and close the carburettor by-pass screw if there is one, then crank the engine around a few times on the starter with the ignition disconnected. The reading ought to be somewhere between 12 and 18 inches. If it's very low (less than 8), then there's probably an air leak into the induction manifold somewhere; if the leak is severe, you'll probably have found it impossible to tune the carburettors properly or get the engine to run steadily at anything other than a fast idle. Air leaks might be through worn spindles in the carburettors themselves, or damaged gaskets, or worn valve guides — or in an old engine, a combination of the lot.

One last tiresome repeat; when you do a vacuum test, make sure the engine is hot. Readings from a lukewarm or cold engine will tell you nothing worth knowing.

Test 4.
Battery & Starter.

Generally people only start worrying about battery problems when it cranks the engine over too slowly to start the car at all. But a faulty battery might start to affect engine performance, particularly at high speed, long before it starts putting out its most obvious symptoms of ill health.

Examine each battery cell with the hydrometer and make a note of the readings. The colour-bands on the float will tell you the state of charge of the battery, and all the cell readings should be more or less the same; if there are big differences between one cell and another it's an ominous sign and the battery should be checked over by a specialist.

If you have the electrical test meter, set it to the voltage scale (on the range 0—15 or 0—20 volts) and measure the voltage across the battery terminals. For a fully charged 12 volt battery, the reading will be slightly higher than the rating, and may even be as high as 14.

If the battery is all right, now we need to know if this healthy voltage is able to get where it ought to go without flagging. Connect the voltmeter between the SW or + terminal of the coil and earth — which can either be a clean bit of the car's metalwork or the earth terminal of the battery. With the ignition switch on, the voltage here ought to be virtually the same as the reading you got from the battery itself. If it drops by more than half a volt there may be a dirty connection somewhere in the control box, main feed or ignition switch, and you should check out all these terminals, clean and re-secure them.

Now check the voltage drop with the starter in operation. Make sure that you get the leads of the test meter connected the right way round depending on whether the car has a negative or positive earthing system. If it's the former, you connect the negative lead from the instrument to the chassis or the battery earth, and the positive lead to the main starter terminal. This is the big nut on the back end of the starter that's insulated from the rest of the motor. Disconnect the ignition by removing the low-voltage supply to the coil so that the engine doesn't fire and operate the starter for ten seconds or so. On a 12 volt system, the meter reading shouldn't drop below 9. If it does, the car would be very likely to be a bad starter in any case, because the current swallowed by the starter itself would be leaving very little over for the coil to provide a suitably hot spark. Check all the electrical connections as described in the earlier Breakdowns section. If you can't improve the reading by cleaning and tightening, then either the battery or the starter needs some close examination, preferably by an auto-electrical specialist. And if there's nothing wrong with them, then there must be some abnormal stiffness in the engine itself, which you can doublecheck by pushing the car in top gear.

Test 5.
Fuel System.

First the S.U. electric fuel pump: early Minis and the like used to carry their petrol pumps under the rear sub-frame where they were exceptionally difficult to service and prone to damage and rusting. Many cars stow the pump in the boot, somewhere near the tank. It's become a more common practice to locate the fuel pump on the bulkhead behind the engine — this kind of pump is designed to suck fuel from the tank, rather than push it, so the pressure ratings are different.

For the low-pressure type fitted close to the engine, you might expect a delivery rate of about a pint a minute. This is easily checked by disconnecting the feed pipe to the carburettors, suspending it in a clean pint bottle, and simply turning on the ignition. Check the flow against the second-hand of your wristwatch, or a stopwatch if you have one. If you can arrange it — possibly by pushing a flexible rubber or plastic extension on to the end of the pipe — get the flow to run with the pipe submerged in the bottle. If there are a lot of air bubbles coming in with the fuel, then you can note the possibility of an air leak somewhere in the supply system. If the rate of flow is really poor (say the pump sends up a pint in something like double the recommended time) try blowing down the supply line to the pump first and listening for bubbling noises in the tank. If there's a lot of resistance, the pipe may be kinked or blocked.

The high pressure S.U. pump, fitted at the tank end of the car should produce a faster delivery rate, something like a pint in three quarters of a minute.

If your car is fitted with a mechanical fuel pump, then testing becomes a bit more complicated since you'll need to crank the engine over to form an impression of its capabilities. It's better to perform this test with the plugs still out of the engine to reduce the compression load on the battery, and the latter needs to be in a reasonable state of charge. Crank the engine for 40 seconds, discharging the fuel into the bottle as before; the pump should supply at least a quarter pint of fuel.

If you have the vacuum gauge and it's fitted with a low-pressure section, then it's possible to take testing of the fuel supply a bit further. All our flow-rate tests tell us is whether the pump works or not; if not, the works manual will describe the overhaul procedure for the particular pump, or you might prefer to go straight to an agent to get an exchange unit. Make sure before you adopt this course that the problem wasn't something trivial in the first place. With the pressure-gauge attached to the outlet pipe, you can measure the pump pressure and compare it with the manufacturer's recommendation — which might be somewhere between ¾ lb./sq. in. and 3 lb./sq. in. You can also measure the suction on the input side of the pump, which ought to be between 6 and 10 inches of mercury. Attaching the gauge line to the pipes or pump unions can sometimes be a bit of a problem,

but if you equip yourself with a variety of rubber tubes of different bores you can generally establish a leakproof joint by forcing one over another.

Pressure and suction tests have to be performed with the engine running but since it only has to idle long enough for the needle to reach its maximum reading it will happily run on the fuel remaining in the float chamber. You switch the engine off when the readings no longer increase, and they should hold steady for at least ten seconds. A rapid drop indicates faulty valves in the pump or a leaky diaphragm. Check with the works manual for the appropriate course of action.

With the electric pump of course, you don't need to run the engine at all but simply turn the ignition on. *Don't* check that the pump feed wire is live by flashing the terminal to earth, always use the circuit tester or the voltmeter. Sparks and petrol vapour are apt to strike up sudden and temperamental relationships. Apart from all the usual ailments of valves and diaphragms that befall any kind of pump, electric pumps can fail because their contact breaker points get dirty or pitted, much like the contact breaker in the ignition system. Clean them up with the file or matchbox edge in exactly the same way.

Test 6.
Ignition System Electrics.

Though the tuning instrument firms market testers for examination of the coil and condenser, investing in them would be taking the whole operation so far that you might as well simply set yourself up as a tuning clinic and have done with it.

We've already established that the voltage at the SW terminal of the coil with the ignition on is more or less the voltage of the battery itself. We then disconnect the wire at the CB terminal and check the voltage at this point. If it's lower or non-existent, the primary windings of the coil are open-circuited, though this wouldn't have happened without a severe effect on the running of the engine having become apparent. Reconnect the CB terminal, open the points or slip a piece of card between them, and take a reading at the same place again. No reading would suggest a short in the points or condenser, but again this would already have caused a partial or total breakdown.

Close the points or remove the card if the CB reading was 12 volts on the last test. The reading should now immediately drop to zero. If it still gives a reading over 0.2v, then the points are dirty or burned, the lead between the distributor and the CB terminal is damaged, or possibly the distributor has a poor earth connection with the engine block.

Check the points by examination of the contact faces, and measure the gap when they're fully open with the feeler gauge. If your electrical test-meter has a 'dwell' scale, take a reading from that with the engine running as per the instructions provided with the instrument. Car manufacturers now supply a correct Dwell Angle with their ignition specification, and it's a much more accurate way of measuring the breaker gap than with a gauge. It might seem like so much blinding with science to be dragging in notions like Dwell Angle, but like most things on the motor car the truth is blissfully simple. The distributor spindle and its associated cam flips the points open four, six or eight times (depending on the number of cylinders in the engine) for every single revolution it makes itself. A single revolution describes an arc of 360 degrees, if you remember anything about first-form geometry. For a proportion of this arc the contact points will be open, for the remainder they'll be closed; on a four-cylinder engine you might expect the points to be closed for 60 degrees per cylinder, on a six-cylinder engine it might be something like 36 degrees. If the points were too far apart then the points would be closed for a smaller proportion of the circle, and if they were too close then they'd be shut for longer. This proportion of 360 degrees that the points are closed is called the *Dwell Angle*, and the dwell scale of a tachometer gives you a reading of it without even taking the cap off the distributor.

One way or the other, you form an impression of the condition and adjustment of the contact points in the course of this test, and make a note of them without interfering with the points or replacing them as yet. The patient may be writhing in agony, but we still need more evidence.

If the points appear to be faulty, then we can put this at the top of the list if one of the car's problems appears to have been weak sparking. If the points are all right, then perform the spark test we used in the Breakdowns section (see p. 103) by directing the high-tension lead from the centre of the coil to the distributor cap to earth and quickly flicking the points apart with the ignition on. If the spark is feeble and the low-tension circuit has been cleared, then we can suspect the high-voltage windings of the coil.

Very burned or pitted points, or points that are repeatedly prone to burning, indicate condenser trouble; and a fat white spark when the contact breaker is opened, instead of a barely perceptible one, supports that diagnosis. Bear it in mind for the tune-up, and clear the low-tension circuit by substitution of the points and condenser if you're in any doubt at all.

Lastly, examine the spark plug leads for perished insulation, oil, grease or moisture. Sometimes ageing high-tension leads will obstruct the spark with a very high resistance in the conductors, and sometimes too the insulation will break down to the point where the spark can hop from one lead to another and finish up in the wrong cylinder. This phenomenon, known as 'cross-fire', can be a

favourite where the leads are closely bound together, or tightly fitted through a tubular metal harness, and it can be a thoroughly elusive source of an intermittent high-speed miss. If you want to establish this for certain before you go out and invest in new leads, disconnect the harness and temporarily rig the leads with string so that they're kept well out of each other's way. If it cures the trouble then new leads and/or a better clipping arrangement is the answer.

Test 7.

Ignition System Timing & Advance Mechanism.

At this point we resort to the timing light, as described on p. 174. Since we're still trying to establish a full catalogue of the engine's habits and eccentricities before trying to improve it, the use of the timing light at this stage is mainly to establish the operation of the ignition advance mechanism. Checking the timing itself before overhauling the distributor components and servicing the plugs isn't a particularly reliable test but it will tell us if the timing is wildly out; this normally wouldn't happen unless someone had already removed the distributor and replaced it in the wrong position.

Find the timing marks by following the directions in the works or instruction manual. Brighten them up by cleaning off any accumulated muck and grease and painting both indicators with white paint — make it a narrow mark with a fine brush rather than a massive blob which will only confuse things. Then connect the timing light between the Number One plug cover and the Number One plug. (This just happens to be the cylinder that's chosen in nine cases out of ten, but check with the manual that it isn't Number Four which is the alternative in some instances). Then get the engine hot and run it at the recommended idling speed for checking the timing, which will normally be around 850 r.p.m. Make a note of the relative positions of the two timing marks; sometimes there are several alternative marks on the 'fixed' pointer, giving different degrees of advance in relation to the crankshaft. Make sure you've marked the one the manufacturer uses as the base position.

To test the automatic advance, disconnect the vacuum line between the distributor and the carburettor if a vacuum advance is fitted to the car, and watch the timing marks as you rev the engine from as slow an idle as possible to whatever speed the centrifugal advance is supposed to be complete. As the speed increases, the two timing marks should move smoothly apart. If they move in jerks, don't move at all, or if the marks already seem to be too far apart and only move slightly further as you rev up, the centrifugal mechanism may be jammed, either in the fully retarded position, or halfway through the advance curve. In the latter case, the ignition would be too far advanced for most running conditions and you would probably notice it in a tendency for the engine to 'pink' — that is, to make a high-pitched, tinny rattle during acceleration.

Lack of experience can sometimes lead you slightly astray in making these tests because — just to make things awkward — the degree of ignition advance you can expect may be quite different in a car fitted with a vacuum unit from one that has a centrifugal mechanism alone. In the latter case, the device may cut in at around 500 r.p.m. and progressively advance the spark up to around 4,500 r.p.m. — the resulting movement of the timing mark on the flywheel or crankshaft pulley might be as much as 30 degrees, which could make the gap between the marks at full advance something like an inch and a half. Where vacuum and centrifugal advance are combined, and in an engine of different design, the centrifugal advance may stop at around 2,500 r.p.m. and only have shifted by 15 degrees or so — maybe half the distance. Beware of these snags, and get some idea of what to expect by studying the ignition specifications in the manual.

If the car has a vacuum advance, check its action by running the engine at 2,000 r.p.m. and noting the relative positions of the timing marks, then repeating the test at the same speed with the vacuum line disconnected. If there's no difference, the device is probably out of action. Occasionally the pipeline blocks or the distributor baseplate jams, but by far the most likely fault is a punctured diaphragm. You can test this with the unit in place by removing the pipeline from the sealed diaphragm unit, and rotating the distributor baseplate against the action of the diaphragm spring. Then wet your forefinger and close the pipeline hole with it; the baseplate will spring back, but only halfway if the unit is OK and will only return to its original position once you remove your finger. If the diaphragm is badly punctured, you can simply blow into the pipeline hole and you'll barely feel any pressure at all. Vacuum units are sealed and can't be repaired, so you have to get another from the agents for the particular vehicle or distributor. They might not look like much, but be warned that the prices of replacements are quite astonishing.

Test 8.
Carburettor Mixture.

Having examined the sparking plugs already, we've been able to collect some information about the ratio of fuel to air being burned by our particular engine. There are various other bits and pieces we can add to this. Listen to the exhaust note with the engine idling; if the engine has a rhythmic misfire that sounds like galloping horses (known appropriately as 'hunting') and there are signs of black smoke

appearing, then the mixture may well be too rich. If it runs irregularly, missing beats at intervals and the needle of an electric rev counter appears to weave up and down, then it may be too weak — the exhaust gas will be colourless and odourless. Rev the engine up sharply and establish whether it will speed up smoothly or with hesitation and misfiring; and if it misses, pull the choke out slightly and repeat the test. An improvement would be a definite indication of the engine running weak. In the case of S.U. carburettors you can go one step further in establishing the state of tune; the instruments are fitted with a lifting pin under the carburettor body and pressing it will slightly raise the piston assembly. Lift the piston by $\frac{1}{16}''$ or so (if the carb is at the back of the engine compartment, you'll have to remove the air cleaner and adapter to get a sight of the piston) and listen to the effect on the exhaust note. If the engine immediately falters, the carburettor is set too weak. If it increases speed rapidly, it is too rich. A slight slowing, followed by a return to the original idling speed, confirms that the carburettor setting is just about right.

Every manufacturer's instruction book provides you with information about how to set your carburettors up, and there's absolutely no reason why it can't be done by ear and common sense since that was good enough for generations of earlier mechanics. But now that cars built for the American market have started to incorporate very strict regulations about gas emission, you could possibly find yourself outside the law in a few years' time for adopting the craftsman's methods. Exhaust gas analysers, capable of measuring the chemical composition of the engine's waste products will be increasingly used for carburettor tuning — though the enterprising Hawk company have already put a portable analyser on the market at around £45. There are, however, much cheaper labour-saving devices available, and it's a variation on a principle that engine-builders and tuners have known about for years. In the early days, they used to tune the Rolls Royce aero engines by the colour of the exhaust flame, and in response to this a few pioneers made up sparking plugs with transparent quartz insulation so that you could see directly into the combustion chamber while the engine was actually running. Just lately Gunsons have picked up the idea again with a device they call the Colortune. It's simply a stunted sparking plug with a thick glass insulator; you substitute it for a normal plug, wire it to the plug lead and check the combustion colour with the engine hot. A white flame indicates a weak mixture, a bunsen-blue flame a normal mixture, an orange flame is over-rich. All you do is adjust the carburettor mixture control until the last of the orange flame disappears and the combustion is all blue. If adjustment doesn't help to get rid of the orange, then the mixture is rich for some other reason, such as a faulty float chamber; if you can't get rid of the white flame or a weak mixture, then there must be air leaks into the induction system somewhere and you can't tune the carburettors until the mechanical problem is solved.

Test 9.
Valve Clearances.

This is normally known as 'checking the tappets' and is a familiar enough feature of any piece of routine engine maintenance. One again, the works manual is the place to look for the checking procedure and the proper clearances; overhead-camshaft engines involve us in a lot more complication when it comes to setting, but measurement is easy enough. Remove the rocker box or valve cover from the engine, and do your best not to tear the gasket though strictly speaking it should be replaced as a matter of course. You then check the clearance between the rocker arm or camshaft lobe and the valve stem on each valve in turn.

The works manual will set out a system for ensuring each valve is fully closed and you should follow that. Find out whether the valve clearances are supposed to be checked with the engine hot or cold, get the engine into the appropriate condition and measure the clearance at each valve with a feeler gauge of suitable dimensions.

Since removing and replacing the rocker box is something of a chore, particularly if we have to use gasket sealer to prevent oil leaks, it's convenient to readjust the valve clearances immediately if any of them seem to be in need of it. With conventional overhead valves this is an easy enough operation for which you need only a screwdriver and a spanner that fits the locknut of the adjuster. Slacken the nut, place the gauge between the rocker arm and the valve stem, screw in the adjuster until the gauge is pinched but not clamped tight, and then retighten the locknut without letting the adjuster move any further. In practice, you generally find that the last turn of the locknut has actually closed the valve clearance slightly and you have to go through it again, but you soon get the hang of it.

With overhead-camshaft engines adjustment becomes more problematic. You can't make simple adjustments, the distance between the camshaft lobes and the tappet that sits on top of the valve stem has to be carefully altered by packing up the tappet with little bits of steel sheet or shims. This is generally reckoned to be one of those little mopping-up operations that you ought to entrust to the car's agents because not only do they have boxfuls of alternative shims to choose from and you don't, but they will also have any special tools that the operation needs.

Whichever way you solve it, getting the tappet adjustment right is a much more significant feature of tuning than amateurs — who frequently neglect

the job from one year's end to the next — ever realize. Over-large valve clearances aren't dangerous, but will inhibit performance in time and make an unpleasant clattering noise anyway. Valve clearances that are too fine, or even non-existent, will eventually lead to the valve burning because it isn't on its seat for long enough for the heat it collects to dissipate into the head. In any case, close valve settings will lower the compression of the engine.

Tuning Up.

We should now be armed with a considerable amount of compromising information about the engine's private life, and a great deal more of it than we might have gleaned from walking round it a couple of times and aimlessly checking for loose wires. As a result of the tests — whether assisted by the full complement of instruments or merely by what you could beg, borrow or steal — it ought to be possible to establish how much of our efforts to improve the performance will be a matter of adjustment and tuning, and how much of it will require actual replacement of parts. We'll know, for instance, if the advance mechanism needs replacement, or the plug leads, or the fuel pump diaphragm. If these problems aren't put right first, then the whole business of tuning the engine at all becomes completely pointless.

Let's say that the tests have cleared the engine, or that we've replaced anything that was faulty. A combination of the compression test procedure and operating faults such as pinking or running on after the ignition is off will have indicated whether or not the engine needs decarbonizing — if it does, then it will be difficult to tune it effectively and the compression test might reveal the problem by showing a reading possibly 10 or 20 lb./sq. in. *higher* than normal. (This is because the build-up of carbon in the combustion chamber is taking up so much space that it's reducing the volume of the chamber and raising the pressure.)

A reliable tune-up procedure, once all these snags have been dealt with, might go like this:
1. Tappet clearances
2. Clean or replace sparking plugs
3. Clean or replace contact points and condenser
4. Ignition timing
5. Carburettors

Tappet Clearances.
The first is self explanatory and has been dealt with in the last section. Stick to the maker's recommended clearances and find out whether the setting is supposed to be made hot or cold.

Sparking Plug.
Replace the plugs at 12,000 mile intervals as a matter of routine, and it's not a bad idea to do it as soon

as you acquire the car unless they're obviously in perfect condition. Make sure you get the right specification for the engine.

Contact Points and Distributor.

Examine the distributor cap as described on p. 105. Replace it if the terminals appear badly burned or corroded or there are cracks in the plastic. Check the carbon brush and the effectiveness of its spring.

Replace the points at 6,000 mile intervals, and if you have to do a laborious amount of filing to clean the old ones up replace them anyway, since you'll be well on the way to filing away the rare metal coating. Clean new points with petrol to get rid of any protective film applied to them and replace them according to the procedure described in the manual. Modern contact points available in bubble packs at the accessory shops are now 'one-piece' units and you merely have to locate the earthed contact over the peg in the distributor baseplate, set the gap and tighten the fixing screw. Some distributors still make use of a variety of points that come in bits, and in this case you have to bend the contact spring right round, locate one end of it on the terminal plate or peg, and push the fibre heel down over the pivot pin. This type of contact set also provides the fibre or plastic washers that insulate the contact spring from the baseplate — but don't lose the old ones until you've finished the job, in case you find you've lost the new ones before you've started it. Again, inexperience can sometimes lead you to miss out one of these washers, or fit the condenser and coil lead in such a way that they accidentally short down the pivot pin. The result is that the ignition is stone dead, and you wish you were. Just remember, the only time electricity is supposed to be conducted from the moving contact arm to the baseplate requires the arm to be set up in such a way that it's electrically isolated from the rest of the distributor, and so is the condenser lead and the coil wire.

If you've had to overhaul the centrifugal mechanism first, then you'll have taken the distributor off the engine altogether and be able to set the points and replace the condenser on the bench. If you've taken the distributor out, don't let the engine turn over for any reason until you've put it back, and if you're really cautious you might even paint a white line on the distributor base and the mounting bracket on the block as a double check.

Ignition Timing.

Time the ignition by hooking up the timing light as already described. Leave the distributor clamp bolt loose and move the instrument both clockwise and anti-clockwise until the timing marks line up. You can set the ignition timing with the vacuum gauge if you prefer it — moving the distributor around until you get the best possible vacuum

reading, and then retarding the ignition very slightly. Whichever method you've opted for, make sure the clamp bolt and nut are properly retightened.

Carburettor.

Adjust the idling mixture of the carburettor by any of the methods already described, or by the Color-tune, or by the vacuum gauge. Most fixed jet carburettors can be adjusted by ear, simply by screwing the mixture control in or out to get the fastest smooth idling speed, then reducing the speed at the throttle stop screw to obtain the idle r.p.m. that seems appropriate for the engine. The workshop manual will describe an appropriate tuning procedure.

Some modern carburettors, particularly the twin-barrelled Weber, don't have their idle speeds adjusted at the throttle stop but by manipulating a by-pass air control that varies the air flow through the idling jet. In this case you attempt to set a smooth tickover with the mixture control, and then bring the speed down with the by-pass screw. Adjusting the throttle stop on these carburretors is meant to be against the rules, because you can upset the position of the throttle plate in relation to the low-speed jets and never know you've done it. These touchy carburettors only really get on well with exhaust gas analysers, so be careful how you deal with them.

The last snag on the subject of tuning carburettors arises where multiple units are fitted. The important consideration then isn't just to get the mixture controls into balance between them, but to ensure that the throttle openings are equal as well so that all the carburettors are sucking the same amount of air. Once again, the workshop manual fills you in, but the procedure will always involve releasing the linkage that connects the throttle together, adjusting the throttle stop screws on each one until they're in balance, and then tightening the interconnections up again without disturbing the adjustment. You can get a rough idea of the air flow past each throttle plate by comparing the volume of the hiss at each one while the engine's running, preferably listening with a rubber tube stuck in your ear and the other end held to the carburettor intake. Carburettor balancers, which indicate the air rate with a pointer on a scale, are a much better bet and are available at the accessory shops. Get the air balance between multiple carburettors right before you start playing around with the mixtures.

Incidentally, don't forget any routine maintenance procedures the carburettor might require, such as topping up the piston damper with engine oil on the S.U. — failure to do this will impede the acceleration. And make sure the acceleration pump works in a fixed jet carburettor that's fitted with such a device. A squirt from the pump jet when you snap the throttle open is fairly conclusive evidence that all is well.

Index.

AA, 58, 74, 84
  test reports, 72
abrasives, 149, 150, 156
acceleration, 36, 38, 70, 71-2, 78, 116, 130, 175, 176
acceleration pump, *see* carburettor
adjustable spanners, 88, 153
advance mechanism, *see* ignition
A.F. spanners, 86, 90
air bleed systems, 34
air-cooled engines, 40, 88, 126
air flow, 33, 34, 36, 109, 130, 175, 183
air leaks and faults, 80, 119, 120, 122, 128, 146, 147, 175, 178, 179, 182
air-pressure gauge, 94, 98
alcohol, 11, 31
Allen keys, 90, 130
alternator, 23, 126, 167, 169
aluminium bodywork, 74, 88
ammeter, 78
annulus, *see* epicyclic gears
anti-freeze, 128, 145
anti-rattle springs, 116
anti-roll bars, 76, 134
anti-smog valve, 144
Armstrong Siddeley, 46
auctions, 74
Autobooks, 83
Automotive Products, 46
axle stands, 97-8, 130, 145, 159
axles, 54, 60, 62, 132
  faults and checks, 76, 78, 117, 121, 122, 146, 161
  shafts, 54, 117
  and suspension, 62, 67, 134

B.A. spanners, 153
baffles, *see* exhaust system
ball-bearings, 117, 118, 160
ball joint taper breaker, 96, 138
ball joints, 58, 96, 121, 134, 136, 138, 148
ball-pein hammer, 92, 151
Bare Metal Stopper, 150
battery, 23, 71, 72, 84, 101-3, 108, 113, 125-6, 154, 167, 169, 178, 179
  casing, 126
  charger, 94, 97, 167, 169
  fluid, 73, 83, 94, 126, 138, 147

jump leads, 98, 102, 113
  main leads, 102, 169
bearing, types of, 56, 58
bench, use of, 97
Bentley, W.O., 34
Benz, C.F., 13, 16, 20
benzene, 31
big-end bearing, 9, 58, 80, 157
blowtorch, 90
bodywork, 62, 67, 74, 88, 149-53
bonnet, 36, 73, 151
boot, 70, 73, 74, 151, 179
Borg-Warner transmission, 54
bottom dead centre, 13
bottom gear, 43
box spanners, 105, 132, 146
brake adjusting tool, 88, 133, 140
brake horse power, 70-1
braking system, 60, 62
  adjuster, 138, 140
  backplate, 119, 138, 140, 147
  bleeding, 94, 119, 142, 147
  disc brakes, 62, 119, 138-42
  drums, 62, 94, 119, 138-40, 142
  fade, 147
  faults and testing, 60, 62, 70, 80, 84, 112, 115, 119, 120, 122, 125, 128, 138-42, 145, 148, 167
  handbrake, 58, 62, 78, 140
  hoses and pipes, 76, 119, 138, 142, 147, 148
  hydraulic fluid and reservoir, 62, 73, 83, 84, 94, 125, 126, 140, 142, 147, 148
  lines, 148
  linings, 119, 121, 128, 138, 140, 142
  master cylinder, 119, 126, 138, 147
  pads, 138, 142
  relining, 72
  self-adjusting, 138, 140
  servo, 46, 54, 120
  shoes, 62, 96, 119, 126, 138-40
  wheel cylinders, 119, 126, 138, 140, 147
breakdowns, 101-23
breathing, 11, 20
British Leyland, 54, 67, 88, 110, 145, 153, 161
bulbs, 98, 111, 167, 171
bump-starting, 102

bumpers, 74
bush, *see* bearing
buying, car, 69-80

Cadillac, 54
calipers, brake, 140, 142
camber, 121
camshaft, 16, 56
  bearings, 56
  chain wheel, 154
  and dismantling, 154
  and ignition, 25-9
  lobes, 16, 132, 182
carburettor, 11, 13, 20, 31-8, 70, 80, 94, 178, 181, 183
  acceleration pump, 34, 58, 110, 146, 183
  air cleaners, 36, 110, 130, 144, 145, 147, 175, 178
  air intake, 33, 109, 110, 183
  balancers, 183
  dampers, 128, 130, 142, 145
  down-draught, 33, 34, 110
  fixed-jet, 110, 146, 183
  float chamber, 33, 34, 36, 38, 109, 110, 114, 142, 145, 146, 153, 179, 181
  fuel filter, 110, 114, 145
  jets, 33-6, 84, 109, 110, 111, 114, 130, 146
  multiple, 183
  side-draught, 34, 36, 110, 130, 142, 146, 181, 183
  spindle, 80, 178
  spray tube, 33, 34
  starter carburettor, 34, 36, 76, 110, 152
  variable jet, 146
  ventilation, 144
  see also choke, fuel mixture, throttle
castor angle, 121
chassis, 62, 67, 76, 122
checks
  weekly, 125-8
  3,000 mile, 128-42
  6,000 mile, 142-5
  12,000 mile, 145-6, 169
  long-term, 146-8
choke, 33-6, 110, 114, 130, 146, 147
  actuating lever, 109

automatic, 36, 109, 110, 146
  choke-depression, 33-4, 38
chrome plating, 73, 149
circuit tester, 92, 108, 110, 112, 113,
  128, 145, 167, 179
Citizen's Advice Bureau, 74
Citroen, 62, 67
clevis, 140
clock, 167
clutch, 40, 43, 46, 54, 73, 78, 84, 88,
  117, 125, 128, 132
  carbon ring bearings, 43, 159
  centre/friction plate, 43, 78, 84,
    116, 117, 132, 159, 160
  diaphragm, 43, 115, 159, 160
  drag, 118, 159
  housing, 102, 169
  hydraulic fluid, 132, 159
  linings, 116, 160, 161
  mechanical, 132
  pedal linkage, 43
  pressure plate, 43, 116, 159, 160
  release, 43, 115, 116, 128, 132,
    159, 160, 161
  reservoir, 126
  slip, 159, 160
  spin, 158
  springs, 115, 159, 160
  vacuum valve, 43, 46
coachwork, *see* bodywork
coefficient of friction, 56
coil, 23, 25, 83, 84, 105, 106, 108,
  113, 167, 179, 180, 183
coil tester, 179
cold-starter device, 34, 36, 76, 110,
  152
collets, 154, 156
Colortune, 181, 183
combustion chambers, 13, 16, 20, 80,
  130, 153, 154, 157, 182
compensating jet system, 33-4
compression and testing, 11, 13, 78,
  80, 84, 142, 144, 152, 154, 156, 157,
  173, 174, 175, 176, 177, 179, 182
condenser, 25, 98, 108, 109, 114, 144,
  145, 180, 182, 183
condenser tester, 179
constant mesh, *see* gears
constant velocity joints, 78, 117, 136,
  161
contact-breaker and gap, 25, 29, 94,
  108, 109, 128, 132, 142, 144, 145,
  176, 179, 180, 183
contact points, 25, 84, 98, 106, 108,
  109, 113, 114, 125, 128, 132, 142,
  144, 179, 180, 182, 183
cooling system, 20, 115, 126, 127,
  142, 145
  see also radiator
copper wire, 98, 112, 113
costs and buying, 69-80
crankcase, 13, 20, 154
  ventilation system, 142, 144
crankpins, 13, 157
crankshaft, 9, 11, 13, 20, 23, 25, 43,
  56, 71, 115, 145, 161, 182

bearings, 56, 88, 158, 160
crash box, 46
crash stops, 138
crossfire, 180
Crypton Company, 125
Cugnot, Joseph, 11
cut and shut cars, 76
cylinder block, 20, 76, 157
cylinder head, 20, 46, 76, 88, 105,
  110, 115, 145, 146, 152, 153-6,
  176
  gasket, 20, 76, 80, 115, 128, 145,
    146, 152, 156, 157, 173, 174,
    177, 178, 182
cylinders, 9-13, 16, 20, 38, 43, 70, 71,
  76, 80, 125, 153, 154, 157, 173,
  174, 180

Daimler, G., 16
dashboard, 73, 78, 84, 167, 171
De Dion tube suspension, 136
decarbonizing (decoking), 78, 84,
  153, 154, 156, 157, 182
decoke gasket set, 152
degreasants, 152
demister, 73
dents, 152
depreciation, 69, 72, 73
detergents, 128
dipper switch, 70, 167
dipsticks, 76, 128, 161
direct drive, *see* top gear
disc brakes, *see* braking system
dismantling and reassembly, 84, 86,
  94, 96, 153-71
displacement, 70
distilled water, 126
distributor, 25, 29, 72, 83, 108, 132,
  144, 183
  advance weights, 142
  baseplate, 109, 144, 181, 183
  brush, 106, 144, 183
  cam, *see* contact-breaker
  cap, 76, 84, 105, 106, 142, 144-5,
    181, 183
  clamp, 145, 183
  cover, 29, 105, 106, 144
  earth, 179
  lead, 179
  pivot pin, 142
  rotor arm, 29, 105, 106, 113, 142,
    144
  spindle, 96, 142, 144, 180
  spring-blade, 132, 144
  see also contact-breaker, contact
    points
domed dolly, 151
doors, 73, 74, 151
double declutching, 46, 52, 70
drive shaft, 78, 117, 128
driving seat, 70, 78
drums, *see* braking system
dry compression figures, 176, 177
dwell angle, 180
dwell meter, 174, 179

dynamo, 23, 56, 71, 84, 126, 130,
  145, 146, 157, 169
earthing, 102, 112, 113, 126, 159,
  161, 162, 167, 168, 178
electrical system, 11, 13, 20-29, 80,
  94, 101, 111, 112, 128, 162-71,
  174, 178
  see also battery, dynamo, earthing,
    indicators, lights, radio, short
    circuits, starter
electrical test meter, 174, 175, 177,
  178, 179
electrolyte, *see* battery fluid
electronic balancer, 123
emery cloth, 126
engine, 46, 73, 76, 78, 80, 103, 113,
  114, 125, 128, 157
  advanced testing, 173-83
  flexibility, 71
  in front, 117, 158
  liner, 20
  at rear, 70, 72
  reconditioning, 78, 157, 158
  side valve, 177
  sump, 20, 56, 73, 76, 125, 128,
    130, 142
  timing chain, 80, 157
  transverse, 54, 58, 70, 88, 110,
    145, 153, 161
  wet-liner, 154
  working clearance, 58
  see also decarbonizing, dismantling,
    fuel, oil, starting, top overhaul,
    tuning
engines, development of, 9, 11, 13, 16
epicyclic gears, 52-4
Evans, Oliver, 11
exhaust system, 13, 20, 38, 40, 71,
  72, 80, 90, 109, 111, 112, 128,
  130, 142, 145, 147, 148, 175,
  177, 181
  back-pressure, 71
  clamps, 148
  dismantling, 154
  downpipe, 153
  expansion chamber, 38, 40
  gas analysis, 181, 183
  mounting straps, 112, 145
  notes, 146, 176, 181
  pipe, 178
  smoke, 80, 146, 147, 176, 182
  valves, 156, 173
extracting tools, 94
Extreme Pressure oil ratings, 56

fan and belt, 7, 40, 98, 101, 111, 112,
  115, 128, 130
fault-tracing charts, 113-23
feeler gauges, 94, 98, 108, 132, 142,
  179, 182
Fiat, 40, 71, 84, 88
fibreglass bodywork, 76
files, use of, 96, 108, 109, 113, 132,
  179, 183

filters, *see* carburettor, fuel, oil
fire extinguishers, 98
flat spot, 38, 103
flexing, 62, 123
flooding, 101, 111, 114, 146
floor pan, 76
flywheel, 11, 13, 20, 43, 46, 54, 88,
    102, 116, 117, 145, 159, 160, 161,
    169
flywheel puller, 161
foreign competition, 72
front-wheel drive, 72, 78, 136, 161
fuel, 9-11, 31-8, 58, 69, 72, 105, 114,
    128, 130, 134, 142, 145, 157, 176,
    177
    feed pipe, 109, 153, 178, 179
    filter, 110, 114, 145
    flow, 31-8, 40, 43, 70, 71, 109,
        178, 179
    gauge, 46, 101
    mixture, 31-4, 38, 109, 115, 130,
        144, 146, 152, 175, 176, 181,
        182, 183
    pump, 36, 38, 109, 110, 111, 114,
        142, 145, 175, 178, 179
fuses, 84, 98, 112, 162, 167, 172

garages, private, 69, 96-8
gas, *see* exhaust system
gaskets, 20, 76, 80, 115, 128, 145,
    146, 152, 156, 157, 173, 174, 177,
    178, 182
gears, gearbox, 40-54, 58, 73, 76, 78,
    96, 118, 130, 142, 145, 161, 162

    automatic change, 46
    constant mesh, 52, 118
    cover, 118, 158, 159, 161
    crownwheel, 54, 117
    differential, 54, 58, 117, 118, 130,
        142, 161
    dismantling, 158, 159-62
    dog clutch, 52, 118
    jumping out, 78, 160
    locking plungers, 118
    output shaft, 43, 52, 54
    ratios, 43-52, 54, 78
    selector mechanism, 118, 159, 160
    shift mechanism, 46, 69, 70, 158
    synchromesh, 52, 78, 118, 161
General Motors, 54
generator, *see* alternator, dynamo
Girling braking systems, 147
glove box, 70
greasing, 58, 60, 94, 96, 134, 140, 142,
    144, 161, 180
Gunsons' equipment, 94, 174, 181

hacksaw, use of, 88, 96, 169
halfshafts, 54, 117
hammers, use of, 92
Hancock, Walter, 11
hand anvil, 151
Hardy-Spicer shafts, 161
Hawk compression testing, 174, 175,
    177

headlamps, *see* lights
heater, car, 73
heating, garage, 98
hoists, 94
horn, 70, 125, 142
horsepower, 70-71
hoses
    brake, 76, 119, 138, 142, 147
    dismantling, 153
    water, 112, 153, 156
hot starting, 111
hub pullers, 96, 161
hubs, 60, 62, 94, 123, 138, 140, 161,
    162
    bearings, 96, 123
    caps, 92, 111
Hydragas suspension, 67
Hydramatic transmission, 46, 54
hydraulic bottle jack, 97
hydraulic fluid, *see* braking system,
    clutch, suspension
hydraulic lift, 97
hydrocarbons, 31, 38
Hydrolastic suspension, 67, 136
hydrometer, 92-4, 126, 167, 178

ignition, 11, 13, 16, 20-29, 36, 38, 76,
    78, 84, 94, 103-9, 113, 114, 125,
    128, 130-32, 142, 167, 171, 177,
    178
    advance-retard, *see* timing
    leads, 113, 142, 144, 145, 177
    switch, 108, 113, 178
    timing, 29, 31, 115, 125, 142, 145,
        156, 157, 174, 175, 180, 181,
        183
    timing light, 115, 174, 175, 180,
        183
    vacuum advance, 29, 31
    warning light, 73, 78, 102, 112
    see also battery, coil, contact
        points, distributor, sparking
        plugs
idling, 80, 117, 146, 147, 157, 176,
    177, 179, 180, 183
inertia-engaged starter, 169
inspection lamp, 97
inspection pit, 97, 98, 145, 159
instrument panel, *see* dashboard
insulating tape, 98, 171
insulation, insulators, 105, 114, 132,
    144, 167, 169, 178, 181
insurance, 69, 78
interference fit, 94
ionization, 106

jacks, use of, 76, 97, 98, 111, 112,
    122, 130, 134, 136, 140, 146, 147,
    159, 160, 161
Jaguar, 71
Jenolite, 149
jets, *see* carburettor

knocking, 157
knuckle bar, 88
Kurust, 149

lamps, *see* lights
Lanchester, 46
Lancia, 71
leaks, *see* air, battery, exhaust, fuel,
    oil, reservoirs, suspension, water
lighting, garage, 97, 98
lights, 73, 78, 113, 125, 142, 145,
    171
    brake, 80
    headlights, 70, 74, 76, 80, 101,
        102, 111, 142, 167, 171
    ignition, 73, 78, 102, 112
    indicator, 80, 148, 171
    oil, 73, 78, 157
    reverse, 159
    side, 74, 111, 167, 171
    stop, 148
little-end bearings, 9, 80, 157
Lockheed brakes, 142, 147
locks, 96
log book, *see* registration documents
low gear, 52
low voltage circuit, 25, 29, 105, 106,
    108, 178, 179, 181
lubrication, 54, 56, 58, 60, 62, 71,
    96, 115, 117, 120, 122, 128, 130,
    134-6, 142, 144, 145, 147, 160,
    161, 169, 181
Lucas equipment, 105
luggage space, 70

machine oil, 96
MacPherson suspension, 134
magnet, use of, 76, 130
maintenance, 69, 72, 125-71
mallets, use of, 92
mandrel, use of, 160
matchbox, use of, 179
metric spanners, use of, 86, 90, 98
M.G. cars, 88
mileage, 58, 72, 73, 76, 84, 125, 152,
    157, 177
minicabs, 74
Minis, 112, 162, 178
misfiring, 103-6, 153, 173, 176
mixture, *see* fuel
mole wrench, use of, 88, 90, 92, 98,
    156
monocoque bodywork, 67
Morgan Co., 67
M.O.T. test, 76-8, 80, 136, 138,
    148-9, 151, 172
muffler systems, *see* exhausts

noise regulations, 38
nuts and bolts, 86, 88-90, 128, 134,
    136

oil, 31, 60, 67, 76, 80, 83, 90, 117,
    118, 119, 121, 122, 128, 130, 134,
    136, 138, 142, 144, 145, 146, 147,
    160, 161, 176
    filters, 56, 58, 76, 128, 130, 142-4
    functions, 54, 56, 58
    multigrades, 56, 58, 96
    oil pressure, 58, 78, 115, 157

pump, 56, 58, 142, 158, 159
   reservoir, 56
open circuit, 167
open-ended spanners, use of, 86,
   134, 152
Otto cycle, 13, 43
overcooling, 115
overdrives, 52
overhead camshaft, 70, 154, 182
overheating, 40, 58, 111, 112, 115
overrun, 78
oversteer, 72

paint and paintwork, 73, 74, 76, 126,
   149-53
panel beating, 92, 151
paraffin, 11, 31, 144
patching bodywork, 152
pedals, 70, 73, 78, 116
petrol, *see* fuel, vaporization as
   cleaner, 146, 147, 155, 169, 170,
   183
petrol pump, *see* fuel pump
petrol tank breather, 114
pinking, 31, 153, 158, 181, 182
pistons, 9, 11, 13, 71, 115, 125, 130,
   145, 153, 155, 158, 174, 181
   bearings, 158
   dampers, 128, 146, 183
   ring clamp, 157
   ring gaps, 94
   rings, 11, 80, 152, 158, 174, 176
   slap, 78, 158
   split skirt, 158
   travel, 70
pit, *see* inspection pit
pliers, use of, 92, 98, 132, 142, 153
plugs, *see* sparking plugs
Plus Gas oil, 90
points, *see* contact points
pollution regulations, 38
poppet valves, *see* valves
Porsche, 174
pouches, 70
power drill, use of, 96, 152, 153, 155
pre-engaged starter, 170
pre-ignition, 31
propeller shaft, 54, 58, 117, 118,
   158, 160, 161
pulling tools, 94
pumps, *see* fuel, oil, S.U., water
punched cards, 154
punctures, 111, 123
push rods, 70, 154, 156
push-starting, 113
putty, *see* stopper

radiator, 40, 73, 76, 112, 115, 125,
   126, 128, 142, 145, 154, 156
radio suppression, 106, 167
ramps, use of, 97, 130, 145, 158
rear wheel drive, 117
reciprocating action, 9, 16
registration documents, 74, 80
Renault, 23
reservoirs, fluid, 56, 120, 125, 126,
   128, 136

resin filler, 152
respray, *see* paint
reverse gear, 43, 54
revolution counter, *see* tachometer
ride height, 132-4, 136, 171
Riley, 46, 58
ring-spanners, use of, 86, 130, 147,
   154, 182
road-holding, 72
road speed, 46
rocker assembly, 70, 94, 144, 153,
   155, 156, 157, 182
Rolls Royce, 54, 67, 71, 181
rotational action, 9, 11, 43
rubber, *see* seals
rust, 67, 72, 73, 74, 76, 86, 90, 96,
   112, 120, 134, 138, 147, 148,
   149, 150, 152, 167, 171, 179
rust-killers, 149

S.A.E. oil ratings, 56
Sale of Goods Act, 74
sales, car, 69-80
sanding, 151
screwdrivers, use of, 84, 88-90, 98,
   105, 111, 134, 136, 140, 142,
   144, 146, 149, 159, 169, 182
screwjack, 97
seals, boots, gaiters, 118, 119, 126,
   128, 136, 138, 140, 144, 145,
   147, 154, 155, 156, 161, 171
seatbelts, 70, 148
secondary circuit, 29-31
second-hand cars, 73-80
self-locking nuts, 90, 92, 158
servicing, *see* maintenance
servo, *see* braking system
shafts, transmission, 9, 11, 13, 16,
   20, 23, 25, 40-58, 70, 71, 78, 88,
   96, 115, 117, 118, 128, 132, 136,
   155, 158, 159, 160, 161, 162, 182
   see also individual shafts
shelving, garage, 97
shims, 142, 182
shock absorbers, *see* suspension
short circuits, 102, 109, 112, 113,
   114, 132, 144, 154, 169, 179,
   183
short engine, 158
sidelamps, *see* lights
silencer bandage, 98, 112
silencers, 38, 40, 76, 84, 112
skew gear, 25
slide-hammer, 152
sliding shaft, 117
small-end, *see* little-end
smoke, 80, 146, 147, 176, 181
snap connectors, 162, 172
snatching, brake, 116, 123
socket set, use of, 86-8, 98, 130, 146,
   152, 153, 161
soldering, 171, 172
solenoid, *see* starter
Solex carburettors, 34, 36, 110
space, inside, 70
spanners, use of, 86-8

spare tyre, 76, 94, 147
spare wheel, 70, 111
spares, 72, 98, 106, 112, 172
spark, function of, 11
sparking plugs, 13, 23, 25, 29, 41,
   76, 80, 84, 98, 103-9, 113, 114,
   125, 132, 142, 144, 145, 154,
   158, 167, 176, 177, 179, 180,
   181, 182
   caps, 106, 142, 180
   electrodes and gaps, 23, 94, 105,
      106, 128, 132, 176
   leads, 105, 106, 180
   sockets, 80, 88, 98, 105, 130, 132
   wrench, 88, 130, 132
speed and checks, 17, 72, 78
speedometer, 78, 158
split pins, use of, 86, 92, 134, 142,
   158, 162
spray paint, 152, *see also* paint
spring dampers (shock absorbers),
   see suspension
springing, *see* suspension
stalling, 111, 146
starter, 84, 101-3, 113, 155, 169,
   171, 176
   bearings, 56, 171
   brushes, 103, 171
   commutator, 169
   motor, 146, 159, 161, 169
   pinion, 102, 103, 113, 169
   solenoid, 102, 103, 110, 113, 169,
starting handle, 177
starting problems, 34-8, 101-14, 169,
   171
static engine timing, 145
steam engines, 9, 11, 40
steel, use of, 56, 67, 74
steering gear, 60, 62, 70, 76-8, 86,
   96, 121, 122, 128, 132-4, 136-8,
   142, 145, 146, 148
   ball joints, 96, 121, 136, 138, 148
   column, 60, 70, 136, 167
   drag link, 60
   drop arms, 136, 138
   lock, 73
   pivots, 58
   rack and pinion, 60, 136, 138
   stub-axle, 60, 92, 136
   swivels, 121, 122, 128, 146, 148
   track rod, 60
   tracking, 106, 121, 144, 145
   universal joints, 136, 161
   worm and nut, 60, 136, 186
stethoscope, use of, 157
Stillson, 90, 156
stolen cars, 74
stop-start driving, 58
stopper (filler), 151
stopping distance, 138
STP, 157
strangler, *see* choke
strap wrench, 144
Stromberg Constant-Depression
   carburettor, 36, 128, 130, 142, 146
stud extractor, 90

S.U. carburettor, 34, 36, 110, 130, 142, 146, 181, 183
S.U. electric pumps, 114, 178, 179
sub-frame, 90, 148
submerged jet system, 33, 34
sump, *see* engine
suspension, 60, 62-7, 72, 76, 78, 80, 92, 117, 120, 121, 128, 132-6, 142, 145, 148, 161
    cart-spring, 62, 134
    coil-spring, 62, 120, 134
    compressed gas, 62, 67
    hydraulic fluid, 67, 120, 128, 136
    independent, 62, 117, 134, 161
    leaf-spring, 62, 67, 80, 92, 134
    shock absorbers, 67, 78, 120, 128, 132, 136
    spring shackles, 62
    torsion bar, 62, 134-6
    wishbones, 62, 134
Sykes-Pickavant Engineering Co., 96
synchromesh, *see* gears

tachometer, 169, 174, 177, 181
tap-cutting bolt set, 90
Tapley meter, 148
tappets, *see* valves
taxation, 69, 78
Tecalemit grease gun, 94
temperature gauge, 78, 115
thermostats
    in automatic chokes, 36, 110, 146
    in cooling systems, 40, 112, 115, 145
throttle, 33, 34, 36, 38, 84, 114, 146, 178, 183
    butterfly-plate, 33, 38, 180, 183
    linkage, 94, 146, 153, 183
    pedal, 78, 109
    spindle, 147
    stop, 80, 183
timing light, stroboscopic, 145
timing marks, engine, 144, 154
tools, 76, 84, 86-96, 97, 98, 125
top dead centre, 13, 145
top gear, 43, 52, 80
    pushing, 106, 108
top overhaul, 153-6
torch, use of, 98, 138, 159
torque, 43, 46, 54, 71, 111, 161
    figures, 43, 71, 130, 156
torque convertor, 46, 54
torque wrench, use of, 84, 86, 88, 153, 157, 158
traction engines, 11
trafficators, *see* indicators
transmission, 40-58, 70, 78, 96, 117, 118, 128, 136, 158, 159, 160, 161
    see also clutch, flywheel, gears, shafts
tuning, 20, 115, 117, 125, 132, 142, 144, 145, 146, 173-5, 179, 181, 182, 183
tyres, 60, 76, 84, 122, 123, 124, 138, 148, 174

pressure, 83, 111, 121, 123, 124, 125, 172
pump, 94, 98, 128
valves, 124

U-bolts, 92, 117, 134
under-inflation, 123
undersealing, 72, 76
underside, 76
understeer, 72
UNF spanners, 98
universal joints, 136, 161
upholstery, 73, 78

vacuum gauge adaptor, 175, 177
vacuum gauge and readings, 147, 175, 177, 178, 179, 183
valves, 13, 16, 20, 84, 94, 125, 153, 154, 156, 157, 174, 177, 178, 179
    bearings, 56
    clearances, 142, 144, 182
    gear, 70, 94, 144, 153, 154, 156, 157, 182
    grinding, 156
    guides, 80, 154, 178
    operating chain, 177
    seats, 154, 156
    springs, 153, 154, 156, 175, 178
    stems, 94, 182
    tappets, 16, 157, 179, 182, 183
    timing design, 71, 178
vaporization, 11, 31-8
vapour lock, 114
Vaseline, 126
Vauxhall, 162
Vee-engines, 177
venturi, *see* choke
vibration, 117, 123, 157
vices, use of, 96, 97
Volkswagen, 16, 23, 36, 40, 54, 70, 88, 140, 142, 174, 178
voltmeter, 169, 174, 178, 179

warranty, 74
water, 56, 58, 76, 83, 114, 115, 128, 130, 156, 157, 180
    in cooling system, 40, 126, 128, 142, 145
    pump, 40, 115, 145, 157
Watt, James, 9
wax polishing, 149
Weber carburettor, 34, 110, 146, 183
welding, 76, 151
wet-and-dry paper, 149, 150, 152
wet compression readings, 176-7
wheels, 43, 58-67, 76-8, 117, 121-3, 134, 138, 140, 147
    arches, 73
    balance, 142, 145
    bearings, 60, 76, 121, 123, 146
    brace, 76, 92, 98, 111
    cylinders, 119, 126, 138, 140, 147
    nuts, 111, 123
    wobble, 121, 123
Whitworth equipment, 86, 90
window winders, 73

windows, 73
windscreen, 72, 98, 112
windscreen washers, 73, 125, 128, 142, 145, 148
windscreen wipers, 70, 73, 80, 125, 128, 142, 145, 148, 167
wings, 151
wire cutter, 98
wiring diagrams, 162
workshops, 96-8

Z-section chassis, 67
Zenith carburettor, 34, 110